JAMES JOYCE, SEXUALITY AND SOCIAL PURITY

In *James Joyce, Sexuality and Social Purity*, Katherine Mullin offers a richly detailed account of Joyce's lifelong battle against censorship. Through prodigious archival research, Mullin shows Joyce responding to Edwardian ideologies of social purity by accentuating the 'contentious' or 'offensive' elements in his work. The censorious ambitions of the social purity movement, Mullin claims, feed directly into Joyce's writing. Paradoxically, his art becomes dependent on the very forces that seek to constrain and neutralise its revolutionary force. Acutely conscious of the dangers censorship presented to publication, Joyce revenged himself by energetically ridiculing purity campaigns throughout his fiction. *Ulysses*, *A Portrait* and *Dubliners* each meticulously subvert purity discourse, as Joyce pastiches both the vice crusaders themselves and the imperilled 'young persons' they sought to protect. This important and highly original book will change the way Joyce is read and offers crucial insights into the sexual politics of Modernism.

KATHERINE MULLIN is Lecturer in Twentieth-Century Literature at the University of Leeds. Her work has appeared in *Semicolonial Joyce* ed. Derek Attridge and Marjorie Howes (Cambridge, 2000) and in *Modernism/Modernity*.

JAMES JOYCE, SEXUALITY AND SOCIAL PURITY

KATHERINE MULLIN

CAMBRIDGE
UNIVERSITY PRESS

PUBLISHED BY THE PRESS SYNDICATE OF THE UNIVERSITY OF CAMBRIDGE
The Pitt Building, Trumpington Street, Cambridge CB2 1RP, United Kingdom

CAMBRIDGE UNIVERSITY PRESS
The Edinburgh Building, Cambridge, CB2 2RU, UK
40 West 20th Street, New York, NY 10011–4211, USA
477 Williamstown Road, Port Melbourne, VIC 3207, Australia
Ruiz de Alarcón 13, 28014 Madrid, Spain
Dock House, The Waterfront, Cape Town 8001, South Africa

http://www.cambridge.org

First published 2003

Printed in the United Kingdom at the University Press, Cambridge

Typeface Adobe Garamond 11/12.5 pt.   *System* LATEX 2ε [TB]

A catalogue record for this book is available from the British Library

ISBN 0 521 82751 5 hardback

For Douglas and Valerie Mullin

I suppose we'll be damn well suppressed if we print the text as it stands. BUT it is damn wellworth it. I see no reason why the nations should sit in darkness merely because Anthony Comstock was horrified at the sight of his grandparents in copulation and there after ran wode in a loin cloth.

Ezra Pound (Letters of James Joyce, vol. II: 414)

Contents

Illustrations

Acknowledgements

First of many thanks are due to John Kelly, who has read drafts and re-drafts of chapters with a patient attentiveness beyond a supervisor's duties, always tempering his perceptive criticisms with a keen appreciation of social purity's moral lessons. I have benefited from the financial support of a British Academy Research Studentship, and the generous assistance of the Denise Skinner Senior Scholarship at St Hugh's College, Oxford. A Research Fellowship at the University College of Chichester removed the terror of a fourth year spent 'writing up', and a second Research Fellowship at Fitzwilliam College, Cambridge allowed me the time and resources to redraft the thesis into a book. Thanks to the staff of the Upper Reading Room at the Bodleian Library, Oxford, the British Library, the Colindale Newspaper Library, London, the National Library of Ireland, Dublin, the Fawcett Library, London Guildhall University, the New York Public Library, the Brooklyn Public Library, New York and the University Library, Cambridge. I am grateful to Bebe Bergsten, author with the late Kemp Niver of *Biograph Bulletins 1897–1908* for her gracious permission to reproduce the image in chapter 5.

When, five years ago, I was eager to start a doctoral thesis on James Joyce, I was warned of the perils of the 'Joyce industry', a daunting collection of individuals who passed a cold eye over graduate students attempting to join their clique. I never met them, but I did encounter an alternative universe of Joyce scholars, at conferences in Miami, Rome, London, Dublin and Trieste, who were welcoming, enthusiastic and kind. I am grateful to Richard Brown and Alastair Stead at the *James Joyce Broadsheet* in Leeds, Andrew Gibson, Robert Hampson, John Wyse Jackson and other members of the Charles Peake Research Seminar on *Ulysses*, London, and Austin Briggs, Susan Sutliff Brown, Anne Fogarty, Marjorie Howes, Clare Hutton, Brandy Kershner, Tim Martin, Mary Power, Lawrence Rainey, and, of course, Fritz Senn. In Ireland, several scholars helped me to surmount difficulties in obtaining information not easily available in England; John

Ryan, who introduced me to the world of Jeremiah O'Donovan studies, and Tadhg Foley, who allowed me invaluable access to his archive of improving pamphlets for the Irish schoolboy. Special thanks to Luke Gibbons, whose painstaking reading of early drafts and suggestions for further research add up to a remarkable generosity of time and scholarship. Maria Luddy and Philip Howell have both shared their research on Irish prostitution regulation, suggesting leads which greatly improved the introduction and chapter 6. My thesis examiners, Derek Attridge and Jeri Johnson, admirably combined kindness with rigour, suggesting many useful ways in which the thesis might be redrafted for publication. The three anonymous readers at Cambridge University Press treated my manuscript with a scrupulousness far from mean, and I am extremely grateful to them for detailed critical comments which greatly improved the final draft. Maureen Leach, my copyeditor, was very helpful. Thanks also to my editor at Cambridge, Ray Ryan, who has guided me through a sometimes daunting process with grace, good sense and wit.

Personal debts are too numerous to list here. E. Ann Gray first introduced me to Joyce, and her inspiring teaching urged me to persevere. Ruth Langley, Peter Barnes and Richard Adams were stoic throughout the first four years, diluting the inevitable wailings and gnashing of teeth with tea, gin and an invaluable sense of perspective. John Holmes and James Thompson indulged me with many delightful conversations on Victorian vice. Stephanie Rains' emails from Dublin, always bristling with her own brand of critical insight, have been a stalwart distraction: any half-finished footnotes are her fault entirely.

This book is dedicated to my parents, Douglas and Valerie Mullin, in gratitude for their loving and unconditional support.

Abbreviations

Quotations from the following works by James Joyce are cited in the text through these abbreviations:

OCPW   *Occasional, Critical and Political Writing*. Ed. Kevin Barry. Translated from the Italian by Conor Deane. Oxford: Oxford University Press, 2000.

D   *Dubliners*. Ed. Terence Brown. London: Penguin, 1992.

FW   *Finnegans Wake*. London: Minerva, 1991.

JJA   *The James Joyce Archive*. 63 vols. Ed. Michael Groden *et al.* New York: Garland, 1978.

L I   *Letters of James Joyce*, vol. I. Ed. Stuart Gilbert. New York: Viking, 1957.

L II   *Letters of James Joyce*, vol. II. Ed. Richard Ellmann. New York: Viking, 1966.

L III   *Letters of James Joyce*, vol. III. Ed. Richard Ellmann. London: Faber and Faber, 1966.

P   *A Portrait of the Artist as a Young Man*. London: Penguin, 1973.

Poems   *Poems and Shorter Writings*. Ed. Richard Ellmann, A. Walton Litz and John Whittier-Ferguson. London: Faber and Faber, 1991.

SH   *Stephen Hero*. London: Jonathan Cape, 1960.

U   *Ulysses: The Corrected Text*. Ed. Hans Walter Gabler with Wolfhard Steppe and Claus Melchior. London: Bodley Head, 1993.

Introduction: provoking the puritysnoopers

The story of my books is very strange. For the publication of *Dubliners* I had to struggle for ten years. The whole first edition of 1000 copies was burnt at Dublin by fraud; some say it was the doing of priests, some of enemies, some of the then Viceroy or his consort, Countess Aberdeen. Altogether it is a mystery...As for the *Portrait*, it was refused by nearly all the publishers in London. Moreover, when the courageous review *The Egoist* decided to publish it, not one printing works in the whole United Kingdom could be found to consent to print it. It was printed in America. The sheets were sent to London and bound there. My new book *Ulysses* was to appear in the *Egoist* of London. The same old story. From the very beginning the printers refused again. It appeared in fragments in the New York *Little Review.* Several times it was taken out of circulation through the post, by the action of the American Government. Now legal action is being taken against it.

(*L* 1: 132–3)

For seven years I have been working at this book – blast it!...No English printer wanted to print a word of it. In America the review was suppressed four times. Now, as I hear, a great movement is being prepared against the publication, initiated by Puritans, English Impe-rialists, Irish Republicans, Catholics – what an alliance! I ought to be given the Nobel Prize for Peace.

(*L* 1: 146–7)

Joyce's publication history is a history of censorship. Plans to place several of the *Dubliners* short stories in the agricultural journal *The Irish Homestead* foundered when the editor refused to publish more than three, telling Joyce 'his readers had complained' (*L* 1: 98). The collection was offered to Grant Richards in 1907, yet, after six months of wrangling, Richards also declined to publish since his printer refused to typeset 'indecent' passages. Five years later, Joyce's contract with Dublin publishing house Maunsel and Co. was similarly fated when the printer John Falconer guillotined the entire print run. Joyce's account of his travails, 'A Curious History', appeared in *Sinn Féin* and the avant-garde review *The Egoist*, the publicity prompting Grant Richards to relent and finally publish *Dubliners* in June 1914. The belated victory, however, presaged troubles to come. Serialisation of *A Portrait of the Artist as a Young Man* in *The Egoist* was impeded by the printer's refusal to typeset 'objectionable' passages.[1] The novel itself was refused by a chorus of publishers, and when Joyce agreed to publish it under the new and untried *Egoist* imprint, no fewer than seven printers declined to set the type, forcing the importation of printed sheets from the United States.[2] Such difficulties in turn anticipated the reception of *Ulysses*. Appearing serially in the New York Modernist magazine *The Little Review*, four numbers carrying extracts from *Ulysses* were seized by the New York Society for the Suppression of Vice. When an extract from 'Nausicaa' was confiscated in August 1920, the vice society had enough evidence to mount a successful obscenity prosecution. On 21 February 1921, *Ulysses* was officially banned from the United States. The ban was effectively duplicated in England, Ireland, Canada and Australia, uniting most of the English-speaking world in opposition.

This brief history of misadventure is a tired one. Joyce's battles against censorship have informed his critical reception to such a degree that Judge John M. Woolsey's judicial statement finding *Ulysses* *not* obscene was appended to many twentieth-century editions, framing the novel as a crucial social document in the war between philistine prudery and artistic freedom.[3] Yet Joyce's reputation as a moral subversive lives on, since recent media appraisals continue to insist upon Joyce as an avatar of sexual freedom, or, conversely, as the author of a dirty book. Typical broadsheet headlines read 'Family upset at "Joyce the foulmouth" ', 'Joyce's heir protests at sexy *Ulysses* show', 'Director of Public Prosecutions waged war on "filthy" *Ulysses*'.[4] This reputation has positioned Joyce at the heart of a potent cultural myth still prevalent today — 'that of the visionary, self-denying artist, who works in splendid isolation and constant jeopardy of suppression by the philistine public'.[5] Richard Ellmann's monumental biography presents

[1] Jane Lidderdale and Mary Nicholson, *Dear Miss Weaver: Harriet Shaw Weaver 1896–1961* (London: Faber and Faber, 1970), 92–3.
[2] *Ibid.*, 114–22.
[3] The Woolsey decision was appended to both the British Bodley Head and USA Random House editions until 1960 and 1986 respectively. Provision for its inclusion in the first USA edition was stipulated in the contract between Random House and Joyce. See Paul Vanderham, *James Joyce and Censorship: The Trials of Ulysses* (London: Macmillan, 1998), 150.
[4] *The Guardian*, 7 May 2000; *The Daily Telegraph*, 31 July 2000; *The Daily Telegraph*, 16 May 1998.
[5] Walter Kendrick, *The Secret Museum: Pornography in Modern Culture* (New York: Viking, 1987), 149.

Joyce as an embattled literary hero, fighting against poverty, illness and meddling censors armed only with genius, self-belief and a coterie of like-minded Modernist friends. Paul Vanderham's study of Joyce and censorship perpetuates this assumption, opening with Joyce's own assertion that Ulysses was 'one of the world-disturbing sailors', and presenting that novel's various court trials as perilous stages on Joyce's own voyage towards literary immortality.[6] This book will query Joyce's implicit passivity within this narrative of artistic struggle against suppression. It will unfold a hitherto ignored and marginalized aspect of the censorship debate to reveal Joyce as neither victim nor hero, but instead, and more interestingly, as an agent provocateur. What will be revealed here is Joyce's fascinating anticipation of his censorship, and his response to that threat through the creative appropriation of prevailing debates about art, morality and sexuality. Within *Dubliners, A Portrait of the Artist as a Young Man* and *Ulysses* are buried many intricate and imaginative subversions of the ideologies and strategies of those *Finnegans Wake* would label 'vice crusaders', 'puritysnooper' and 'watch warriors of the vigilance committee' (*FW* 434: 36, 254: 21, 34: 4). The complex agility of these subversions must modify the established conception of Joyce as a hapless victim of belated Victorian prudes. Instead, Joyce's fiction daringly incited the cultural conflict which would make him notorious.

I

How and when did this cultural conflict between art and the censors emerge? As Walter Kendrick suggests, 'it was when contemporary art joined in the pornographic battle' that the contest between visionary, self-denying artist and philistine public can be said to begin.[7] The war between art and morality may be loosely dated from 1857, a watershed year critical to the history of literary censorship. The year 1857 saw the publication of Baudelaire's *Les Fleurs du Mal* and Flaubert's *Madame Bovary*, the former convicted, the latter acquitted of offences against public morality. In Britain, John, Lord Campbell and his Society for the Suppression of Vice successfully campaigned for the Obscene Publications Act (1857), granted after four decades of that society's efforts against 'the sale of poison more deadly than prussic acid, strychnine or arsenic – the sale of obscene publications and indecent books'.[8] Campbell produced Dumas' *La Dame aux Camélias* in

---

[6] Vanderham, *James Joyce and Censorship*, 1.   [7] Kendrick, *The Secret Museum*, 149.
[8] Lord Campbell quoted in Morris L. Ernst, *To The Pure: A Study of Obscenity and the Censor* (London: Cape, 1929), 116.

Parliament to support his case: the debate 'pitted self-conscious artistry against self-righteous conventionality. Both sides were aware that the encounter was taking place on the leading edge of literary innovation.'[9] Whilst the membership, funds and activities of the Society for the Suppression of Vice waned over the next twenty-five years, in the early 1880s, the policing of the obscene underwent a sudden revival with the rise of a late-Victorian reform movement broadly known as social purity.

Richard Brown's groundbreaking study *James Joyce and Sexuality* compellingly argues for Joyce's creative engagement with the new theories of sexuality emerging at the turn of the nineteenth century. He persuasively suggests that Joyce's views of sexuality are informed by the contemporary discourses on sex flourishing as part of the *fin de siècle* 'discursive explosion' identified by Michel Foucault. Brown illustrates Joyce's borrowings from such diverse contemporary writings on sexuality as anthropological investigations of global marriage customs, 'free love' polemics, birth control manuals, novels by Balzac and Tolstoy, plays by Ibsen and Shaw, and the 'new sexology' of Freud, Otto Weininger, Richard Krafft-Ebing and Havelock Ellis. Such writings are pointedly 'highbrow', written and read by a self-consciously progressive cultural elite. Yet, as this study will show, they existed in counterpoint with a similarly voluble and far more populist sexual discourse which, crucially for Joyce, had the suppression of sexually explicit fiction at the heart of its project. Social purity was a formidable branch of the elaborate network of moral reform which flourished at the close of the nineteenth and the early decades of the twentieth centuries. Like the urban explorers and temperance campaigners who were their natural allies, social purists were well-organised and politically active. Their crusades to raise the moral tone of the nation were both remarkably influential and sustained into the 1920s.

In the USA, the principal social purity society was the New York Society for the Suppression of Vice, the prosecutor of *The Little Review* and *Ulysses* in 1921. Founded in 1873 by Anthony Comstock, it spawned a network of affiliated vice societies across the United States, including the Boston Watch and Ward Society, the Philadelphia Society for the Suppression of Vice, the Illinois Vigilance Association and the Chicago Vice Commission.[10] In Britain and Ireland, the largest purity group was the National Vigilance Association, presided over by the vice-regents of Ireland, the Earl and Countess Aberdeen. Others included the Moral Reform Union, the Gospel

---

9 Kendrick, *The Secret Museum*, 115–18.
10 Paul Boyer, *Purity in Print: The Vice Society Movement and Book Censorship in America* (New York: Charles Scribner's Sons, 1968), 5.

Purity League, the Social Purity Alliance, the White Cross League and the Church of England Purity Society. These organisations campaigned for a high standard of 'purity' in literature and art by boycotting, intimidating and occasionally even prosecuting the purveyors of sexually explicit material, and agitating for further legislation against 'indecent publications'. In the United States, the vice societies were still more closely entangled with the state apparatus, since Anthony Comstock and his New York Society for the Suppression of Vice were granted a federal charter empowering them to police the passage of 'obscenity' through the mails.[11] Such formidable opponents had moral subversives like Joyce in their sights. Their determination to cleanse their nations of highbrow smut was matched by the determination of the liberal intelligentsia to resist and ridicule their attempts.

The tone of the conflict was summarised in Anthony Comstock's 1883 polemic, *Traps for the Young*. Chapter xi, 'Artistic and Classical Traps', asserted

'Art' and 'classic' are made to gild some of the most obscene representations and foulest matters in literature, regardless of their results to immature minds... Authors whose pens seemed dipped in the sunlight of eloquence have vividly portrayed scenes of licentiousness; or satirically personated the life of the libertine and his conquests; or recorded the histories of ancient rakes; or gratified their own low-born and degraded natures by making pen-pictures of their own lascivious imaginings.[12]

This outburst explained how, to social purists, the 'artistic merit' defence of a morally dubious work was no defence at all, but instead compounded the crime. As the New York Society for the Suppression of Vice noted,

The grosser publications being measurably suppressed, there are appearing in their place publications of a less gross, but more insidious and equally dangerous

---

[11] *Ibid.*, 9. The distinctions between the British and American social purity movements have been outlined elsewhere. To summarise, in Britain the alliance between suffrage feminism and social purity was more pronounced than in the USA; British purity movements enjoyed a more socially inclusive constituency than their American counterparts; British purists sought more energetically to police working-class sexual disorders. Nevertheless, in many respects, social purity was an international and, particularly, transatlantic phenomenon, as British organisations like the National Vigilance Association, and United States groups like the New York Society for the Suppression of Vice communicated with each other and borrowed one another's strategies. White Cross Armies on both sides of the Atlantic urged young men to club together and pledge themselves to chastity; social purity organisations in both Britain and America were convulsed with anxieties over 'white slavery' or procured prostitution; in both countries, 'obscenity' in all its diverse forms was vigorously pursued. See Alan Hunt, *Governing Morals: A Social History of Moral Regulation* (Cambridge: Cambridge University Press, 1999), especially pages 121–30 for a fuller exposition of these distinctions and similarities.

[12] Anthony Comstock, *Traps for the Young*, ed. Robert Bremner (Cambridge, Mass.: Harvard University Press, 1967), 168–9.

character. This class is defended by many as 'classic' or 'artistic', and free circulation is claimed for them on these grounds. The Board cannot yield to this claim. One 'classic' for which exemption is claimed is an attempt to clothe the most sensual thoughts with the flowers and fancies of poetry, making the lascivious conception only the more insidious and demoralising. No, the 'classic' plea is misleading and fallacious.[13]

Vigilance societies on both sides of the Atlantic accordingly achieved their greatest notoriety not primarily for the prosecution of the authors, publishers and vendors of the 'grosser publications', underground pornographic classics such as *The Lustful Turk* or *Fanny Hill*, but for their onslaught upon writing with literary or avant-garde aspirations, an 'insidious' form of demoralisation. One London convention of purity societies issued a statement in 1910 castigating the modern trend for 'immoral, unhealthy and objectionable books professedly treating of the sex problem', in other words, 'serious' fiction.[14] It was an onslaught forcibly brought to the attention of English and Irish publishers in 1888, when the National Vigilance Association instigated the first high-profile prosecution of a publisher of 'sex problem' novels.

   The trial of Henry Vizetelly both inaugurated and exemplified that conflict between social purity moralism and artistic integrity which would later overshadow Joyce's travails with so many reluctant publishers. Vizetelly specialised in translations of novels by Gogol, Dostoevsky, Tolstoy, Balzac, Flaubert and Zola, and had founded the Mermaid Series of Elizabethan and Jacobean dramatists, all unexpurgated and under the general editorship of the sexologist Havelock Ellis. He was well aware that 'English literature, like English journalism, was under the thumb of Mrs Grundy', yet his cautiously expurgated editions of Zola's *La Terre* and *Nana* aroused the purists' wrath.[15] Vizetelly personified what many social purists dreaded; his decadent foreign fiction polluted the nation whilst, as Anthony Comstock alleged, sheltering behind the terms 'Art' and 'classic'.[16] These objections were first taken up in the House of Commons by the stalwart social purity

---

[13] New York Society for the Suppression of Vice, 'The Semi-Classic', *Annual Report* 8 (1882), 6. The 'classic' specified was probably Walt Whitman's *Leaves of Grass*, issued in a cheap edition a year earlier.

[14] Statement of the Committee of Representatives of London Societies Interested in Public Morality, delivered in January 1910 and quoted in Samuel Lynn Hynes, *The Edwardian Turn of Mind* (Princeton: Princeton University Press, 1968), 293.

[15] Mrs Grundy was, of course, the Victorian personification of the prudish censor. Vizetelly quoted in Edward de Grazia, *Girls Lean Back Everywhere: The Law of Obscenity and the Assault on Genius* (London: Constable, 1992), 42.

[16] See 'A Judicial Murder', in de Grazia, *Girls Lean Back*, 40–53 for a fuller account of the Vizetelly trials.

MP, Samuel Smith. Pointedly erasing cultural hierarchies, Smith mounted a pre-emptive strike against the 'artistic merit' defence, grouping Zola together with 'penny dreadfuls', quack remedies for sexually transmitted diseases, erotic postcards and lurid tabloid divorce-court reports. He alleged that certain shops in London were supplying 'young girls' with copies of *Nana*, in league with 'houses of the worst class to which the girls, when their minds were sufficiently polluted and degraded, were consigned'.[17]

Vizetelly retaliated with the classic 'artistic merit' defence, publishing and sending the Home Secretary an eighty-page pamphlet of 'obscene' passages from the Bible, Chaucer and Shakespeare.[18] This defence failed, and he was fined £250 and ordered to pay the Association's costs. In spring 1889, Vizetelly was once more dragged through the courts by the National Vigilance Association, this time accused of publishing more 'obscene' foreign classics, including eight more Zola novels and a translation of *Madame Bovary*. Nearing bankruptcy, sixty-nine years old and failing in health, he pleaded guilty and, unable to pay another fine, served three months imprisonment with hard labour, a sentence which almost certainly contributed to his death shortly after his release. For the National Vigilance Association, however, Vizetelly was a pornographer and his second conviction a triumph. In 1889, they published Samuel Smith's Commons oratory in a pamphlet prefaced with an appeal for 'a healthy public opinion' necessary 'to enable this Association to set the law in motion'.[19]

One Home Office official described the Vizetelly trials as 'epoch-making', and certainly they highlighted the rising power of the purity associations.[20] For printers like John Falconer and publishers like Grant Richards and George Roberts, the Vizetelly case functioned as a cautionary tale; his example, as the National Vigilance Association hoped, deterring many from issuing 'sex problem' fiction. Organisations such as, in Britain and Ireland, the National Council for Public Morals, the Pure Literature Society and the Forward Movement for Purity, and in the USA the New York Society for the Suppression of Vice, the Boston Watch and Ward Society and the Women's Christian Temperance Union Department for the Suppression of Impure Literature kept the threat of financially crippling

---

[17] National Vigilance Association, *Pernicious Literature* (London: National Vigilance Association, 1889), 6, 8, 11.

[18] Henry Vizetelly, *Extracts Principally from the English Classics, showing that the legal suppression of M. Zola's Novels would logically involve the Bowdlerising of some of the greatest works in English Literature* (London: Vizetelly and Co, 1888).

[19] National Vigilance Association, *Pernicious Literature*, i.

[20] Edward Bristow, *Vice and Vigilance: Purity Movements in Britain since 1700* (Dublin: Gill and Macmillan, 1977), 207.

prosecutions uppermost in publishers' minds. Together, these vigilantes mounted an indiscriminate assault upon low and high culture, and naturally, their persecutions of novels to which others were willing to ascribe artistic merit were most widely disputed. In Britain, 'pernicious literature' included works of established literary repute by Rabelais, Maupassant and Dostoevsky and Richard Burton's translation of *The Arabian Nights* as well as novels by contemporary writers. George Moore, Thomas Hardy, H. G. Wells, D. H. Lawrence, Compton Mackenzie and Hall Caine were just a few writing fiction classed as 'The Sex Novel, an epidemic of a most objectionable or in some cases indecent form of a novel purporting to deal with the sex problem'.[21] In the USA, the New York Society for the Suppression of Vice and its allies would similarly question and in many cases ban established classics, including Aristophanes' *Lysistrata*, Boccaccio's *Decameron*, Ovid's *Art of Love*, *The Arabian Nights*, Voltaire's *Candide*, Rousseau's *Confessions* and the complete works of Rabelais.[22] Yet it more readily pursued modern 'sex problem' works by Gabriele D'Annunzio, Oscar Wilde, Leo Tolstoy, George Bernard Shaw, George Moore, D. H. Lawrence, Upton Sinclair, Sinclair Lewis, Aldous Huxley, Arthur Schnitzler, Theodore Dreiser, Radclyffe Hall and Joyce himself.[23]

The scale and high profile of this loudly proclaimed and commercially intimidating war upon 'indecent' writing provoked two distinct stages of response, both of significant impact upon Joyce's troubled literary career. The first was the inevitable production of a climate of auto-censorship, where publishers, printers, editors, libraries and newspapers were inhibited from risking anything that might be deemed 'pernicious' by litigious vigilantes. The second was an eruption of reactive protest, as writers mobilised to defend themselves from the threat social purity posed to creative autonomy. In the decades following the Vizetelly trial, artists and vice crusaders would become increasingly polarised.

Auto-censorship was a natural response by publishers and printers not only to the legal threat posed by vigilantes, but to the considerable popular support their campaign attracted. The second edition of the National Vigilance Association account of the Vizetelly trials, *Pernicious Literature*,

[21] Ernst, *To The Pure*, 58; Nicolas Hiley, 'Can't you find me something nasty?': Circulating Libraries and Literary Censorship in Britain from the 1890s to the 1910s', in *Censorship and the Control of Print in England and France 1600–1910*, ed. Robin Myers and Michael Harris (Winchester: St Paul's Bibliographies, 1992), 128; National Vigilance Association, *Pernicious Literature*, i.

[22] Boyer, *Purity in Print*, 35, 209–10.

[23] William Coote, *The Romance of Philanthropy* (London: National Vigilance Association, 1916), 24; Hiley, 'Can't you find me something nasty?', 130; Boyer, *Purity in Print*, 15, 29, 185–7, 210.

contains an appendix quoting praise for the campaign from *The Guardian,
The Times, The Whitehall Review, The Pall Mall Gazette, The Spectator*
and *The Tablet*.[24] Such support was substantiated when, for instance, several British newspapers orchestrated specific purity crusades themselves.
In 1907, *The Daily Chronicle* mounted a letter-writing campaign against
'Sordid Fiction'; in 1909, *The Spectator* began a crusade against 'Poisonous
Literature' exemplified by H. G. Wells' *Ann Veronica*, and urged readers
to contribute to a fighting fund to launch private prosecutions against
'objectionable' books.[25] If this was the 'healthy public opinion' social purists
sought, then those involved in the book trade were forced to respond.
George Moore was one of the first victims of a shift in cultural climate
when, five years after the Vizetelly trials, Britain's two principal circulating
libraries, Mudies and W. H. Smith's, declined to stock his *Esther Waters*
(1894), a portrait of a working-class single mother.[26] To be boycotted by
the libraries was a heavy blow to any author, since their purchasing power
permitted them to cover the publishing costs of a novel: often books with
a print run of 50,000 would sell 10,000 to libraries.[27] By January 1910,
the libraries were so in accord with the vice societies that a committee of
'Representatives of London Societies Interested in Public Morality' issued
a statement thanking the Circulating Libraries Association for its help in
'combining to prevent the circulation of immoral, unhealthy or objectionable books'.[28] Such activities naturally influenced publishers and printers,
who feared not only the threat of vigilante prosecutions, but also the less
direct but commercially damaging effects of boycotting.

Such highly organised and successful attempts to suppress 'sex-problem'
fiction was unsurprisingly strenuously resisted by the cultural elite the purity movement targeted. George Moore began the fight back with an emotive protest against Vizetelly's fatal imprisonment, *The New Censorship of*

[24] National Vigilance Association, *Pernicious Literature*, 23–46; de Grazia, *Girls Lean Back*, 700–1.
[25] 'Sordid Fiction', *The Daily Chronicle*, 9 July 1907; *The Spectator* damned *Ann Veronica* for Wells'
portrait of 'a community of scuffling stoats and ferrets, unenlightened by a ray of duty or abnegation'
('A Poisonous Book', *The Spectator*, 20 November 1909, 846–7). In response, purity campaigner Revd
Herbert Bull proposed a fighting fund 'to be used under proper legal advice for the prosecution of
those who are responsible, whether as authors, publishers or distributors, for the dissemination of
poisonous literature' ('Poisonous Literature', *The Spectator*, 27 November 1909, 876). *The Spectator's*
subsequent appeal eventually raised £720 18s. ('The Guarantee Fund', *The Spectator*, 25 December
1909, 1100).
[26] Hiley, 'Can't you find me something nasty?', 128.
[27] For the economic influence of the circulating libraries on the book trade, see Hiley, 'Can't you find
me something nasty?', 124–30.
[28] Hynes, *The Edwardian Turn of Mind*, 293.

Literature, serialised in *The New York Herald* where he accused the National Vigilance Association of 'judicial murder'.[29] When the New York Public Library banned George Bernard Shaw's *Man and Superman* on Vice Society advice, Shaw retaliated by coining the term 'comstockery' which, with a curious disregard for similar zeal in Britain, he defined as 'the world's standing joke at the expense of the United States'.[30] In London, John Galsworthy started a debate in *The Times*, protesting 'if something is not done, there will be not a dog's chance in this country for any outspoken work of art'.[31] In 1916, the Author's League of America formed an international petition in support of Theodore Dreiser, whose novel *A 'Genius'* was the latest victim of comstockery.[32] As Dreiser himself suggested

A band of wasp-like censors has appeared and is attempting to put the quietus on our literature which is at last showing signs of breaking the bond of Puritanism under which it has long struggled in vain...A literary reign of terror is being attempted. Where will it end?[33]

Such appeals were in part answered by an alternative publishing network, circulating around a number of literary journals and Modernist little magazines which were vociferous in their condemnation of purity interventions in literary experimentation, including Frank Harris' *Pearson's Weekly*, H. L. Mencken's *Smart Set, The Era, The Little Review* and *The Egoist*.[34] These journals and the publishing enterprises connected with them sought to circumvent social purity's stranglehold upon a cautiously self-regulating mainstream press by issuing those 'outspoken works of art' and thus defying social purity's 'literary reign of terror'.

In this climate of purity censorship and avant-garde dissidence, Joyce's sexually radical writings were of particular significance. Contemporary reviews, whether squeamish or celebratory, bore witness. *Vanity Fair* reminded readers that *A Portrait*, 'perhaps not a book for *la jeune fille*', was 'refused by publisher after publisher in London, ostensibly because of the frankness with which certain episodes were treated'; yet suggested it

[29] George Moore, 'The New Censorship of Literature', *New York Herald*, 28 July 1889, 5.

[30] Modern dictionaries still define the word in terms of its opposition to art and culture. *The American College Dictionary* (1963) gives us 'overzealous censorship of the fine arts and literature, often mistaking outspokenly honest works for salacious ones', *The American Heritage Dictionary* (1975) as 'overzealous censorship of literature and the other arts because of alleged immorality'. Cited in Kendrick, *The Secret Museum*, 147; George Bernard Shaw, 'Shaw to Comstock: You Can't Scare Me', *New York Times*, 27 October 1905, 559.

[31] John Galsworthy, 'Library Censorship', *The Times*, 3 October 1913, 9.

[32] Ezra Pound, 'The Dreiser Protest', *The Egoist*, October 1916, 159.

[33] Richard Lingerman, *Theodore Dreiser*, II: *An American Journey* (New York: Puttnam, 1990), 135.

[34] De Grazia, *Girls Lean Back*, 122.

was 'bracing, hard and clean' in comparison to 'such a soft and false and dangerous book as H. G. Wells' *Ann Veronica*'.[35] *Ulysses* attracted similar comparisons with infamous authors: 'Compared with Joyce, Zola is respectable and George Moore merely mincing', '*Ulysses* would have been boycotted in the palmiest days of Holywell Street'.[36] Other reviewers interpreted the novel as a significant assault on censorship. For *The New Age*, *Ulysses*' suppression demonstrated 'the apprehension expressed in Mr Ezra Pound's *bon mot* that the USA should be renamed the YMCA...Not a flower will grow upon the soil of Comstock'.[37] *The Chicago Tribune* concurred, warning that a writer 'hailed a genius by several of our very capable cognoscenti' had 'generally been condemned, both in Great Britain and the United States, by that highly moral yet unperceiving element of Comstockery that reigns with an iron hand'.[38] As one commentator later put it, the 1934 Woolsey decision constituted 'a victory dance over the graves of Bowdler, Anthony Comstock and Mrs Grundy'.[39] The alacrity with which Joyce and his fiction was conscripted into Modernism's war on social purity was unsurprising since Joyce's own experience of publication closely corresponded to the sequential pattern outlined above of social purity pressure, commercial auto-censorship and Modernist reactive protest. To rehearse Joyce's troubled publication history is to unravel a sequence of negotiations with the literary climate the purists were determined to enforce.

II

Joyce's earliest forays into print fell victim to anxieties about the perceived sexual impropriety of his writing. His 1901 student essay 'The Day of The Rabblement' was omitted from *St Stephen's Magazine* for its discussion of D'Annunzio's novel *Il Fuoco* (1900), which had been placed on the Vatican's Index of Prohibited Books and was simultaneously vigorously pursued by

[35] John Quinn, 'James Joyce, A New Irish Novelist', *Vanity Fair* 8: 3 (May 1917), 48, 128. See also *The Athenaeum's* comparison of Joyce with the banned George Moore and Zola (20 June 1914), or *The Irish Book Lover's* protest that 'no clean-minded person could possibly allow it to remain within reach of his wife, his sons or daughters' (*The Irish Book Lover*, April–May 1917, 113).

[36] Holbrook Jackson, '*Ulysses* à la Joyce', *To-Day* 9 (June 1922), 47–9; 'Aramis', 'The Scandal of *Ulysses*', *The Sporting Times*, no. 34, 1 April 1922, 4. Holywell Street in London gained mid-Victorian notoriety for its bookshops selling clandestine pornography. It was the target of a Society for the Suppression of Vice clean up, and dwindled after the passage of the Obscene Publications Act 1857. See Bristow, *Vice and Vigilance*, 47–50.

[37] 'R.H.C.', 'Readers and Writers', *The New Age*, 28 April 1921, 89.

[38] *Chicago Tribune* (European edition), 13 February 1922, 2.

[39] Ben Ray Redman, 'Obscenity and Censorship', *Scribner's Magazine*, May 1934, 344.

social purists in Britain.[40] Submitting stories to *The Irish Homestead* in 1904, Joyce was advised by the literary editor George Russell to stick to material which would not 'shock the readers' (*L* II: 43); nonetheless versions of the first three *Dubliners* stories prompted 'many letters of complaint from readers in both the country and the city' and the series to be abruptly terminated.[41] Yet Joyce's first explicit statement of hostility towards the sexual politics of social purity can be traced in letters written during October and September 1906. Curiously enough, the immediate impetus for Joyce's wrath was that most unlikely moral zealot, Oliver StJohn Gogarty, Joyce's one-time whoring companion and the prototype for Buck Mulligan, who ventriloquized purity rhetoric in a series of articles in Arthur Griffith's journal *Sinn Féin*:

It is this English monster that demands and supports whatever indecencies Paris can produce. He has published a book – too sordid and too lost to see his own hypocrisy – wherein are statistics to prove, if proof be needed, that his own army is rottener and more immoral than any or all the armies in Europe put together . . . The Army [is] a body of men who, as their own statistics show, are already more than half-leprous from venereal excess.[42]

Joyce, reading copies of the paper sent to him in Rome by his brother Stanislaus, found this too much to bear:

I wish some unkind person would publish a book about the venereal condition of the Irish; since they pride themselves so much on their immunity. It must be rather worse than England, I think. I know very little of the subject but it seems to me to be a disease like any other disease, caused by anti-hygienic conditions. I don't see where the judgement of God comes into it nor do I see what the word 'excess' means in this connection. Perhaps Gogarty has some meaning of his own for this word. I would prefer the unscientific expression 'venereal ill-luck'. Am I the only honest person to have come out of Ireland in our time? How dusty their phrases are! (*L* II: 170–1)

Significantly, Joyce swiftly digresses from Gogarty's contentious theorisation of a fundamental distinction between English and Irish sexual conduct

---

[40] J. R. Woodhouse, 'Victorian Verecundity: D'Annunzio's Prudish Public', in *Moving in Measure: Essays in Honour of Brian Moloney*, ed. Judith Bryce and Douglas Thompson (Hull: Hull University Press, 1989), 107–21.

[41] Richard Ellmann, *James Joyce* (Oxford: Oxford University Press, 1983), 165.

[42] Oliver StJohn Gogarty, 'Ugly England I', *Sinn Féin*, 15 September 1906, 3. Gogarty was following Griffith's lead, since earlier that year the editor had enlivened his campaign against the recruitment of Irish soldiers into the British Army by disclosing an Army Blue Book report into the sexual health of troops stationed in Dublin. Observing that the report showed that 'more that one half of the British Army are annually treated for the foulest of diseases', Griffith urged 'Irishmen of clean bodies and clean minds' to refuse to enlist, since 'three fourths of them return from that army moral degenerates' (Arthur Griffith, 'The British Army', *Sinn Féin*, 7 July 1906, 2).

to focus instead upon his inflection of social purity rhetoric to suit *Sinn Féin's* agenda. Furthermore, Joyce's frustration is not merely passive irritation at purity discourse, a personal protest against a friend's hypocrisy he intends to confine to the private domain of a letter to a favourite brother. A month later, appalled that 'they are still at the venereal excess cry in *Sinn Féin*', a second letter sets out plans for 'my novel' as a blunt response to such 'lying drivel about pure men and pure women and spiritual love and love for ever: blatant lying in the face of the truth' (*L* II: 191–2). On the threshhold of his literary career, Joyce was self-consciously imagining his fiction as an articulate, 'honest' and creative rebuttal of social purity pieties.

It is surely no coincidence, then, that Joyce fumed over Gogarty's diatribe against 'venereal excess' in the immediate aftermath of the collapse of precarious negotiations to bring out *Dubliners* through the London publisher Grant Richards. For Richards had provisionally accepted the manuscript of *Dubliners* on 17 February 1906, but soon regretted that acceptance, writing on 1 May to explain that his printer had refused to set 'Two Gallants', and was furthermore insisting that questionable allusions in 'Counterparts' and 'Grace' be omitted:

I told you what the printer had said not because I cared about his opinion as his opinion, or cared a bit about his scruples, but because if a printer takes that view you can be quite sure that the booksellers will take it, that the libraries will take it, and that an inconveniently large section of the general public will take it. You told me frankly that you look to your future being helped by your literary work. The best way of retarding that result will most certainly be to persist in the publishing of stories which – I speak commercially not artistically – will get you a name for doing work which most people will regret.[43]

Later that month, Richards wrote again to add 'On consideration I should *like* to leave out altogether "The Encounter" [*sic*]', since his recent bankruptcy and struggle to re-establish his business in his wife's name made his firm 'peculiarly liable to attack'.[44] Joyce's response was vehement, naïve and oddly prescient: 'You will not be prosecuted for publishing it. The worst that will happen, I suppose, is that some critic will allude to me as "The Irish Zola"!' (*L* II: 137) He continued

Critics (I think) are fonder of attacking writers than publishers; and I assure you their attacks on me would in no way hasten my death. Moreover, from the point of view of financial success it seems to me more than probable that an attack, even a fierce and organised attack, on the book by the press would have the effect

[43] Robert Scholes, 'Grant Richards to James Joyce', *Studies in Bibliography* 16 (1963), 145.
[44] *Ibid.*, 147.

of interesting the public in it to much better purpose that the tired chorus of imprimaturs with which the critical body greets the appearance of every book which is not dangerous to faith or morals. (*L* I: 62)

Joyce's flippant hopes of financial success from notoriety display his ignorance of the specific pressures placed upon publishers and printers. Richards, however, knew too well how a successful vice society prosecution might lead to punitive fines, imprisonment and a second bankruptcy. On 19 June and again on the 26th he wrote to Joyce emphasising the danger: 'look inside any book where you will find a printer's imprint. This is necessary. If a book is attacked as indecent the printer suffers also from the attack; and if it is sufficiently indecent he also is prosecuted.'[45] By the end of September, Richards was in retreat, recommending 'some other publisher less timid than this house, for instance Mr John Long'; a more established firm with the financial stability to take the risk.[46] Few publishers, as Joyce would learn, were 'less timid', since all were inconveniently alert to the perils of prosecution.

This early lesson in the very real threat social purists posed to publishers and printers was repeated in August 1909 when Joyce signed a contract with George Roberts to bring the collection out in Dublin through Maunsel and Co.[47] After three years procrastination, it seemed that plans to publish *Dubliners* had been shelved, and Roberts' colleague Joseph Hone later suggested that Lady Aberdeen, the president of the National Vigilance Association and one of the firm's most valued clients, had insisted that *Dubliners* be quietly dropped.[48] In an attempt to break the deadlock, on 20 August 1912 Joyce's solicitor John Lidwell was requested to write a letter assessing 'whether certain paragraphs...are of such a character as would leave the Author and Printer and Publisher liable to a criminal prosecution' (*L* II: 306). Lidwell's letter, however, advised him to 'either delete or entirely alter the paragraphs in question', since 'there is at present in existence in this city a Vigilance Committee whose object is to seek out and suppress all writings of immoral tendencies' (*L* II: 306), a response which provoked Joyce 'to think on the subject all night' (*L* II: 304). This assessment was particularly devastating since Roberts was on the hunt for further evidence of potential obscenity:

---

45 *Ibid.*, 149–50.   46 *Ibid.*, 151.   47 Ellmann, *James Joyce*, 289.

48 'As I look back, it occurs to me that the firm's hesitation . . . may have been due to a desire not to prejudice itself with Lady Aberdeen, the then Lord Lieutenant's wife, by whom it had been commissioned to publish tracts relative to her anti-tuberculosis campaign', Joseph Hone, 'Recollections of James Joyce', *Envoy* 5 (April 1951), 44. This was a charge denied by Roberts, yet clearly believed by Joyce, as his complaint to Carlo Linati cited earlier demonstrates: 'some say it was the doing of priests, some of enemies, some of the then Viceroy or his consort, Countess Aberdeen' (*L* I: 132).

He asked me very narrowly was there sodomy also in *The Sisters* and what was 'simony' and if the priest was suspended only for the breaking of the chalice. He asked me also was there more in *The Dead* than appeared. (*L* II: 305–6)

Suppressing this first letter, Joyce visited Lidwell again and extorted a second, which blandly stated 'As the passages you have shown me are not likely to be taken serious notice of by the Advisors of the Crown, they would not interfere with the publication, nor do I consider a conviction could be easily obtained' (*L* II: 309). This did not convince Roberts, and cannot have reassured Joyce, since on 21 August he promised 'to close with your proposal' (*L* II: 309) in omitting 'An Encounter' entirely from the collection. Roberts, however, was obdurate, driving Joyce to arrange to purchase the sheets directly from Roberts' printer, John Falconer, and to publish the first edition of a thousand copies privately under the imprint of 'The Liffey Press'. Yet Falconer refused to give up the sheets, unconvinced by Joyce's protests that his scheme would leave the printer 'free from all responsibility in the matter' (*L* II: 319), and they were destroyed, in Joyce's account by symbolic fire, in Roberts' by the more prosaic guillotine. Joyce's satirical broadside 'Gas from a Burner' bore witness to the baneful influence of purity pressure in its initial title, 'Mr Falconer Addresses the Vigilance Committee' (*JJA* I: 287). For a second time, the publication of *Dubliners* had been halted by the unspoken yet potent threat of social purity retribution.

Social purity thus appears as a silent presence on the margins of each of Joyce's abortive attempts to publish *Dubliners*. These drawn-out difficulties demonstrate how the sexual suggestiveness of Joyce's work made it too high a risk for commercial publishers, and accordingly *A Portrait of the Artist as a Young Man* and *Ulysses* would issue from presses which, like Joyce's own proposed 'Liffey Press', were peripheral to the mainstream publishing industry and dedicated to evading the strictures imposed by 'comstockery'. These were the little magazines and hastily assembled private publishing houses of avant-garde Modernism, and their interest in Joyce was initially piqued by his open letter on the *Dubliners* travails, 'A Curious History', which appeared in January 1914 in place of Ezra Pound's usual column on the arts in *The Egoist*. Joyce, as yet unpublished and unknown, was announced as a victim of an interminable and familiar censorship, and consequently, the year Richard Ellmann has described as Joyce's 'annus mirabilis' saw both Grant Richards' belated publication of *Dubliners* and *The Egoist*'s serialisation of *A Portrait of the Artist as a Young Man*. Predictable difficulties, however, soon beset the new serial story. Printer after printer declined to set Joyce's 'indecent' passages, and a bowdlerised version eventually concluded in September 1915. To issue the novel as an unexpurgated book was the next challenge and, after seven rejections from established publishers, the journal's editor, Harriet Shaw Weaver, undertook to release it under a new imprint, *The Egoist Limited*.[49] After six months fruitless hunting for a co-operative printer, Pound's desperate suggestion that 'largish blank spaces be left where passages are cut out', allowing him to 'if necessary paste [the excisions] in myself. And damn the censors' was seriously contemplated.[50] The forthcoming novel was announced in the editorial page of *The Egoist*, where Weaver noted that 'to penetrate with cool analysis and innocent of suggestiveness' into sexual matters is to 'raise a hullabaloo which brings police and pale swarms of terrified protectors of orthodox Morality rushing to the spot':

Had Mr Joyce consented to bow to the taste of publishers' 'readers' and alter or delete certain words and phrases and re-write certain sections in order to bring his work a little nearer the popular level, it would have been published 'through the trade'. But Mr Joyce refused to comply with these requirements, with the result that no publisher would touch the book. Accordingly, we decided to publish it ourselves. Even so the same difficulties cropped up again, and the printer declined to print except subject to certain excisions. Happily, a printer has now been found* who is willing to print without deletions, and it is hoped that Mr Joyce's work will at last, and without further difficulties, see the light of publication in the shape which he conceived it to take.[51]

Weaver's narrative of triumph over adversity, however, had a sting in the tale which seems more artful than inadvertent. A small asterisk alerted readers to a footnote:

* Since the above was written we are informed that, on reflection and on the same grounds as other printers, the printer here referred to declines to print. We shall not, however, relax our efforts in the matter-Ed.

The very announcement of *A Portrait*'s debut was thus shaped into a highly political narrative of conflict, defeat and defiance. When Weaver finally managed to circumvent recalcitrant English printers by importing the sheets from New York, Pound triumphantly wrote 'James Joyce – At Last the Novel Appears', reminding readers that success came 'despite the jobbing of bigots and of their sectarian publishing houses'.[52] *The Egoist* drew readers into the

---

[49] *A Portrait* was turned down by Grant Richards, Duckworth, John Lane, T. Werner Laurie, the Yale University Press, John Marshall and William Heinemann. See Lidderdale and Nicholson, *Dear Miss Weaver*, 102–22.

[50] *Ibid.*, 122.   [51] 'H.S.W', 'Editorial', *The Egoist*, 1 March 1916, 34–5.

[52] Ezra Pound, 'James Joyce – At Last the Novel Appears', *The Egoist*, February 1917, 21.

drama of that defiance, transforming the publication of *A Portrait* into a symbolic act of cultural rebellion.

Theatricality similarly characterised the next instalment in the adventure of issuing Joyce through Modernism's peripheral and precarious minor presses. When plans arose to serialise *Ulysses* simultaneously in New York through *The Little Review* and in London through *The Egoist*, the melodrama of publication became still more intense. Monthly bulletins in *The Egoist* updated readers:

A new novel by Mr James Joyce, *Ulysses*, will start in the March issue. Mr Joyce's new novel *Ulysses* has been unavoidably postponed owing to unexpected difficulties in regard to the printing.

As our efforts to find a British printer willing to print the complete text of Mr Joyce's new novel *Ulysses* have been unsuccessful, we regretfully abandon the proposal to bring that work out as a separately printed supplement.

As printing difficulties have made it impossible to publish *Ulysses* in full in serial form, a series of extracts from it will be printed in *The Egoist* during the next few months.[53]

Meanwhile in New York, *Little Review* editors Margaret Anderson and Jane Heap were similarly flamboyant in their response to the encroaching threat of the New York Society for the Suppression of Vice, which was implementing its federal powers to prevent the transmission of 'obscenity' through the mails. The bravado of a magazine determined to 'enjoy that untrammelled liberty which is the life of Art' and subtitled 'A Magazine of the Arts – Making No Compromise With The Public Taste' was clear.[54] Here, for instance, is Anderson's apology for bowdlerising part of the 'Scylla and Charybdis' episode in May 1919:

The Post Office objected to certain passages in the January instalment of *Ulysses*, which prevents our mailing any more copies of that issue. To avoid similar interference, I have ruined Mr Joyce's story by cutting certain passages in which he mentions certain natural facts known to everyone.[55]

This typical editorial declaration of endurance under attrition was sustained throughout the magazine's travails with the vigilantes. Such statements insist that *Ulysses* was not only, as Anderson put it, 'the most beautiful thing we'll ever have': its publication was an integral aspect of high Modernism's public fight against social purity. Joyce's fiction, sexually pungent, certainly,

[53] 'Announcements', *The Egoist*, January 1918, 15; 'Announcements', *The Egoist*, March 1918, 47; 'Notices', *The Egoist*, November–December 1918, 139; 'Episode Two of Mr Joyce's *Ulysses*', *The Egoist*, January–February 1919, 11.
[54] *The Little Review* 1: 1 (March 1914), 2; *The Little Review* 5: 9 (January 1919), 1.
[55] *The Little Review* 6: 1 (May 1919), 21.

yet also the product of 'an intelligence abnormally acute and observant, an accomplished literary craftsman who sets down no phrase or line without its meaning for the creation as a whole' was the ideal focus for the avant-garde crusade.[56] To read these exhilarated, often passionate, invariably defiant bulletins from Modernism's little magazines is to participate in a heady atmosphere of anticipation, frustration, triumph, disappointment and, above all, ideological mission. Social purity's heavy-handed opposition evidently added a certain piquancy to the adventure of publication, and this struggle with the vigilantes helped to determine both the reception and, we will see, the shape of Joyce's writing.

III

What precisely was this formidable opponent, and how did it gain its influence over the social and cultural life of the early twentieth century? The social purity movement was far more complicated and diverse than the necessarily brief and partial picture given above would suggest. A glimpse of this diversity can be given by simply listing some of the many organisations classed as social purist; the National Vigilance Association, the Social Purity Alliance, the Gospel Purity Association, the White Cross League, the Moral Reform Union, the Ladies' National Association, the Church of England Purity Society, the Women's Christian Temperance Union, the Young Men's Christian Association, the New York Society for the Suppression of Vice, the Boston Watch and Ward Society, the Chicago Vice Commission, the Travellers' Aid Society, the National Council for Public Morals, the American Purity Alliance, the Jewish Association for the Protection of Girls and Women, the Leeds Rational Recreation Society, the Dublin White Cross Vigilance Association, the American Federation for Sex Hygiene, the British Social Hygiene Council. From this tangle can be discerned a network of distinct and even competing allegiances. Some organisations stress national identity in their titles, ('National', 'American', 'British'), others emphasise a more local focus ('New York', 'Boston', 'Chicago', 'Leeds', 'Dublin'). Some stress repression ('The New York Society for the Suppression of Vice', 'The National Vigilance Association'); others use the language of consensus and aspiration to suggest a more positive approach ('The American Federation for Sex Hygiene', 'The National Council for Public Morals'). Several state a religious allegiance ('Church of England', 'Jewish Association', 'Gospel Purity', 'Women's Christian Temperance

[56] 'Notice to Readers', *The Egoist*, December 1919, 70.

Union', 'Young Men's Christian Association'). Some are explicitly female in their membership and, by implication, feminist in their sexual politics ('The Ladies National Association', 'The Women's Christian Temperance Union'); others imply their attitude to women is more conservative ('Jewish Association for the Protection of Girls and Women'). Some declare their focus upon specific aspects of moral regulation; travelling, or 'rational recreation'. The range of foci suggested in these names offers a snapshot of the variety of different organisations sheltering under the umbrella of 'social purity'. As we will see, the movement was more potent and significant than its historically occluded and frequently trivialised status as a collection of belated Victorian 'prudes on the prowl' suggests.[57]

This study will focus in the main upon one particular branch of this diverse and international social purity movement; the evangelical Protestant strain which dominated the United Kingdom under the principal direction of the National Vigilance Association. This was the branch active in Dublin during Joyce's adolescence and young manhood; it helped to shape the sexual context of Joyce's fiction. At first glance, my central hypothesis that Joyce's writing is provocatively engaged with a Protestant evangelical social purity campaign which threatened his chances of publication might seem suspiciously counter-intuitive. For, as other scholars have abundantly shown, the regulation of sexuality in Joyce's fiction is, time and again, the province of the Irish Catholic Church.[58] Priests, from the priest who helps to bully Bob Doran into marriage in 'The Boarding House', to the Father Corrigan who elicits from the adolescent Molly Bloom the information that her lover touched her 'on the canal bank' (*U* 18: 108) are the ubiquitous policemen of sex, and confession is their chief instrument of moral discipline. The persistence with which Joyce connects the church with the disciplining of sex is predictable enough in the context of the post-Famine 'Devotional Revolution', where the church sought to inhibit a boisterous popular sexual culture most blatantly manifest at wakes, patterns and fairs.[59] However, whilst it is not possible to marginalise the indisputable role of Catholicism

---

[57] *The Daily Telegraph* and *Punch* ran a satirical series, 'Prudes on the Prowl' during 1894, attacking the National Vigilance Association and, in particular, their secretary, Laura Chant, who had closed down the Empire music-hall theatre, a notorious rendezvous for prostitutes and their clients. See Lucy Bland, *Banishing the Beast: English Feminism and Sexual Morality 1885–1914* (London: Penguin, 1995), 95, 105–8.

[58] See Robert Boyle, SJ, *James Joyce's Pauline Vision: A Catholic Exposition* (Carbondale and Edwardsville: Southern Illinois Press, 1978); Mary Lowe-Evans, 'Sex and Confession in the Joyce Canon: Some Historical Parallels', *Journal of Modern Literature* 16: 4 (Spring 1990), 563–76; Mary Lowe-Evans, *Crimes Against Fecundity: James Joyce and Population Control* (Syracuse: Syracuse University Press, 1989).

[59] Sean O Súilleabháin, *Irish Wake Amusements* (Cork: Mercier Press, 1967), 23–45.

in Joyce's portrait of sexuality, it must also be emphasised that there are two distinct forms of moral regulation at work in Joyce's Dublin. The first is confined to the spiritual sphere of pulpit and confessional, and is tirelessly carried out by the Catholic church. The second, though, is both more secular and more public, utilising far more socially pervasive techniques such as street patrols, agitation for legislation, confiscation and prosecution. This additional strand of moral policing was carried out by social purists and, whilst Joyce, declaring 'non serviam', attempted to secede from the former, he found the latter resolute and inescapable.

This division between private spiritual Catholic and public secular Protestant sexual regulation is founded upon an intriguing anomaly. Surprisingly, there was no home-grown Catholic version of the English Protestant social purity project flourishing in Ireland prior to Joyce's departure in 1904. In 1902, for instance, the anti-Catholic polemicist Michael McCarthy protested that Dublin's blatant red-light area notably lacked a Catholic purity patrol, although 'nearly nine tenths of the denizens of this region are Catholics and the region itself is in the parish of the Pro-Cathedral', Catholic Dublin's principal place of worship. Furthermore, the Catholic clergy 'refused to co-operate in any movement to reclaim the area' with the Dublin White Cross Vigilance Association, the British National Vigilance Association's local branch, who had set up midnight patrols and a drop-in centre to evangelise the prostitutes.[60] McCarthy's blatant sectarianism was, in this case, substantiated since curiously, despite a predictable overlap between Catholic discourse on sexual morality and social purity ideology, there were no Catholic-sponsored attempts at direct action until as late as 1911. 'Catholic and non-political in programme and membership' and 'dedicated to preserving the high traditional moral standard of the Irish people', the Irish Vigilance Association was founded in that year, yet remained dwarfed in both size and political influence by its Protestant counterpart until the foundation of the Free State in 1922.[61] Only then, together with the Legion of Mary, did it successfully close down the red-light area and begin to oversee censorship as part of the new state's Committee on Evil Literature.[62]

[60] Michael McCarthy, *Priests and People in Ireland* (London: Hodder and Stoughton, 1908), 285–7. Nationalist opposition to the Dublin White Cross Vigilance Association will be discussed below in chapter 2.

[61] Irish Vigilance Association, *Constitution* (Dublin: Brindley and Son, n.d.). I am extremely grateful to Maria Luddy for providing me with a photocopy of this rare publication.

[62] In February 1923, Frank Duff eventually responded to Michael McCarthy's complaint two decades earlier that the Catholic church in Dublin, in particular the Pro-Cathedral parish, did nothing to ameliorate the moral condition of Monto, the red-light district of Dublin in the north-east of the

The Irish Catholic purity movement was, then, oddly belated, and its reticence seems inextricably tied up with the character of the state. Only when a Catholic Free State was established did a Catholic purity movement thrive in Ireland; conversely, before 1922, purity work was in the main carried out by a Protestant evangelical satellite of a British organisation. This intimate relationship between the state and social purity in Ireland is consonant with social purity's increasingly vocal demands for state interventions into the traditionally designated 'private' sphere of sexual morality. For, as Frank Mort and others have explored, social purity's 'emphasis upon using the state to promote morality marked an important shift away from the traditional [mid-Victorian] strategies of private philanthropy and rescue work'.[63] A reliance upon Parliament, political lobbying and the law is summarised in the National Vigilance Association's insistence that 'the law is schoolmaster to the whole community, preventing wrong by whipping most of the citizens into a condition of obedience'.[64] As Jeffrey Weeks further notes, social purity thus challenged the widespread late-Victorian assumption that 'the function of the state, local and national, was to regulate the public sphere and not the private'.[65] In pre-Free State Ireland, therefore, where social purity was a predominately evangelical Protestant movement, imported from England and presided over by the Viceregents Aberdeen, social purity could readily be construed as another branch of that intrusive state presence Joyce so eloquently documents. In other words, that policing of the public sphere by the British state so evident on the streets of Joyce's Dublin, which swarm with policemen in uniform and in plain clothes, their informers, the military and other service personnel, is extended by social purists into the occluded private sphere of sexuality. The Englishness of social purity in an Ireland Joyce so shrewdly designated 'semicolonial' (*FW* 152: 16) is a crucial aspect of his subversion.[66]

city. Duff founded the Legion of Mary, and, following the example set by the Dublin White Cross Vigilance Association, patrolled the area with a small band of followers, picketing brothels and placing prostitutes in rescue homes. Within six months, Monto was cleared. For an account of the Legion's work with prostitutes, see Joseph O'Brien, *Dear, Dirty Dublin: A City In Distress 1899–1916* (London: University of California Press, 1982), 23–6. For a detailed exploration of post-1921 purity initiatives, see Philip Howell, 'Venereal Disease and the Politics of Prostitution in the Irish Free State', forthcoming in *Irish Historical Studies*. I am indebted to Dr Howell for allowing me advance access to this important essay.

[63] Frank Mort, 'Purity, Feminism and the State', in *Crises in the British State*, ed. M. Langan and B. Schwartz (London: Hutchinson, 1985), 209.

[64] William Coote, 'Law and Morality', in *Public Morals*, ed. James Marchant (London: Morgan and Scott, 1902), 45–6, 69–70.

[65] Jeffrey Weeks, *Sex, Politics and Society* (London: Longman, 1981), 83.

[66] For a selection of essays on the 'semicolonial' aspects of Joyce's work, see *Semicolonial Joyce*, ed. Derek Attridge and Marjorie Howes (Cambridge: Cambridge University Press, 2000).

It is, therefore, the British branch of the social purity movement, imported into Ireland through satellite groups working in close alliance with parent organisations in England, which formed part of the cultural landscape of Joyce's Dublin. This British social purity movement originated from Josephine Butler's campaign to defend the civil liberties of prostitute women in the early 1870s.[67] Butler founded her Ladies National Association to campaign for the repeal of the several Contagious Diseases Acts of the 1860s and 70s, Acts which provided for the fortnightly gynaecological inspection of women deemed 'known prostitutes', who were confined in 'lock hospitals' if they were found to be infected with a sexually transmitted disease. The Acts were supported by most medics, the military authorities and the majority of politicians, who hoped to protect soldiers, sailors and eventually the general male population from infection. They were, however, strenuously opposed by Josephine Butler and her feminist libertarian allies, who were outraged at the way the legislation clarified the meaning of the double standard whilst, as Judith Walkowitz has shown, creating an 'outcast group' of 'inscribed' women.[68] The repeal movement produced over a thousand public meetings in protest against the state sanctioning of 'vice', the intimidation of prostitutes and the injustice, hypocrisy and medical inefficacy of examining prostitute women yet not their clients.[69] To defeat the Acts, Butler's feminist libertarians allied themselves with two popular constituencies, firstly 'the more educated artisans, clerks, warehousemen and tradesmen who study politics and are honest devotees of justice to all classes and races', and secondly 'those with whom religion takes the lead, and with whom virtue and the law of God are the paramount interest'.[70] This broad coalition allied feminists with other late-Victorian pressure groups – the Quakers and Methodists of the 'nonconformist conscience', some Anglican clergy, evangelicals, the Salvation Army, Chartists and trade unionists, and the 50,000 members of the Working Men's National League.[71] Butler's

---

[67] There are several accounts of the transition from the repeal movement to social purity. See the chapter 'Against the Double Standard: From the Contagious Diseases Acts to White Slavery', in Bristow, *Vice and Vigilance*, 75–93; chapter 3, 'Purifying the Public World', in Bland, *Banishing the Beast*, 95–123.

[68] Judith R. Walkowitz, *Prostitution and Victorian Society: Women, Class and the State* (Cambridge: Cambridge University Press, 1980), 76–8, 128.

[69] *Ibid.*, 104.

[70] First Annual Report of the Ladies National Association, quoted in Walkowitz, *Prostitution*, 94.

[71] *Ibid.* The class politics of the social purity campaigns have provoked much contention, since the diversity of the movement itself invites a range of contradictory readings. For Frank Mort, notwithstanding Butler's initial appeal to 'working men', subsequent British purity movements were 'shot through with class divisions', since 'purists could be utterly ruthless about the menace working-class immorality posed to the middle-class home', *Dangerous Sexualities: Medico-Moral*

religious zeal, personal charisma, feminism and class rhetoric that prostitution was the consequence of dissolute aristocrats violating the 'daughters of the poor' managed to sustain this uneasy alliance.[72] The repeal movement's constituency, its insistence that male sexual morality be raised to the standard expected of women and its progressive demands to break the 'conspiracy of silence' protecting sexual misconduct and hypocrisy from disclosure would be carried forth into the social purity movement it spawned.

The moment of transition from the radical, anti-state sexual politics espoused by Butler and her colleagues, and the more conservative and regulationist ideologies of the mainstream social purity movement is difficult to discern. Whilst not the subject of this study, it might be loosely located at some point between the suspension of the Contagious Diseases Acts in 1883 and the passage in 1885 of the Criminal Law Amendment Act, social purity's first legislative triumph.[73] In league with the Salvation Army, Butler's band of repealers had for some years attempted to propel such a statute through Parliament in an attempt to raise the female age of consent from twelve to sixteen or eighteen, thus criminalising men who had sex with juvenile prostitutes, rather than the prostitutes themselves.[74] Their eventual success in 1885 was largely impelled by W. T. Stead, the flamboyant crusading editor of *The Pall Mall Gazette*. To support Butler's campaign, Stead published 'The Maiden Tribute of Modern Babylon' in early July that year, a series of articles sensationally exposing child prostitution in London.[75] His revelations provoked riots outside *The Pall Mall Gazette* offices, a mass demonstration in Hyde Park and a petition to Parliament bearing over 400,000 signatures.[76] The Criminal Law Amendment Act was passed within three months, with additional repressive clauses relating to brothel keepers, pimps, the act of soliciting, and, notoriously, the Labouchere Amendment prohibiting any sexual contact between men. With the considerable profits from 'The Maiden Tribute's' immense sales, Stead founded the National Vigilance

---

Politics in England since 1830 (London: Routledge and Kegan Paul, 1987), 124. Mort's thesis that the urban lower classes were 'the real target of purity action' is significantly qualified by Nicola Beisel and Alan Hunt, who both insist that, whilst working-class sexual disorder was certainly one target of vigilance activity, the primary thrust of both the British and United States campaigns was 'directed at fostering the self-regulation of the respectable classes' and thereby ensuring the reproduction of bourgeois values and status in the next generation. See Hunt, *Governing Morals*, 98; Nicola Beisel, *Imperilled Innocents: Anthony Comstock and Family Reproduction in Victorian America* (Princeton: Princeton University Press, 1997), 9.

[72] Walkowitz, *Prostitution*, 141–3.   [73] For such a study, see Bland, *Banishing the Beast*, 95–122.
[74] Bristow, *Vice and Vigilance*: 89–91.
[75] An excellent account of the 'Maiden Tribute' controversy, and its wideranging cultural significance, is given in chapters 3 and 4 of Judith R. Walkowitz, *City of Dreadful Delight: Narratives of Sexual Danger in Late-Victorian London* (London: Virago, 1998), 81–135.
[76] *Ibid.*, 104. Bristow, *Vice and Vigilance*, 89–91.

Association, Britain and Ireland's most powerful social purity league.[77] Its initial purpose was to ensure the enforcement of the new law, but its many branches would also disseminate propaganda, collect evidence for the police, initiate private prosecutions, attack 'pernicious literature' and campaign vociferously for further legislation.[78]

The National Vigilance Association, ably supported by a number of affiliated purity leagues, immediately set in motion a variety of campaigns to mobilise the 'calm steady voice of righteous public opinion'.[79] Firstly, the rising generation were to be educated to resist temptation, since if boys were taught 'self-control' and girls warned of the dangers of extra-marital sex, the social evils of illegitimate birth, prostitution and sexually transmitted disease might be tackled at source. Best-selling sex education manuals such as *Damaged Pearls* for girls and *True Manliness* for boys reached print runs of several million copies, and adolescents were energetically recruited for a variety of chastity leagues. Secondly, and more coercively, other morality statutes would follow the 1885 Criminal Law Amendment Act. These included the 1889 Indecent Advertisements Act, prohibiting the promotion of contraceptives and remedies for sexually transmitted diseases, the 1898 Vagrancy Act, tightening the penalties for streetwalking and living off immoral earnings, the 1908 Incest Act, and the 1912 Criminal Law Amendment Act against 'white slavery'. The scope of this legislation gives a broad indication of the scale and diversity of the purity project. In the drive to 'chain the devil of impurity by fear of law', vigilantes combined propaganda and legislation to fight against the rising tide of modern 'demoralisation'.[80]

Potential demoralisation was to be found in a broad range of cultural phenomena, from 'serious literature' to smutty postcards. Some social purists set up 'midnight missions' to survey and police red-light zones by infiltrating brothels and accosting streetwalkers. Others campaigned against the music-halls, designated 'highways of ruin to the young, licensed opportunities for the vicious'.[81] As the purists were swift to discover, contemporary culture

---

[77] *Ibid.*, 116–17.

[78] Butler, although a nominal member, was disquieted by the new Association's emphasis upon the repression of brothels, and soon resigned her membership, complaining 'Beware of Purity Societies, ready to accept and endorse any amount of inequity in the laws, any amount of coercive and degrading treatment of their fellow creatures in the fatuous belief that you can oblige human beings to be moral by force and in so doing promote social purity.' Quoted in Bland, *Banishing the Beast*, 100. William Coote, the chairman of the National Vigilance Association, was ironically one of Butler's disciples from the Working Men's League, persuaded to focus on social purity by Butler's powers of oratory. However, she did not return the admiration: 'Coote is most unsound . . . Coote loves coercion'. See Bristow, *Vice and Vigilance*, 117.

[79] Laura Chant, *Why We Attacked the Empire* (London: Horace Marshall and Son, 1895), 5.

[80] Coote, 'Law and Morality', 69.

[81] Laura Chant, 'Music Hall Vice', *Woman's Signal*, 1 November 1894, 5.

was riddled with such highways and opportunities. The National Vigilance Association campaigned for legislation prohibiting the reporting of details in divorce trials, a staple form of titillation for readers of *The News Of The World* or *The Illustrated Police Gazette*.[82] It lobbied Parliament to prohibit 'demoralising' mutoscopes, a peepshow precursor of cinema notorious for its 'racy' flickercards showing undressing women.[83] The *fin-de-siècle* fashion for *tableaux vivants*, or 'living pictures', posed tableaux of 'classical' subjects usually accomplished by actors in flesh-tights, similarly prompted protest, whilst adverts for 'rubber goods', contraceptive advice, 'female pills' promising to induce 'late' menstruation, or cures for syphilis were vigorously monitored in popular journals.[84] Titillating men's magazines such as *Photo-Bits*, *Bits of Fun* or *Illustrated Bits*, precursors of modern photography magazines with their images of young women in 'artistic' stages of undress, were under constant threat of suppression.[85] Flirting with the barmaid was subject to purity censure, as pressure was put on the state to outlaw bar work for women on account of its 'demoralising' effects.[86] Even the undraped classical statues gracing the front of the new British Medical Association offices on the Strand caused a committee of London purity leagues to agitate for their removal.[87] The diversity and sheer determination of this war on every imaginable kind of smut is best summarised by Emile de Laveleye, a Belgian social purist addressing the National League. Purity leagues were needed to fight this 'inundation of immorality, a contagion of satyriasis which infects alike our books, our journals, engravings, photographs, and extends from our fine art exhibitions down to our allumette boxes'.[88]

IV

These various interwoven complexities, we will see, inform the many imaginative, subversive, subtle and creative ways in which Joyce incorporates social purity discourses and campaigns into his fiction. For now, however, it

---

[82] *The Pioneer: The Journal of the Social Purity Alliance*, 1 March 1887, 1 April 1887. A bill to prohibit the publication of divorce court details was introduced into Parliament in July 1887 by Henry Vizetelly's persecutor and indefatigable National Vigilance Association lobbyist Samuel Smith MP, but was defeated (*The Pioneer*, 1 August 1887). Interestingly, although the National Vigilance Association supported the bill, the Social Purity Alliance and the Moral Reform Union were opposed, arguing that 'it was to the welfare of the country that deeds of darkness should be brought forth to the light' (*The Pioneer*, 1 April 1887).

[83] The purity crusade against the mutoscope will be discussed in greater detail in chapter 5 below.

[84] Bristow, *Vice and Vigilance*, 212–13, 203.   [85] *Ibid.*, 216.

[86] See Joint Committee on the Employment of Barmaids, *Women as Barmaids* (London: P. S. King and Son, 1905).

[87] *The Vigilance Record*, November 1908, 3.   [88] *The National League Journal*, November 1882.

is enough to emphasise how precisely the social purity campaigns outlined briefly above collided with and attempted to inhibit that sexually ebullient popular culture that Joyce so eloquently documents. Tracing Leopold Bloom's perambulations through Dublin on 16 June 1904 makes clear how frequently his desires, observations and urban encounters coincide with the disparate targets of social purity intervention. Bloom has pinned a picture of *Photo-Bits* erotica, *The Bath of the Nymph*, over his bed; he notes how advertisements for 'That quack doctor for the clap' (*U* 8: 96) have recently vanished from public lavatories; he examines the backsides of the statues in the National Library, as picturesquely undraped as those outside the British Medical Association; he watches acquaintances flirt with the barmaids in the Ormond Hotel; he thinks of saucy mutoscope films as he watches Gerty MacDowell; he visits a brothel in 'Circe'; he remembers salacious details of famous divorce cases; he owns a pornographic picture of a 'dirty bitch in that Spanish photo' (*U* 18: 564) and has ordered an illicit 'French letter' (*U* 18: 1235) from an advertisement with a Charing Cross address. To note these correlations between Bloom and contemporary social purity preoccupations is to recognise the extent to which Joyce's fiction is saturated with sidelong allusions to the vice crusades. The wealth of these allusions suggest how disingenuous was Joyce's artful masquerade to Carlo Linati and others as a hapless victim of 'prudes on the prowl'. For this proclaimed passivity is as playfully misleading as one might suspect. As we shall see, Joyce moved beyond simple reaction against the threat of censorship to weave such frustrations and proscriptions into the fabric of his art.

The six chapters which follow will explore two key issues of central importance to Joyce's subversive assault upon social purity. As we have seen, vice crusaders ardently desired to protect the 'young person', the child or adolescent boy or girl, from corruption. Ideas of imperilled youth and innocence lay at the heart of their drive to moralise the public sphere, outlaw impure representations in art, literature and popular culture, and impose laws regulating sexual behaviour. Accordingly, the first half of this study examines Joyce's portraits of several 'young persons', children and adolescents in sexual danger. We begin with the boys in 'An Encounter', morally threatened both by their 'improper' reading matter, and by the only dimly understood overtures of the 'queer old josser'. The second chapter concerns Eveline Hill, considering a high-risk emigration to Buenos Ayres with a shady lover whose promises of marriage and respectability are uncertain. Chapter 3 explores the childhood and adolescence of Stephen Dedalus in the first four chapters of *A Portrait of the Artist as a Young Man* to argue that Stephen is the masturbating boy of the purity imagination, corroded and overwhelmed by a sexual guilt imposed upon him by popular chastity league propaganda castigating the 'solitary vice'.

The second half of the book addresses more explicitly the second implication of my argument, that Joyce was deliberately provoking and inciting the eventual vice society intervention into the publication of *Ulysses* in 1921 which would win him worldwide notoriety. It examines three chapters crucial to the trials of *Ulysses* in *The Little Review*. 'Scylla and Charybdis' was suppressed by the New York Society for the Suppression of Vice in January 1919. Through an analysis of Joyce's redraftings during and after that suppression, Stephen's assault on the theosophists in the National Library can be read as an allegory for Joyce's own complex attack upon the sexual politics of the social purity movement, a sexual politics borrowed by the theosophy movement in its veneration of a celibate spirituality. Chapter 5 examines 'Nausicaa', the chapter concerning an older man's voyeuristic encounter with the 'winsome specimen of Irish girlhood', Gerty MacDowell, which allowed the Vice Society its legal victory over *Ulysses*. Gerty's masquerade as the ideal 'young person' of the social purity imagination is fatefully compromised by her appropriation of techniques of sexual display from the mutoscope, which warranted a social purity campaign of its own. The final chapter explores 'Circe', not only set in Dublin's notorious red-light zone, but also largely drafted and revised as *The Little Review* trial drew to its inevitable conclusion in February 1921. Leopold Bloom, 'down here in the haunts of sin' (*U* 15: 395) and masquerading as one attempting the 'Rescue of fallen women' (*U* 15: 402), is Joyce's most sustained and devastating portrait of the compromised purity reformer, fatally fascinated by the vice he would discipline.

What follows will trace how intimately Joyce's fiction appropriated and engaged with social purity's various campaigns against 'vice' in its myriad contemporary forms. *Dubliners*, *A Portrait of the Artist as a Young Man* and *Ulysses* all meticulously document the deadening effects of the social purity movement upon Edwardian culture, anticipating and inciting that notorious cultural moment, the suppression of *Ulysses* by the USA's most potent vice society in February 1921. Accordingly, the intertextual presence of social purity discourse in Joyce's fiction transcends the status of incidental detail to take on a political eloquence of its own. By unravelling the ideological work such intertexts perform, we might dismantle the pervasive myth, so teasingly deployed by Joyce himself, of artistic martyrdom in the face of philistine prudery.

CHAPTER I

'Works which boys couldn't read': reading and regulation in 'An Encounter'

> It would be well to remember that although these paragraphs might possibly escape notice there is at present in existence in this city a Vigilance Committee whose object is to seek out and suppress all writings of immoral tendencies and I am of opinion that if the attention of the Authorities be drawn to these passages it is likely they would yield to the pressure of this body and prosecute. Whether a conviction could be obtained is another matter altogether. But I would advise you to take no risks, and under the circumstances either delete or entirely alter the paragraphs in question.
>
> (*L* II: 306)

On 21 August 1912, Joyce reluctantly acceded to the demands of his recalcitrant publisher George Roberts. 'An Encounter', Joyce agreed, would be omitted from the forthcoming edition of *Dubliners*, on condition that its absence would be duly stated in 'the following note placed by me before the first story: *This book in this form is incomplete. The scheme of the book, as framed by me includes a story entitled An Encounter which stands between the first and second stories in this edition*' (*L* II: 309). Six years earlier, the story had been a sticking point for Grant Richards also, since Joyce had unwisely alerted him to its impropriety: 'The more subtle inquisitor will denounce *An Encounter*, the enormity of which the printer cannot see because he is, as I said, a plain blunt man' (*L* II: 134). At last, however, in August 1912, Joyce had capitulated, intimidated by a consultation with his solicitor John Lidwell, who not only castigated the story's depiction of 'this most odious vice of which modesty rejects the name and nature abominates the idea' (*L* II: 306), but also alluded to 'a Vigilance Committee', the Dublin White Cross Vigilance Association, Ireland's most active social purity league. As Joyce knew, this Vigilance Committee was presided over by the Vicereine Lady Aberdeen, one of Maunsel and Co.'s most valued customers with a lively interest in new Irish writing.[1] This veiled yet potent threat, then, was

---

[1] See above, Introduction, note 43.

28

plausible enough to persuade Joyce to reduce 'An Encounter' to an indexed absence in the collection, a gnomic commemoration of a forced silencing. The withdrawal of 'An Encounter' from Maunsel and Co.'s proposed edition of *Dubliners* was Joyce's first reluctant and coerced capitulation to the cultural climate social purists had induced.

What precisely was the nature of 'An Encounter's' challenge to purity proprieties? The protests of Joyce's publishers, printers and legal advisors suggest that the blatantly implied sexual act at the close of the story was to blame for its suppression, the queer old josser's insinuated if never quite confirmed public masturbation compromising the innocence of the two young boys in much the same way as, later, Leopold Bloom's indecent exposure would besmirch the 'winsome Irish girlhood' (*U* 13: 81) of Gerty MacDowell. For Joyce's schoolfriend Thomas Kettle, the story's explicitness placed it 'beyond anything in its outspokenness he had ever read'.[2] However, this quality of flagrance can only be uneasily attributed to 'An Encounter', a story which baffles on account of its deliberate manipulation of ideas of innocence, ignorance, uncertainty and insinuation. Whatever might be obscene in 'An Encounter' is literally so – *ob scena*, offstage, carried out under the startled gaze of Mahoney ('I say! Look what he's doing!...I say...He's a queer old josser!' – *D* 18), but deliberately not witnessed by the narrator, who 'neither answered nor raised my eyes' (*D* 18). This veiled yet oddly explicit sexual threat, an 'enormity' which after all Joyce suggested would evade all but the 'more subtle inquisitor' is only the most obvious example of 'An Encounter's' diffuse assault upon contemporary proprieties. It is rather the story's bewildering narrative logic, its inexplicable silences; specifically, its 'off-scene' or 'ob-scene' intertexts, the partly submerged allusions which Joyce expected his 'more subtle' contemporaries to excavate for themselves, which together make up 'An Encounter's' curious subversiveness.

Some readers were puzzled by this intertextual obscurity, easily interpreted as a perverse resistance to interpretation. The story's earliest critic, Stanislaus Joyce, demanded

But what is the meaning of writing one half of a story about 'Joe and Leo Dillon' and the other half about a sodomite, named by me for convenience sake 'the captain of fifty'? To call it 'An Encounter' will hardly link the two parts together. (*L* 11: 115)

Stanislaus' confusion depends upon his inability to connect the first part of the story, about the Dillon brothers and their entrancing halfpenny library of boys' magazine fiction, with the second, about another two boys' meeting

---

[2] Richard Ellmann, *James Joyce* (Oxford: Oxford University Press, 1983), 329.

with a paedophile in a deserted field. Yet, in the context of Joyce's own publication difficulties, 'An Encounter' emerges as an ideologically weighted
parable exploring a frequently posited link between youthful reading and
moral danger. The story, as R. B. Kershner notes, is the first in *Dubliners*
to be 'framed intertextually by popular literature', and consequently, the
Dillon brothers' 'little library made up of old numbers of *The Union Jack,
Pluck* and *The Halfpenny Marvel*' (*D* 11) is significantly the first explicitly
placed intertextual allusion we encounter in the collection.[3] At the start
of the story, the boy-narrator is fascinated by his transgressive reading. He
relishes 'the adventures related in the literature of the Wild West', stories
he defensively tells us, 'remote from my nature', since he is 'studious', but
opening 'doors of escape' (*D* 11), a portal of significance in paralytic Dublin.
The defensive note continues; 'Though there was nothing wrong in these
stories and though their intention was sometimes literary they were circulated secretly at school' (*D* 12). After Father Butler's classroom humiliation
of Leo Dillon, the boy's remarks are curiously suggestive of addiction; the
'restraining influence of the school . . . at a distance, I began to hunger again
for wild sensations, for the escape which these chronicles of disorder alone
seemed to offer me' (*D* 12). Reading in 'An Encounter' is clearly a dangerous pleasure, a message enforced when the narrator meets a 'queer old
josser' (*D* 18) in a field, who begins to talk to him 'of school and of books'
(*D* 17). Their discussion, and the boy's pretence 'that I had read *every* book
he mentioned' (*D* 17) leads him into a second encounter with forbidden
literature, the mysterious 'Lord Lytton's works which boys couldn't read'
(*D* 17). This second transgression allows the old man to begin his paralytic monologue about 'rough boys' and the 'nice warm whipping' (*D* 19)
he longs to administer. Through a series of superficially illogical narrative
leaps, then, 'An Encounter' bafflingly progresses from 'bad reading' to flagellation, a narrative glissade which on the surface indeed fails 'to link the
two parts together'. Yet, Joyce's dogged connection of reading and beating invites that 'more subtle reader' he required to link the two together
through metaphor, as a story about reading segues into a story about discipline. Reading and perverse fantasies of proscription are shadily elided in
'An Encounter', in a narrative illogic which signals the story's status as a
richly allusive fable about policing the reading of the young.

    Those vigilance committees John Lidwell warned Joyce against had, as
Nicola Beisel amply documents, the young person as the primary focus

---

[3] R. B. Kershner, *Joyce, Bahktin and Popular Literature: Chronicles of Disorder* (London: University of
   North Carolina Press, 1989), 31.

of their concern.[4] Evil reading was bad enough in the hands of adults, but children and adolescents were its innocent victims, indelibly morally corroded by what they read. Accordingly, social purity campaigners were swift to concern themselves with the reading aimed at the very young, and in particular they constructed the kind of unsupervised reading the Dillons and their schoolfellows relish as a threat to the innocence and moral character of juveniles. This strand of the broader crusade against 'pernicious literature' that endangered Joyce asserted that children could be corrupted by bad books, as well as by bad people; and that one might well lead to another. A well-organised chorus of moral crusaders relentlessly insisted that the kinds of magazines the boys read, innocuous as they might seem now, imperilled youth. These magazines were known as 'penny dreadfuls', a term coming into popular use around 1830 to denote adult broadsides about folk villains such as Spring-Heeled Jack, Eugene Aram and Sweeney Todd, but by the late nineteenth century applying almost exclusively to boys' magazines of the cheapest class.[5] The decades following the 1870 Education Act saw an unprecedented explosion in the number and circulation of juvenile periodicals. In 1824, there were five magazines for boys in the United Kingdom; in 1900 there were 160, and no fewer that 307 commercial boys' papers were launched between 1880 and 1918.[6] Priced at a penny or halfpence, they were affordable to almost all. The most successful had weekly circulations running into millions, and their editors boasted how copies were frequently, as in 'An Encounter', shared amongst friends.[7] The ubiquity of cheap boys' magazines in bookstores, newsagents and railway news stands thus coincided with the late-Victorian interest in urban reform, philanthropy and juvenile delinquency. Specifically, the explosion of the youth publication market was simultaneous with the growth of support for social purity, a movement with a declared mission to protect the young from 'impure' stimuli. When *Punch* suggested in 1898 that 'Philanthropy is continually busying itself about the education of the young – here is something practical for it to do – let it look to the quality of imaginative literature', its advice was oddly belated.[8] Social purists had been busying themselves about penny dreadfuls for a good two decades, creating a moral crusade which has been described as

---

[4] Nicola Beisel, *Imperilled Innocents: Anthony Comstock and Family Reproduction in Victorian America* (Princeton: Princeton University Press, 1997), 161–8.

[5] Patrick A. Duane, 'Penny Dreadfuls: Boys' Literature and Crime', *Victorian Studies* 22: 2 (1979), 135.

[6] Claudia Nelson, 'Mixed Messages: Authoring and Authority in British Boys' Magazines', *The Lion And The Unicorn* 22: 1 (January 1997), 1.

[7] Circulation figures from Claudia Nelson, 'Mixed Messages', 2.   [8] *Punch*, 20 February 1886, 96.

'arguably one of the most emotionally charged social campaigns of the period'.[9]

If one man can be said to have inaugurated this campaign, that man would be the notorious New York social purist Anthony Comstock, state censor of the United States mails and founder of the New York Society for the Suppression of Vice. Comstock's polemic *Traps for the Young* (1883) is prefaced with a lengthy diatribe against 'demoralising' youth fiction which summarises social purity objection to penny dreadfuls:

Each birth begins a history. The pages are filled out, one by one, by the records of daily life. The mind is the source of action. Thoughts are the aliment on which it feeds. We assimilate what we read. The pages of printed matter become our companions. Memory unites them indissolubly, so that, unlike an enemy, we cannot get away from them. They are constant attendants to quicken thought and influence action.

Good reading refines, elevates, ennobles and stimulates the ambition to lofty purposes. It points upward. Evil reading debases, degrades, perverts and turns away from lofty aims to follow examples of corruption and criminality. This book is designed to awaken thought upon the subject of *Evil Reading* and to expose to the minds of parents, teachers, guardians and pastors some of the mighty forces for evil which are today exerting a controlling influence over the young. There is a shameful recklessness in many homes as to what the children read. The community is cursed by pernicious literature.

Our youth are in danger; mentally and morally they are cursed by a literature that is a disgrace to the nineteenth century. The spirit of evil environs them. Let no man be henceforth indifferent. Read, reflect, act.[10]

Comstock articulates a paranoid yet complex theory of reading. The child is initially imagined as a text or 'history', its 'pages' inscribed as it grows to maturity 'by the records of daily life'. Suddenly, Comstock inverts his metaphor. If the child is the book, then the book is also the child: 'memory' converts the printed page into personified thoughts which, 'unlike an enemy', we cannot escape. This elision of the boundaries between reading, action and identity, between the corrupting text and the corrupted child, was the characteristic and central strategy of the social purity crusade against 'demoralising' books. The 'young person' was the imagined consumer of such writing: youths of both genders were figured as susceptible, passive and easily influenced, *tabula rasa* upon whom the effects of 'evil reading' were fatally inscribed.

---

[9] Duane, 'Penny Dreadfuls', 151.
[10] Anthony Comstock, *Traps for the Young*, ed. Robert Bremner (Cambridge, Mass.: Harvard University Press, 1967), 1.

Comstock was no isolated extremist, since his claims that young people were menaced as severely by 'pernicious literature' as they were by actual sexual assaults were also voiced by a chorus of reformers, both in the USA and in Britain. In the United Kingdom and Ireland, anxiety over the reading habits of the 'young person' had intensified in the wake of the 1870 Education Act, which brought widespread literacy to the working class. The perceived dangers of mass literacy preoccupied many conservative commentators, such as the Revd Freeman Wills:

The Education Act of 1870, which was looked upon as the Abolition of Ignorance, has ... left darkness grosser by the revolt of those educated under compulsion. The education it has enforced is worthless, a mere capacity to read which leaves its possessor brutal and uncultured. It has depraved youthful minds to a taste for highly spiced criminal excitements.[11]

The Pure Literature Society was more specific:

Newspapers furnish us with the painful proofs of the sad effect of reading the pernicious stories contained in the low class of serials which sell so frequently throughout the country. These papers are mostly embellished with engravings of a sensational character, and chiefly devoted to the representation of crime. The wide diffusion of education through our elementary schools has given an impetus to the sale of these publications, and the newsvendors say that their customers are boys and girls. ... The effects of these journals seems to break out like an epidemic amongst boys. Some romance of a highwayman has intoxicated them with its lawless spirit: their hero is a thief or a cut-throat, and forthwith every variety of crime is bred among the ignorant and ardent for adventure.[12]

Such anxieties explicitly placed mass literacy, and the affiliated rise in sensational juvenile fiction, as moral dangers in and of themselves. However, the literature those anxious about youth corruption concerned themselves with was not sexually explicit or conventionally 'obscene' – the underground pornography covertly circulated throughout the Victorian era. Rather, social purity concern was curiously centred on the kinds of stories 'circulated secretly at school': cheap illustrated weekly magazines for pre-pubescent boys emphasising adventure, foreign travel and exploration, and featuring boisterous bloodshed.

What objections did social purity reformers make to these boys' papers? *Punch*'s anxiety over 'imaginative literature' betrayed the reformers' primary concern over the unsupervised, illicit reading of juveniles: it would infect the imagination. The corruption of the imagination through secret reading

[11] Revd Freeman Wills, 'Recreative Evening Schools', *Nineteenth Century* 20 (July 1886), 133.
[12] The Pure Literature Society, *Annual Report* 12 (1886), 2.

was melodramatically outlined by the New York Society for the Suppression of Vice:

A malignant disorder is everywhere prevalent, a disease of the mind which for the lack of a better name we term

IMMORAL IMAGINATIONALISM.

When the re-imaging power of the mind is connected with the emotional nature by evil reading or vile pictures, forces for evil are awakened which goad the soul to misery and ruin.[13]

At first glance, 'immoral imaginationalism' might obviously apply to the re-lationship between erotic or pornographic stimuli and sexual fantasy. How-ever, the society's definition here explicitly included its theorised connection between penny dreadfuls and juvenile delinquency. Indeed, pornography and the penny dreadful were viewed as symbiotic dangers to youth, since the penny dreadful, aimed at the pre-pubescent boy, inculcated habits of 'immoral' and furtive reading which could easily lead to reading sexually titillating material during adolescence. 'A sabbath school attendant writes of Boys' Story Papers "I believe that this kind of literature does as much if not more damage than the baser sort" ', commented the New York Society for the Suppression of Vice in 1880.[14] The vice societies' war on obscene literature and penny dreadfuls alike relied upon this concept of 'immoral imaginationalism' at the heart of its naive understanding of how youths read. Rather than recognise that the fantasies of adventure and escape which popular literature for the young inspired were little more than fantasy, re-formers repeatedly insisted that juveniles exposed to 'pernicious' stories of lawlessness would be moved to mimic the exploits they were seduced into admiring. The connection between the penny dreadful and delinquent youth was similar to that more commonly theorised between pornography and sexual acts or crime. As 'obscene' books led to erotic dreams, mastur-bation, prostitution or sexual assault, so criminal boys' story papers led to 'our courtrooms thronged with infant criminals, with baby felons'.[15]

This kinetic model of reading was assumed by most social purity campaigners against 'pernicious' juvenile adventure stories. The theory that young people were drawn to mimic what they read found constant

---

[13] New York Society for the Suppression of Vice, *Annual Report* 21 (1894), 8.
[14] New York Society for the Suppression of Vice, *Annual Report* 6 (1880), 10. The New York Society for the Suppression of Vice frequently grouped boys' papers together with sexually explicit material as twinned threats to youth: 'If obscene books, criminal story papers and lewd pictures are permitted to be distributed amongst the young, then must State prisons, penitentiaries, jails and reformatories be erected and supported at the taxpayer's expense' commented *Annual Report* 8 (1882), 19.
[15] New York Society for the Suppression of Vice, *Annual Report* 6 (1880), 7.

reiteration. The New York Society for the Suppression of Vice's claim that boys' papers led directly to juvenile crime was supported by lurid tales of young offenders who, when caught by the Vice Society or the police, were quick to confess the source of their ruin.[16] One chapter of Comstock's *Traps for the Young* was wholly dedicated to 'Half-Dime Novels and Story Papers', where social purity claims about the deleterious effects of penny dreadfuls on the young were apparently supported by a series of melodramatic confessions. One sixteen year old youth planned to 'rob his employer's safe in accordance with the deception in the story', confessing 'I never thought of stealing until I began to read these stories.'[17] Another delinquent adolescent, arrested by Comstock for running a mail-order pornography business from his parents' home, produced 'a pile of these vile five-cent story papers' from his room, declaring 'There! That's what has cursed me! That has brought me to this!'[18] A third, a 'judge's son' from Mississippi, told how adventure stories had led him to run away from home and, eventually, to become fatally injured in a drunken brawl. 'Warn all young people who you know to let these foolish books alone', he told his rescuer. 'They're very silly, but they do harm to many. They take you one step down a bad road, and the rest comes quick and easy.'[19] Social purity invective against the penny dreadful successfully percolated into the mainstream, in the United Kingdom and the United States alike. One of the most influential and frequently cited assaults on penny dreadfuls was G. A. Salmon's 1886 *Fortnightly Review* study, 'What Boys Read'. Salmon noted that boys' papers were 'patronized almost exclusively by the working class' and characterised by 'stories of blood and revenge, of passion and cruelty, as improbable and almost impossible in plot as they are contemptible in literary execution'.[20] Not only were these stories farfetched and badly written, to Salmon as to Comstock, they inexorably led to the juvenile courtroom. As in *Traps for the Young*, Salmon supplied a list of youthful criminals who blamed 'bad reading' for their downfall; a youth who 'was so maddened by the tales provided for his entertainment that he shot dead his father and his brother', another 'apprehended on a charge of keeping firearms in his room', a third, implausibly enough, who planned to rob his employer's safe by 'mewing like a cat at his door and awaiting his exit with a handkerchief charged

---

[16] See for example, New York Society for the Suppression of Vice, 'Boys' Papers', *Annual Report* 6 (1880), 6–8 for a series of 'case histories' of boys incited to criminality by their magazines; *Annual Report* 8 (1882), 18–9 for an account of 'the advancing army of young criminals recruited by these infamous devices'.

[17] Comstock, *Traps for the Young*, 34.   [18] *Ibid.*, 28–9.   [19] *Ibid.*, 32.

[20] G. A. Salmon, 'What Boys Read', *The Fortnightly Review* 45 (February 1886), 256.

with chloroform'.[21] Like many other commentators, Salmon deemed the pernicious state of popular periodicals 'of such vital moment in the social economy of the masses as to justify high-handed action on the part of the State', demanding the extension of the Obscene Publications Act of 1857 'to check the veiled incentive to crime which many boys' journals now supply'.[22] To social purists and their sympathisers, juvenile magazine fiction was both a cause and a symptom of the mass moral degeneration they diagnosed.

This theory of juveniles' kinetic response to 'demoralising' fiction is satirised in 'An Encounter'. There too, the boy finds his reading of adventure stories incites in him sensations which seem distinctly unwholesome: 'a spirit of unruliness diffused itself among us' (*D* 11), 'I began to hunger again for wild sensations, for the escape which those chronicles of disorder alone seemed to offer me' (*D* 12). Although he does not attempt petty theft, highway robbery or patricide like the young delinquents in *Traps for the Young* or *The Fortnightly Review*, he does join in a less ambitious scheme of mischief in his plan to play truant for a day. His reading distracts him from his normal bookish diligence: as Kershner notes, to be 'studious' (*D* 11), within the code of masculinity boys' papers create, is a source of shame.[23] Instead of 'the routine of school', he craves 'real adventures to happen to myself', even though his reading has taught him that 'real adventures . . . do not happen to people who remain at home: they must be sought abroad' (*D* 12). What 'An Encounter' ostensibly traces, therefore, is precisely the same trajectory of fantasy, corruption and fall set out in reforming critiques of the kinetic effects of 'bad stories'. Like the disgruntled apprentices and bored middle-class adolescents who rob their employers or flee their parents' homes to seek 'adventure' in the pool halls, saloons and gambling dens of the big city, Joyce's protagonist is a dissatisfied fantasist desperate to explore beyond the parameters of his own confined life. Significantly, like the judge's son in *Traps for the Young* who transgresses class boundaries to brawl in working-class saloons, the first 'adventure' Mahoney and the protagonist seek involves 'slumming it' in one of Dublin's tenement districts, where they 'arranged a siege' with 'the ragged troop' (*D* 14) of local children. They move on to the quays, a space displaying a magnetic connection with the 'abroad' that juvenile fiction celebrated as the locus of adventure. Here, individual fantasies emerge: Mahoney remarks 'it would be right skit to run away to sea on one of those big ships', and the protagonist adds 'I, looking at the high masts, saw, or imagined, the geography which had been scantily dosed

[21] *Ibid*.   [22] *Ibid*., 258.   [23] Kershner, *Joyce, Bakhtin*, 35.

to me at school gradually taking substance under my eyes' (*D* 15). These dreams create the very dislocation from the steadying influences of family and school that reformers predicted: 'School and home seemed to recede from us and their influences on us seemed to wane' (*D* 15). Through this study of reading, fantasy, imagination and influence, Joyce appears to flesh out the clichéd panic narratives characteristic of the prolonged campaign against penny dreadfuls, transforming a cautionary tale into something rich and strange.

II

One source of this complexity is the obvious distinction between Joyce's story and the prototype narrative of reading that the critics of boys' magazines supplied. That distinction is between reforming melodrama and Joycean realism: importantly, the boys' attempts to mimic what they read are futile, as dreams of running away to sea are substituted by more pedestrian and local adventures aspiring towards, although never reaching, Dublin's Pigeon House. 'An Encounter' thus sardonically undercuts the kinetic theory of reading that moral reformers insisted on: whilst Joyce's juvenile readers certainly share in the longings for escape, adventure and estrangement from school and home commonly ascribed to susceptible delinquents, they are not impelled by their reading towards the magistrates' court. 'An Encounter' thus illustrates the argument of another contemporary commentator upon the vice societies' distorted rhetoric. G. K. Chesterton's 1904 polemic 'A Defence of Penny Dreadfuls' savaged the 'utterly ridiculous exaggeration and misconception' characterising earnest contemporary debate over the effects of 'pernicious reading'.[24] Noting 'It is the custom, particularly amongst magistrates, to ascribe half the crimes of the Metropolis to cheap novelettes' and that 'it is firmly fixed in the mind of most people that gutter boys, unlike everybody else in the community, find their principal motives for conduct in printed books', Chesterton contends 'this wild life is contemplated with pleasure by the young, not because it is like their own life, but because it is different from it'.[25] 'An Encounter' dramatises Chesterton's exasperated common sense. In the face of 'penny dreadful' hysteria, Joyce presents us with two juveniles whose ideas of 'adventure' and 'escape' are disappointingly different from the exhilarating Wild West stories they read. Their excursion is badly planned and disappointing, its

[24] G. K.Chesterton, 'A Defence of Penny Dreadfuls', *The Defendant* (London: 1901), 9.
[25] *Ibid.*, 11, 13.

failings only emphasised by the glamorised expectations of the protagonist's imagination; 'wild sensations', 'spirit of unruliness', 'chronicles of disorder'. In place of the melodramas of disgrace offered by reformers, Joyce offers only bathetic realism.

A second source of complexity, however, inheres in the cultural implications of the specific boys' magazines Joyce chose. R. B. Kershner has expertly recovered their precise contemporary connotations: as Edwardian readers would immediately recognise, Joe Dillon's 'little library made up of old numbers of *The Union Jack, Pluck*, and *The Halfpenny Marvel*' (*D* 11) belonged to a very particular class of boys' journals; the supposedly 'wholesome' halfpenny magazines launched in the early 1890s by newspaper magnate Alfred Harmsworth. As Kershner observes

Ironically for a magazine generally regarded as cheaply sensational, [*The Halfpenny Marvel*] claimed the intent of counteracting the influence of unhealthy sensationalism aimed at children, announcing in the first issue, 'No more penny dreadfuls! These healthy stories of mystery and adventure will kill them.' Soon the magazine began printing testimonials such as that of the Reverend C. N. Barnham expressing pleasure that the magazine was so 'pure and wholesome in tone'. On the front cover of that issue was a man being tortured, with the caption, 'The gaoler screwed up the horrible machine until the brigand's bones were nearly broken and he shrieked aloud for mercy, though none was shown.'[26]

Such obvious disingenuity was one response to social purity agitation over the demoralizing effects of 'penny dreadfuls' on the young. Although G. A. Salmon was one of many reformers demanding the extension of the 1857 Obscene Publications Act, most critics recognised that since boys' papers were seldom sexually explicit, successful prosecutions would be extremely difficult to orchestrate, and that other methods of suppression were required.[27] The Pure Literature Society maintained 'the best way to supplant bad literature is to supply good'; the Religious Tract Society achieved strong circulation for its *Boys' Own Paper*, designed to offer 'sound and healthy fare'; social reformer Henry Mayhew longed to 'supply a higher class of literature for youths than the present pernicious trash now provided for

[26] Kershner, *Joyce, Bahktin*, 33.
[27] Another reformer attempting to legislate against the dreadful was Lord Shaftesbury, who in 1879 attempted to steer a bill banning pernicious juvenile fiction through the House of Lords. See Duane, 'Penny Dreadfuls', 140. Harmsworth himself shrewdly acknowledged the impossibility of legislation against the penny dreadful: 'while we have no law to prevent the trash being published, there is only one way of stopping the further spread of their sinful influence – that is by bringing high-class, healthy and at the same time exciting tales within the reach of all', 'Why This Paper is Published and What It Is Going To Do', *Pluck* 1 (1894), 2.

them'.[28] Statements like these offered a standing invitation to an enter-prising publisher to seize an eager and ideologically committed market. Accordingly, Harmsworth's boys' papers were carefully pitched to cash in on social purity anxieties over children's reading. Editorials ventriloquised 'penny dreadful' debates, jostling for position with other papers in a fiercely competitive market by mimicking social purity rhetoric and deflecting it towards their rivals. 'You need not be ashamed reading this!', 'Nothing but pure healthy literature', 'No More Penny Dreadfuls: These Healthy Stories of Mystery and Adventure Will Kill Them' and 'A Schoolmaster to the Editor: *The Marvel* I consider to be one of the very best and health-iest books for boys' were the taglines for the Harmsworth boys' papers.[29] In its inaugural article 'Why this Paper is Published', *Pluck* was eager to convert its young readers to the purity crusade against penny dreadfuls, noting

Young people devour the trash ravenously, not because they really like it, but because they must read something in these reading days. A bitter cry for healthy literature comes every day from the police courts. Each week dozens of boys and lads have to pay the penalty of offences and crimes they would never have committed but for the reading of penny dreadfuls. Surely there can be no better plea for better books than a woman's tears?[30]

Such moralising, an ubiquitous refrain in all Harmsworth's papers, blatantly appropriated the language and arguments of social reform – 'a bitter cry' here directly lifts a phrase from a classic of the genre, Andrew Mearns' 'The Bitter Cry of Outcast London' – in order to appeal both to boys reluctant to be seen reading 'trash', and to their parents, teachers and guardians. Behind the scenes, however, Harmsworth's strategy was explicit enough, since his brother Harold initially suggested 'we call *The Marvel* "The Boys' Weekly Reader" since that sounds respectable and would act as a cloak for some fiery stories'.[31] The disguise convinced few: to A. A. Milne, 'Harmsworth killed the penny dreadful by producing the ha-penny dreadfuller'.[32]

[28] Pure Literature Society, *Annual Reports* (1886), 15; circulation figures for *Boys' Own Paper* cited in Patrick A. Duane, 'Boys' Literature and the Idea of Empire, 1870–1914', *Victorian Studies* 24: 1 (1980), 84; unpublished letter from Henry Mayhew, dated 19 October 1872 and quoted in Duane, 'Penny Dreadfuls', 146.

[29] For examples, see *Union Jack* (1894), vol. 1, issue 1, front cover; *Union Jack* (1895), vol. 2, issue 2, 4; *Pluck* (1894), vol. 1, issue 5, 4; *The Halfpenny Marvel* (1904), vol. 13, no. 2, front cover.

[30] *Pluck*, vol. 1, issue 1, 2.

[31] Paul Ferris, *The House of Northcliffe: The Harmsworths of Fleet Street* (London: Weidenfield and Nicolson, 1971), 60.

[32] Kirsten Dromer, *English Children and Their Magazines, 1751–1945* (New Haven: Yale University Press, 1988), 126.

To contemporary adult observers, it was obvious that Harmsworth manipulated the social purity crusade to censor and suppress 'corrupting' juvenile fiction into a unique selling point. To juvenile readers, however, Harmsworth's marketing strategy cannot have been so clear. The Harmsworth boys' papers offered puzzling moral messages to their young readers, parading their 'wholesomeness' whilst offering precisely the kind of reading pleasures that made the 'penny dreadfuls' notorious. Father Butler's outburst neatly summarises this conflict to Leo Dillon and his classmates, since his attack upon the 'wretched stuff' written by 'some wretched scribbler that writes these things for a drink' (*D* 12) is in striking contrast to the *Marvel's* frequent pedagogical endorsements. In 1894, for instance, an unnamed 'Schoolmaster' wrote in to the editor, explaining

Notwithstanding my vigilance, I have sometimes found boys under my care with copies of penny dreadfuls in their possession. However, they willingly gave them up and eagerly took *The Halfpenny Marvel* instead. I read your numbers myself, as I have no doubt do many adults, and allow them to circulate freely in my school, and I am sure they can only influence for the good.[33]

Father Butler not only directly contradicts this 'Schoolmaster', he makes precisely the same objections to the *Marvel* that Harmsworth's papers habitually deflected towards their rivals. One editorial in the inaugural number of *The Marvel's* sister-paper, *The Boy's Friend*, titled 'The Penny Dreadful and the Scoundrels who Write It' attacked 'the miserable beer-swilling wretches who "write", if such a word can be applied – the stupid lying stories they contain – drunken sodden creatures whose lives have been one unbroken catalogue of failure'.[34] This association between the dreadfuls and the drunken hack was frequently reiterated in the Harmsworth papers, and in 'An Encounter' Joyce transfers it to Father Butler, no doubt to the confusion of those boys who have allowed themselves to be reassured by their papers' claims to schoolmasterly sanction. 'Confusion' is, indeed, the sensation the narrator ascribes to Leo Dillon who, when reprimanded by Father Butler, shows a 'confused puffy face' (*D* 12) to his classmates, and 'confusion' can be perceived behind the narrator's defensive claim that 'Though there was nothing wrong in these stories and though their intention was sometimes literary they were circulated secretly at school' (*D* 12). As the boy shamefacedly recognises, these stories are not 'literary', despite their loudly proclaimed 'intention'; hence the secrecy of their circulation. The liminal status of Harmsworth's papers – supposedly distanced from the

[33] 'The Editor Speaks', *The Halfpenny Marvel* (1894), vol. 5, 16.
[34] 'The Penny Dreadful and the Scoundrels Who Write It', *The Boys' Friend*, 29 January 1895, 2.

'dreadful' yet in essence very similar in tone, recommended by the school-masters within their pages, yet condemned in the boy's own classroom – muddies the rhetoric about juvenile reading with which 'An Encounter' is concerned.

III

The Harmsworth boys' papers are the first of several radically unstable in-tertexts in 'An Encounter' to blur the boundaries between texts condemned and texts recommended by adult guardians of youth. This confusion persists when the queer old josser introduces himself to the children by initiating a conversation about suitable reading for the young:

Then he began to talk of school and of books. He asked us whether we had read the poetry of Thomas Moore or the works of Sir Walter Scott and Lord Lytton. I pretended that I had read every book he mentioned so that in the end he said:

– Ah, I can see you are a bookwork like myself. Now, he added, pointing to Mahoney who was regarding us with open eyes, he is different; he goes in for games.

He said he had all Sir Walter Scott's works and all Lord Lytton's works at home and never tired of reading them. Of course, he said, there were some of Lord Lytton's works which boys couldn't read. Mahoney asked why couldn't boys read them – a question which agitated and pained me because I was afraid the man would think I was as stupid as Mahoney. The man, however, only smiled. I saw that he had great gaps in his mouth between his yellow teeth. (*D* 17)

The old man's 'talk of books' closely coincides with a second strand of the social purity campaign against 'demoralising' youth fiction. Alongside the rise of Harmsworth's 'penny healthfuls' in the early 1890s grew a par-allel effort to supply children and adolescents with cheap copies of classic fiction. This optimistic attempt to wean juveniles away from sensational story papers towards the kind of books that would inculcate the virtues of Christian manliness assumed a simple moral and social divide between books and magazines. To G. A. Salmon, 'Boys' books are on the whole morally unimpeachable; boys' magazines, with a few notable exceptions, are in every way objectionable', a state of affairs all the more regrettable since 'Books are purchased by the well-to-do. Magazines, on the other hand, are patronised almost exclusively by the working class.'[35] This distinction between elevating children's 'classics' and demoralising magazines was en-thusiastically taken up by the prominent social purist and founder of the

---

[35] Salmon, 'What Boys Read', 256.

National Vigilance Association, W. T. Stead. In the 1890s, Stead launched a
'Masterpiece Library', a series of abridged popular classics priced at a penny
a volume to compete with the 'dreadfuls' for children's pocket money. Those
selected were middlebrow adventure novels, and sales reached a million in
three months.[36] The first, selling 250,000 copies of the first edition, was
Rider Haggard's *She*; later bestsellers included Dumas' *Count of Monte
Cristo*, Scott's *Ivanhoe*, Edward Bulwer-Lytton's *The Last Days of Pompeii*,
James Fenimore Cooper's *Last of the Mohicans*, Harriet Beecher Stowe's
Uncle Tom's Cabin, Henry Fielding's *Tom Jones*, Jules Verne's *Around the
World in Eighty Days* and Bret Harte's *Gabriel Conroy*. Girl readers were
offered *Pride and Prejudice, Jane Eyre, Little Women* and Mrs Henry Wood's
East Lynne.[37] One of the abridgers, Grant Richards, the first of Joyce's publishers to object to 'An Encounter', noted that the task of 'boiling down
the great novels of the world into sixty four pages was not one that did
credit to any one of us'.[38] An improvement in the moral tone, rather than
an increase in the artistic sensibility of the nation was, however, Stead's
priority. Soliciting testimonials from 'the most distinguished personages of
the Empire', Stead made clear the ameliorating effects this diet of bracing
popular classics was to have on children previously limited to 'penny dreadfuls and penny novelettes... the trash that now holds possession of so large
a portion of the field'.[39]

Coincidently, this is the class of improving reading recommended by the
queer old josser, who names alongside the safely patriotic choice, Thomas
Moore, two staple authors in the Masterpiece Library series, Scott and
Lytton. The old man's literary taste is not just staid, mid-Victorian and
middlebrow; significantly, his recommendations complement the moral
panic over 'penny dreadfuls' disclosed in the first half of 'An Encounter'
by suggesting alternative 'elevating' reading to his young listeners. The
structural parallels between the old man's recommendation and Father
Butler's prohibition are asserted to the child-narrator by the queer old
josser's claim to have 'all Sir Walter Scott's and all Lord Lytton's works at
home' (*D* 17). This boast throws into relief the earlier description of the
Dillon boys' collection of magazines as a 'little library' (*D* 11), a retrospective
piece of irony which helps to sustain the moral contrast between 'good'
books and 'bad' boys' papers. The story's two superficially irreconcilable

[36] See Joseph O' Baylen, 'Stead's Penny Masterpiece Library', *Journal of Popular Culture* 9: 3, 710–25.
[37] Information taken from British Library catalogue.
[38] Grant Richards, *Memoirs of a Misspent Youth, 1872–1896* (London: Grant Richards, 1932), 332.
[39] W. T. Stead, *A Plea for the Revival of Reading With a Plan of Campaign* (London: Review of Reviews, 1906), 77.

halves are knitted together through these two complementary strands of social purity rhetoric about juvenile reading, as the boy-narrator encounters two older men instructing him on what he should and shouldn't read. Father Butler's prohibition, enforced with a vague threat of the cane ('Now Dillon, I advise you strongly, get at your work or...' – *D* 12) is mirrored by the queer old josser's recommendations of elevating fiction, advice which soon modulates into a fantasy on whipping boys. Furthermore, the boy is as eager to win the approval of the strange old man, pretending 'I had read every book he mentioned' (*D* 17), as he is earlier to recommend himself to Father Butler through his 'studious' habits. This connection between the benign schoolmaster and the deviant old man, figures Joyce associates with complementary strands of the contemporary crusade to sanitise children's reading, further compromises the black and white clarity of social purity rhetoric. For 'An Encounter' suggests through these structurally paralleled instances of advice on reading that the respectable Father Butler and the perverse queer old josser are underneath dangerously similar.

IV

This disturbing of the binary purity certainties about good and bad reading is continued when the queer old josser qualifies his recommendation with the disclosure 'there were some of Lord Lytton's works which boys couldn't read' (*D* 17). For Joyce's use of Lytton here is intriguing, since if the queer old josser is an old man in the mid 1890s, then it would seem he refers back to Lytton's 'unsuitable' novels as a rough equivalent of the Halfpenny Marvels of his youth. To explore this faultline in greater depth, it is necessary to identify and to unravel the precise intertextual nuances of Lytton's fiction in 'An Encounter'. For Kershner, the novel Joyce meant was *The Last Days of Pompeii*, the most popular of Lytton's novels and the only one listed in Joyce's Trieste library. As Kershner's persuasive reading shows, *The Last Days of Pompeii* anticipates key themes of 'An Encounter', since a young boy is seduced by a sinister older man in a story saturated with 'mingled strains of paedophilia, sodomy and sadomasochism'.[40] Compelling though this identification is, Joyce elsewhere implies a broader knowledge of Lytton than Kershner suggests, allowing Myles Crawford to quote from Lytton's play *Richelieu* in 'Aeolus' and Molly Bloom to remember Lytton's novel *Eugene Aram* as a favourite of her youth.[41] More importantly, *The Last Days*

[40] Kershner, *Joyce, Bahktin*, 42.
[41] 'You can do it. I see it in your face. *In the lexicon of youth...*' (*U* 7: 617); 'I lent him afterwards with Mulveys photo in it so as he see I wasnt without and Lord Lytton Eugene Aram' (*U* 18: 656).

of Pompeii, as its inclusion in Stead's Masterpiece Library surely suggests, was relatively respectable reading in contrast to Lytton's other novels. It made a relatively blameless appearance in the midst of a decade convulsed by a literary and cultural controversy that closely compares to the later campaign against 'penny dreadfuls'. This controversy circulated around the so-called 'Newgate novels', crime fictions in which lawless protagonists flaunted their moral ambiguity. The genre flourished from 1830 to 1846, and Lytton was both its pioneer, and integral to the widespread cultural disquiet it provoked.[42] Marking 'the threshold of a new literary period', his highwayman novel *Paul Clifford* (1830) was swiftly followed by three more best-sellers; a fictionalised biography of a notorious scholar-murderer, *Eugene Aram* (1832), *Night and Morning* (1841), featuring William Gawtrey, a coiner and forger, and *Lucretia* (1846), a composite portrait of a female poisoner.[43]

Loosely based upon a celebrated murder trial of 1759, *Eugene Aram* became 'the storm centre of the Newgate controversy', fixing Lytton's reputation as the writer of fiction both unsuitable yet compelling for the young.[44] Aram was regarded as the first to discover the relationship between Celtic and European languages and still commanded widespread scholarly respect at the close of the nineteenth century.[45] Yet he was also responsible for a brutal and mercenary murder, a psychological abnormality which fascinated Lytton whilst infuriating his critics. Taking 'the common and fair licence of writers of fiction', Lytton transformed the historical Aram into a tragic hero, elevating his rank from village-schoolmaster to gentleman-scholar, erasing the wife and seven children whom Aram abandoned, substituting a virginal heroine as love-interest, blackening the character of Aram's victim and finally altering the second edition to suggest that Aram was, after all, innocent.[46] *Fraser's Magazine* led the assault, suggesting that, to the young and susceptible, such a book might induce imitation: 'We dislike altogether this awakening sympathy with interesting criminals and wasting sensibilities on the scaffold and the gaol. It is a modern, a depraved, a corrupting taste.'[47] To *The Spectator*, Lytton's crime fiction revealed a 'mortal

---

[42] Keith Hollingsworth and Juliet John each argue convincingly for Lytton's status as the pioneer of the Newgate genre. See Keith Hollingsworth, *The Newgate Novel, 1830–1847: Bulwer, Ainsworth, Dickens and Thackeray* (Detroit: Wayne State University Press, 1963), 15–20; *Cult Criminals: The Newgate Novels, 1830–1847*, ed. Juliet John (London: Routledge, 1998), ix–xii.

[43] Hollingsworth, *The Newgate Novel*, 69.   [44] *Ibid.*, 82.

[45] Leslie Stephen, 'Lytton, Edward George Earle Lytton Bulwer, first Baron Lytton 1803–1873', *Dictionary of National Biography* (London: n.p., 1912).

[46] Juliet John, preface to Edward Bulwer-Lytton, *Eugene Aram*, ed. Juliet John (London: Routledge, 1998), vii.

[47] *Fraser's Magazine* 5 (February 1832), 112.

unhealthiness of mind', and *The Times*, in a review of *Lucretia*, summarised fifteen years of attack:

He had dallied so long with crime and criminals, had thrown so sickly a halo around the forms of vice, had taken such pleasure in the tricking out of naturally repulsive thoughts that we knew it to be impossible for the man to depart forever without some crowning work of hideousness and strangely morbid fancy. It is here – unredeemed and unredeemable – a disgrace to the writer, a shame to us all![48]

The tone of such commentary suggests that the 'works of Lord Lytton' the queer old josser and Joyce had in mind were almost certainly plural. Alongside *The Last Days of Pompeii* stood a body of work castigated for decades for its fascination with vice and crime, and its corrupting influence upon the young. Newgate novels were perceived to appeal to precisely the audience that would later be in thrall to 'penny dreadfuls': young boys and adolescents, tempted into imitation by glamorised criminal biographies. Henry Mayhew's reform classic *London Labour and the London Poor* frequently describes teenaged thieves and prostitutes who found in 'Newgate novels' their motive for criminality; John Binny, author of the 'Thieves and Swindlers' section of Mayhew's study, interviewed a former pickpocket who, he noted, had read Lytton; Bracebridge Hemyng, writing on prostitution, was similarly keen to trace the reading matter of young girls who became prostitutes, noting that the Newgate stories of criminal life were a 'very fruitful source of early demoralisation'.[49] An 1852 House of Commons Select Committee on Criminal and Destitute Juveniles is riddled with testimony from young criminals that Newgate fiction 'has been my ruin', doubtless, as Hollingsworth notes, a response to leading questions by boys eager to 'lay hold of an acceptable excuse'.[50] Lytton's crime fiction induced these anxieties, as his writing became immediately associated with the demoralisation of young people. As one of Lytton's less reputable correspondents, the celebrated courtesan Harriette Wilson explained, *Eugene Aram* was 'the favourite of the boarding school miss'.[51]

The threat Lytton posed to these imperilled innocents is easy to discern. *Eugene Aram* is the paradigmatic and self-referential example of Lytton's technique of masking 'immorality' behind erudition: the protagonist himself, incongruously combining intellectual virtuosity with criminality, shadows his creator, since Lytton himself blended conspicuous learning

---

[48] *The Spectator*, 12 December 1846, 1190; *The Times*, 17 December 1846, 7.
[49] See Hollingsworth, *The Newgate Novel*, 220–1.   [50] *Ibid*., 222.
[51] Quoted in Michael Sadleir, *Bulwer, A Panorama. I. Edward and Rosina, 1803–1836* (London: Constable, 1931), 245.

with a 'low' fascination with crime. For Lytton's 'Newgate' fiction uneasily subtends sensational accounts of criminal adventures with his notoriously florid prose style signposting its status as 'high art'. Here, for instance, is Eugene Aram at the murderous moment:

I had wrapped myself above fear into a high and preternatural madness of mind. *I looked upon the deed I was about to commit as a great and solemn sacrifice to knowledge, whose Priest I was.* The very silence breathed to me of a stern and awful sanctity – the repose, not of the charnel-house, but of the altar.[52]

The italics, the diction – 'preternatural', 'sanctity', 'repose', 'charnel-house' – and the metaphor of the murderer as a priest of knowledge are clearly designed to demarcate the novel not as cheaply sensationalist, but as the reading of persons of culture. Lytton's insistence that his tales of low life were high art is also manifest in his prefaces to *Eugene Aram* and other Newgate fictions, which meditate upon the relationship between art and criminality, propose social reforms and make serious claims for the novel as a prestigious genre.[53] In this context, Lytton is revealed as an ideologically laden intertextual presence in 'An Encounter'. His works are another instance of those duplicitous, morally ambiguous texts which seduce and compromise the boy-narrator. As Harmsworth used declarations of the 'wholesomeness' and 'pure tone' of his boys' stories in an attempt to mask their fundamental similarities to the dreadfuls, so the corrupting tendencies of Lytton's Newgate fiction was partly modified, partly masked by its aura of cultural elevation.

Amid these ambiguous, conflicting messages about what children should read, no wonder Joyce's boy-protagonist is at sea. The crisp polarities presented in the story between Roman History, Walter Scott, Thomas Moore, Lord Lytton and 'high culture' on the one hand, and the 'penny dreadfuls' of the Dillons' library on the other are relentlessly destabilised. The Harmsworth papers which the boys pour over confusingly present themselves as the wholesome choice of schoolmasters and parents, yet are scathingly denounced by Father Butler as no better than the 'penny dreadfuls' they ostentatiously condemned. Similarly, Lytton, presented as an elevating alternative to the Dillons' 'little library' and supposedly bestowing cultural capital upon his readers, is puzzlingly classed as the writer of certain books 'boys can't read', books which are precariously proximate in subject and reputation to the penny dreadfuls proscribed in the opening section of the story. The culturally volatile nature of these slippery intertexts is at the heart of Joyce's complex subversion of campaigns to police the reading of the young, campaigns which, as the controversies over *Dubliners'* publication demonstrate, had 'An Encounter' in its sights. For these volatile intertexts stand in allegorical relation to the perplexingly perverse figure of the queer old josser. Through the distorting lens of Joyce's story, the old man is revealed as a figure oddly like Harmsworth or Lytton – one who disingenuously adopts a role as an educator or elevator of youth, whilst covertly attempting to demoralise. Lytton's verbose and ostentatiously 'cultivated' prose style, Harmsworth's persistent claims to 'wholesomeness' each correlate within 'An Encounter' to the queer old josser's deeply suspect attempts to gain authority over and intimacy with the boys through the adoption of a familiar role – that of the adult supervisor of children's reading.

'An Encounter's' troubling intertexts, situated as they are on the faultlines of debates about what children should and should not read, thus correlate to the equally baffling and borderline figure of the queer old josser. For the old man is simultaneously social purity's propagandist and its threat. He attempts to establish his credentials as a friend and guide to youth through a discussion of 'good' and 'bad' books, recommending appropriately 'elevating' fiction whilst warning that 'of course...there were some of Lord Lytton's works which boys couldn't read' (*D* 17). He masquerades as that familiar figure, an overseer of children's reading, as another Father Butler, or as a comstockian vice crusader, eager to censor or sanction juvenile fiction. Joyce's masterstroke is to make the queer old josser simultaneously a child-protector and a would-be child-abuser, for his recommendation of Scott, Moore and Lytton, and his sudden warning about certain mysterious books boys cannot read is, of course, also a seduction. Whilst the old man's sentimental platitudes, 'He said that the happiest time of one's life was undoubtedly one's schoolboy days', leave his listeners 'bored' and 'silent' (*D* 17), his talk of books and reading immediately prompts both boys to confide, show off and ask questions. His claim that certain of Lytton's novels are unsuitable for the young is thus an assertion of enticing cultural power inextricably bound up with his later attempt to lure the narrator into that most improper knowledge of all – the plea 'that I should understand him' (*D* 20) and the desires which, after all, Joyce's contemporary John Lidwell designated 'this most odious vice of which modesty rejects the name and nature abominates the idea' (*L* II: 306). The old man's taboo longings are disguised beneath a familiar brand of censorious bibliophilia, where he initially suggests the addictive pleasures of reading ('He said he had all Sir Walter Scott's works and all Lord Lytton's works at home and never tired of reading them' – *D* 17), then vaguely insinuates the dangers of 'works which boys couldn't read' (*D* 17). The way his 'talk of books' veers between recommendation and censure draws attention once more to the fragility of the boundary between pleasure and its policing. 'An Encounter' thus presents in a particularly economic, compact form Joyce's central hypothesis about those who would erase all traces of 'impropriety' from fiction. Through the queer old josser's mimicry of a rhetoric highly suggestive of contemporary purity campaigns, Joyce suggestively connects desire and its discipline.

V

The closing paragraphs of 'An Encounter' elaborate the ideological argument about reading and censorship that the story's various compromising intertexts insinuate. For, if the queer old josser is Joyce's particularly savage burlesque of the child-protecting social purist, then as his monologue progresses, he reveals the extent of the pleasure he finds in prohibition. The boy is puzzled by the old man's sudden post-orgasmic veer away from his initial 'reasonable' (*D* 18) discourse 'of school and of books' (*D* 17) and 'about boys and sweethearts' (*D* 18), and towards 'the subject of chastising boys', where 'He seemed to have forgotten his recent liberalism' and insists that 'if ever he found a boy talking to girls or having a girl for a sweetheart he would whip him and whip him' (*D* 19). Yet, as the pattern of the old man's speech betrays, these apparent polarities of opinion are underneath the same. As the boy observes, when talking about girls, their 'nice white hands' and 'beautiful soft hair', the old man is 'magnetised by some words of his own speech, his mind was slowly circulating round and round in the same orbit', and he 'spoke mysteriously as if he were telling us something secret which he did not wish others to overhear' (*D* 18). When he turns to whipping, the tone, the boy recognises, is curiously similar: 'His mind, as if magnetised again by his speech, seemed to circle slowly round and round its new centre' (*D* 19). The paralytic tone of his two apparently contradictory monologues underlines, even to a child, the disconcerting continuity between vice and its control. Joyce's intertextual enunciation of a fragile, permeable and frequently breached boundary between the policing and the inciting of vice is symbolised by the specific nature of the queer old josser's sexual quirk.

As Colleen Lamos has already explored in relation to Joyce, flagellation occupied two ostensibly contradictory roles in late-Victorian culture, being both the punishment meted out to children and criminals, and a particularly popular sexual practice. Whipping collapsed the precarious distinction between pleasure and punishment, vice and its control in a particularly symbolic and explicit manner:

The crucial yet often indistinguishable difference between the uses of whipping for punishment and pleasure, or between the application of the rod for moral correction and moral corruption, points to the collaborative relation between desire and its censorship.[54]

Joyce's use of whipping to stand in allegorical relation to the pleasure intrinsic to discipline is typically culturally nuanced. Bizarrely, flagellation played a contentious role in a range of highly compromised social purity attempts to police sexual behaviour. Prior to the rise of the social purity movement in the mid 1880s, corporal punishment of adults was a relatively rare penalty for a narrow range of offences.[55] The decline in the popularity of corporal punishment during the mid-Victorian period made the renaissance of whipping statutes for sexual offences at the turn of the century particularly striking. The first, the 1885 Criminal Law Amendment Act to raise the female age of consent to sixteen, provided for the whipping of boys under sixteen convicted of sex with underage girls. An amendment prescribing corporal punishment for adult offenders was only narrowly defeated.[56] In 1898 a social purity-sponsored attempt to extend the 1824 Vagrancy Act succeeded, meaning that men living on a prostitute's earnings, or convicted of procuring women for 'immoral purposes' were to be classed as 'incorrigible rogues' and flogged. Social purity enthusiasm for flogging became still more intense during the decade leading up to the passing of the second Criminal Law Amendment Act of 1912, a legislative response to the widespread anxiety about 'White Slavery' or enforced prostitution. The president of the National Vigilance Association, the Earl of Aberdeen, won a standing ovation when at a social purity rally in December 1911 he explained 'he was not an advocate of flogging in the Army and Navy, but he would advocate it in the case of procurers'.[57] In the House of Commons, supporters of the 1912 Criminal Law Amendment Act insisted that any foreign procurer be deported forthwith 'with the hall-mark of some British muscle on his back', and MPs voted overwhelmingly in favour of a flogging clause by

---

54 Colleen Lamos, 'James Joyce and the English Vice', in *Novel: A Forum on Fiction* 29: 1 (1995), 19–26.
55 The only three British statutes prescribing flogging were the 1824 Vagabond Act, providing for the whipping of 'incorrigible rogues', vagrants receiving a second or subsequent conviction for begging; the Treason Act of 1842, allowing flogging for those convicted of attacks on the Sovereign; and the Security from Violence Act 1863, allowing the birching of armed robbers. The Whipping Act (1862) abolished corporal punishment of adults for all other offences.
56 Details from debates on Criminal Law Amendment (White Slavery) Act (1912), *Hansard*, 1 November 1912, cols. 776–90.
57 *The Vigilance Record*, December 1911.

297 votes to 44.[58] Elsewhere, social purists tried and failed to get flogging on the statute book for other offences. In 1889 and again in 1900, a short-lived Corporal Punishment bill was introduced by a group of MPs affiliated to the National Vigilance Association, which provided for the birching of child rapists, 'sodomites' and those convicted of bestiality.[59] The New York Society for the Suppression of Vice even called for the punishment for those responsible for 'penny dreadfuls': 'We want the whipping post and that old-fashioned implement of torture, the cat, for the men who publish this kind of paper.'[60] In this context, the National Vigilance Association's chairman William Coote's declaration that 'the law is schoolmaster to the whole community, preventing wrong by whipping most of the citizens into a condition of obedience' displayed a particularly appropriate metaphoric choice.[61] Whipping was integral to the social purity crusade to outlaw vice.

The queer old josser's monologue about whipping covertly alludes to the sexual practices social purists were eager to proscribe:

He said that if ever he found a boy talking to girls or having a girl for a sweetheart he would whip him and whip him; and that would teach him not to be talking to girls. And if a boy had a girl for a sweetheart and told lies about it then he would give him such a whipping as no boy ever got in this world. He said there was nothing in this world he would like so well as that. (*D* 19)

This hypothesised scenario is couched in saccharine euphemisms which perhaps conceals from his young listener the nature of the offence he discusses. Any sexual activity between juveniles was a source of great anxiety to purity workers, since how were they to proceed when the seducer of a girl under was not the dissolute gentleman of melodrama, but instead the boy next door? Middle-class reformers, from Andrew Mearns, author of *The Bitter Cry of Outcast London*, to Alfred Dyer of the National Vigilance Association and Ellice Hopkins of the White Cross League discovered amongst the 'submerged tenth' of the urban working class moral codes and conduct radically different from their own. In particular, they struggled to make sense of a precocious sexual culture where juveniles became sexually active at a far earlier stage of adolescence.[62] Joyce's narrator, of course, is

[58] *Hansard*, 1 November 1912, cols. 786; 784.
[59] Ian Gibson, *The English Vice: Beating, Sex and Shame in Victorian England And After* (London: Duckworth, 1979), 155–8.
[60] The New York Society for the Suppression of Vice, *Annual Report 6* (1880), 24.
[61] William Coote, 'Law and Morality', in *Public Morals*, ed. James Marchant (London: Morgan and Scott, 1902), 45–6, 69–70.
[62] See Edward Bristow, *Vice and Vigilance: Purity Movements in Britain since 1700* (Dublin: Gill and Macmillan, 1977), 92–7.

priggishly middle class, indignant at being mistaken for 'National School boys, to be *whipped*, as he called it' (*D* 19), yet the old man is curiously insensitive to the class signals the boys give out. Perhaps because of their deliberately 'adventurous' dress and behaviour; he remarks 'my friend was a very rough boy', adding 'When a boy was rough and unruly there was nothing would do him any good but a good sound whipping' (*D* 19). The queer old josser's talk of rough boys, sweethearts and whipping shadows the moral anxiety which can be glimpsed in one clause of the 1885 Criminal Law Amendment Act. Boys convicted of a sexual relationship with an underage girl, in the queer old josser's euphemistic term, 'having a girl for a sweetheart' escaped the prison sentence reserved for adults, but were instead punished by twelve strokes of the birch.

Social purists' enthusiasm for the corporal punishment of offenders against sexuality statutes was curious since the connection between flagellation and sexual arousal was widely acknowledged. Sexologists such as Ivan Block, Havelock Ellis and Richard Krafft-Ebing were busy diagnosing sadism and masochism as discrete sexual disorders, whilst, as Stephen Marcus has shown, underground booksellers circulated a 'vast literature of flagellation', a pornography closely connected to the nineteenth century's thriving flagellant brothels.[63] Ironically enough W. T. Stead's 'Maiden Tribute of Modern Babylon', the exposé which precipitated the 1885 Criminal Law Amendment Act and funded the National Vigilance Association, disclosed

Flogging, both of men and women, goes on regularly in ordinary rooms, but the cry of the bleeding subject never attracts attention from the outside world . . . When means of stifling a cry – a pillow, a sheet, or even a pocket handkerchief lie all around, there is practically no danger. To some men, however, the shriek of torture is the essence of their delight, and they would not silence by a single note the cry of agony over which they gloat.[64]

'Massage parlours' freely advertised 'discipline treatment' for 'poor circulation' (erectile dysfunction) in popular papers such as *Reynold's News*, whilst periodicals as respectable as *Notes and Queries* and *The Englishwoman's Domestic Magazine* published lengthy correspondences on the 'birching

---

[63] For a summary of early 'sexological' and later psychoanalytical investigations into flagellation, see Gibson, 'Towards an Understanding of Sexual Flagellation', chapter 8 of *The English Vice*, 234–87. For Victorian flagellant pornography and brothels, see Stephen Marcus, 'A Child is Being Beaten', chapter 6 of *The Other Victorians: A Study of Sexuality and Pornography in Mid-Nineteenth Century England* (London: Weidenfeld and Nicolson, 1970), 252–65.

[64] W. T. Stead, 'The Maiden Tribute of Modern Babylon', *The Pall Mall Gazette*, 7 July 1885, 5.

question'.[65] Those still too innocent to recognise the erotic implications of flagellation were alerted by sporadic birching scandals, such as the first prosecution under the 1898 Vagrancy Amendment Act, of the Marylebone Road Massage Parlour, an institution specialising in 'the treatment of rheumatism by dry hot-air baths, massage and discipline', or a 1904 police raid on a massage parlour in St John's Wood, which found birches, restraints and other paraphernalia.[66] Both cases were high-profile triumphs for the National Vigilance Association, since they had carried out preliminary investigations, tipped off the police and pushed through the laws criminalizing such behaviour.[67] Whipping was thus simultaneously integral to what the social purists wanted to repress, and their favoured mode of repression, an irony which played into the hands of anti-flogging campaigners.

These ambiguities were exploited by social purity's vocal opponents, in particular the coalition of liberal reformers grouped around the Humanitarian League who campaigned against all forms of corporal punishment in schools, the military and the police courts.[68] Between them, the social purists and the humanitarians made flagellation a hotly contested issue throughout the first decade of the nineteenth century. The 1908 Corporal Punishment Restriction bill, attempting to abolish flogging for all adults over sixteen, failed after a second reading, but the Children's Act of that year reduced the maximum number of strokes for juvenile offenders from twelve to six. Public birching was finally abolished for naval cadets in 1906, to be replaced by caning. The frequency of flogging punishments – between 1900 and 1911, 28,781 young offenders were flogged in England and Wales – combined with a series of brutal prison birchings to help the anti-flogging campaign further.[69] However, the most powerful argument that humanitarians could employ was the insinuation that flogging was an unwholesome

---

[65] For instance, in 1903 *Home Chat* ran an article on the chastisement of children, which coyly noted that birching 'is used by the professional masseuse, who treats some patients with a gentle application of the rod to stimulate sluggish circulation' ('Flogging is Back in Fashion', *Home Chat*, January 1903, 5). For other birching correspondences in 'family' journals, see Gibson, 'The Flagellant Correspondence Column in Nineteenth Century England', chapter 5 of *The English Vice*, 165–94.

[66] Henry Salt, *The Flogging Craze: A Statement of the Case Against Corporeal Punishment* (London: Allen and Unwin, 1916), 82–3.

[67] *The Vigilance Record*, November 1899, 4; August 1904, 7.

[68] The Humanitarian League's campaign against flogging was threatening enough to provoke the foundation of a specifically pro-flogging organisation, the Duty and Discipline Movement, which published a series of essays on flagellation during the 1900s, collected as *Anarchy or Order?* (London: Duty and Discipline Movement, 1914). Their views were presented, or perhaps spoofed, in a single issue of a magazine *The Brutalitarian: A Journal for the Sane and Strong*, published in October 1904.

[69] The Humanitarian League was quick to publicise cases such as the birching of four boys under nine for petty offences in October 1901, or the flogging of elderly tramps classed as 'incorrigible rogues' under the 1824 Vagrancy Act. See Salt, *The Flogging Craze*, 15–20.

punishment, a manifestation of the perverse sexuality it intended to repress. George Bernard Shaw, a stalwart of the Humanitarian League and a fierce critic of social purity pieties, was particularly vociferous. In the wake of the 1898 Vagrancy Amendment Act, Shaw pointed out

White slaves make money for themselves and their employers by allowing men to flog them. Whenever a flogging is described in the papers they have a rush of custom. The literature of their trade is full of flogging. Men actually pay women to flog them. 'Russian Flagellation' is impudently announced on posters... Why, then, is flogging chosen? Why do people frantically keep protesting that it is the only punishment that these people fear? The answer is obvious. The Act is a final triumph of the vice it pretends to suppress.[70]

Shaw boldly stated a truth which must have been universally acknowledged, and his argument was frequently reiterated. For Joseph Collinson in 1905, the Humanitarian League's secretary, recent investigations by 'sexologists' proved that 'flagellomania is a real and widespread disease... birching has come to be regarded among medical men in France, Germany and other parts of the Continent as a sensuous gratification for people of morbid tastes'.[71] His colleague Henry Salt stated the case even more explicitly in his 1916 polemic *The Flogging Craze*, where a whole chapter on 'The Lash As Purifier' ridiculed the 'strange hallucinations' of social purists who 'believe that the lash, and especially the birch, can be used as a penalty for sexual offences and as an instrument for moral reform'.[72] Following Shaw in diagnosing 'flagellomania... a real and very mischievous disease', Salt summarised two decades' work of the humanitarian League by directly comparing social purity's enthusiasm for flogging with a parallel enthusiasm catered for in contemporary brothels.[73] The anti-flagellation campaign exploited widespread cultural unease about the meaning of the punishment in a society saturated by highly visible intimations of an explicitly sadomasochistic sexuality.

Joyce's sympathies with this campaign against flogging can be safely assumed. Firstly, his opposition to corporal punishment is explicit in the second chapter of *A Portrait of the Artist as a Young Man*, and, unusually for the

---

[70] *Ibid.*, 88.
[71] Joseph Collinson, *Facts About Flogging* (London: Humanitarian League, 1905), 6–7, 13.
[72] Salt, *The Flogging Craze*, 79.
[73] Disquiet about flogging's erotic implications even affected some of the more moderate social purists. W. T. Stead ran a campaign against flogging in the *Pall Mall Gazette* in 1887. The Revd Edward Lyttelton, a stalwart of the Social Purity Alliance and the Church of England Purity Society, who had published a popular pamphlet *On The Training of the Young in Laws of Sex*, quietly replaced birching on the bare buttocks with caning on the hand when he became headmaster at Eton in 1911. See Gibson, *The English Vice*, 149, 136–7.

time, he refused to smack either of his children, arguing 'Children must be educated by love, not punishment.'[74] Secondly, as Lamos observes, his own sexual tastes seem to have corroborated the theorised connection between whipping and desire.[75] Bloom's Circean confrontations with Mrs Mervyn Talboys and her comrades clearly draw upon encounters with flagellant heroines such as Lady Termagant Flaybum in popular flagellant pornography, whilst his defence 'Refined birching to stimulate the circulation' (*U* 15: 1096) seems to quote directly from the advertising copy of a massage parlour. 'An Encounter', however, is Joyce's most pointed creative incursion into the fiercely contested debates upon flagellation which dominated the decade of the story's composition. The story transforms the humanitarian argument against social purity's commitment to corporal punishment into a parable of remarkable cultural precision, as Joyce, like Shaw, construes flogging as 'the final triumph of the vice it pretends to suppress'. Yet, Joyce goes further than liberal anti-flogging campaigners like Shaw who, whilst pointing out the connections between flagellation and sexual fetish, never quite suggested that social purists themselves were concealing their own sadistic desires behind their philanthropy. Instead, Joyce insinuates that his elderly, paralytic pederast represents the dark underbelly of the social purity enthusiasm for flagellation. Whilst the fetishistic qualities of the queer old josser's desire to punish are unmistakeable, so too, to contemporary readers, would have been his unnerving subscription to two key social purity articles of faith; the first that there are certain books 'which boys couldn't read', the second that 'rough boys' displaying signs of precocious sexuality should be whipped. The queer old josser is thus, as his comments on reading earlier suggest, a devastating caricature of the vice crusaders who were threatening, and would continue to threaten Joyce's work.

Joyce's anticipatory assault upon social purity goes beyond his story's complex, slippery nature which makes its 'moral' so difficult to discern. If 'the more subtle inquisitor will denounce *An Encounter*, the enormity of which the printer cannot see because he is, as I said, a plain blunt man' (*L* II: 134), the story's 'enormity' to would-be censors is not just that what the old man does in the corner of the field is insinuated but never stated, an obscenity literally off stage. Its enormity also lies in the way the story opens up through its off-stage intertexts those questions about children, their reading, their sexuality and their punishment that the vigilance leagues attempted to close down. The vice organisations who would eventually pursue Joyce were preoccupied with the imposition of a series of categories

---

[74] Ellmann, *James Joyce*, 434.   [75] Lamos, 'James Joyce and the English Vice', 20–5.

by which morality could be governed. 'An Encounter' relentlessly queries these rigidly demarcated categories, introducing uncertainties, confusions, breached boundaries and grey areas into the moral questions social purists regarded as fixed. Joyce's loaded cultural allusions to a sequence of borderline texts – the penny dreadfuls and Harmsworth boys' papers, the 'elevating' Lytton novels which are simultaneously pernicious – map out the continuities between the vicious and the virtuous to imply that the former is integral to the latter. Nowhere is this argument more symbolically freighted than in Joyce's portrait of whipping as simultaneously punitive and perverse. For whipping was not only the social purist's favoured mode of legislative enforcement. As William Coote's claim that 'the law is schoolmaster to the whole community, preventing wrong by whipping most of the citizens into a condition of obedience' suggests, whipping metonymically stands for the purity campaign's reliance upon coercion to enforce, restrict and discipline the public, and its writers, into a state of virtue. In 'An Encounter', Joyce allows flagellation to take on these meanings, and by isolating and displaying the fundamental perversity behind the queer old josser's mania for whipping, he insinuates, in a way which must have been unmistakeable to those 'more subtle' contemporary readers he sought, the compromises, ambiguities and murky motives he ascribes to those who would censor his writing. 'An Encounter' thus functions as a playful, devastating and intricate pre-emptive strike against the various Vigilance Committees 'whose object it is to seek out and suppress all writings of immoral tendencies' that John Lidwell warned him against. The story appears in *Dubliners* as the first such anticipation; it would not be the last.

CHAPTER 2

'Don't cry for me, Argentina': 'Eveline', white slavery and the seductions of propaganda

It finally got to her that Buenos Ayres was her own private prison.
That's when she decided to run away.[1]

'Eveline' seems to be straightforward enough, a five-page story about a young woman's choice between home and abroad, entrapment and escape, duty and love. Eveline has a 'hard life' (*D* 31) working in a department store for seven shillings a week, whilst keeping house for her violent and threatening father, bound to a promise made to her dying mother to 'keep the home together as long as she could' (*D* 33). Into this dismal existence comes Frank, 'very kind, manly, openhearted' (*D* 31), a sailor 'over to the old country just for a holiday' (*D* 32). Frank has prospects: 'She was to go away with him by the night-boat to be his wife and to live with him in Buenos Ayres where he had a home waiting for her' (*D* 31). Yet at the North Wall quay Eveline offers her lover 'no sign of love or farewell or recognition' (*D* 34) as she watches him board alone the steamer which will separate them forever. Why does Eveline refuse her chance of escape? For Hugh Kenner, she is unconsciously wise to do so, since her story seethes with latent sexual danger. Noting Dublin night-boats all left for Liverpool, where travellers caught further steamers, he reads Frank as a 'bounder with a glib line trying to pick himself up a piece of skirt'. Had Eveline left Dublin, Kenner speculates she would have been seduced and abandoned in Liverpool: as it is, the tragedy of Joyce's story is that she will spend the rest of her life 're-gretting her great refusal'.[2] Kenner's concern was shared by contemporary social purists, who similarly constructed the risk Eveline contemplates as a fatal error. Young women like Eveline, city-dwelling, working outside the home, estranged from parents, virginal yet eager for romance, courtship

---

[1] *Gilda*, dir. Charles Vidor, 1947. In 1904, Argentina's capital, Buenos Aires, was spelt Buenos Ayres. To avoid confusion, I have adopted the Edwardian spelling, also used by Joyce in 'Eveline' and by the contemporary sources cited here.

[2] Hugh Kenner, *The Pound Era* (London: Pimlico, 1991), 37.

56

and marriage provoked an epidemic of social purity anxieties. As we have seen, vigilantes ardently desired to protect the 'young person', the child or adolescent, from the many corruptions of modern society. Whilst, for schoolboys, those corruptions might be 'criminal' boys' papers, for girls like Eveline, wavering between adolescence and womanhood, the danger was more commonly theorised as unscrupulous men. In particular, these anxieties were exacerbated by the surge in young single female migration from around 1880 through to 1920. What would become of these vulnerable young women, travelling unprotected from the countryside to city, or, worse still, from one country to another in search of work and better social opportunities? In 'Eveline', Joyce produces a story of frustrated emigration and potential sexual danger which subversively alludes to this cultural unease and thus acts as an elaborate pastiche of one of social purity's most potent propagandas. Eveline's paralytic inability to board the steamer that will carry her to the 'clean air' of a new life is Joyce's dramatisation of the impact of social purity propaganda upon a bewildered, vulnerable adolescent. In this early story, Joyce's fascination with contemporary attempts to discipline vice is foregrounded as he inserts a notorious scare-story within a deceptively simple frame.

I

The germ of Joyce's subversion lies in the process of 'Eveline's' commission. In July 1904, Joyce was living precariously in Dublin and attempting to scrape together the money for two steamer passages for his planned flight to Europe with Nora Barnacle. George Russell, the literary editor of *The Irish Homestead*, was sympathetic to his poverty and suggested

Look at the story in this paper The Irish Homestead. Could you write anything simple, rural?, livemaking?, pathos?, which could be inserted so as not to shock the readers. If you could furnish a short story about 1800 words suitable for insertion the editor will pay £1. It is easily earned money if you can write fluently and don't mind playing to the common understanding and liking for once in a way. You can sign it any name you like as a pseudonym. (*L* II: 43)

The Irish Homestead, or 'the pigs paper', as Joyce derisively termed it, was the journal of the Irish co-operative farming movement, and its literary pages specialised in 'simple, rural' Celtic twilight fictions of national identity.[3] It was at the forefront of a contemporary nationalist initiative to slow the rate of emigration, explaining schemes to 'Brighten Rural Life' in its editorials

---

[3] Richard Ellmann, *James Joyce* (Oxford: Oxford University Press, 1983), 164.

and holding an annual 'Stop Emigration' competition which offered a cash prize to 'the co-operative society which shall have done the most to make their parish a place from which no Irishman would want to emigrate'.[4] Its proprietor, Horace Plunkett, described emigration as 'the symptom of a low national vitality...which not only depletes our population, but drains it of those elements that can least be spared'.[5] Arguing that 'we cannot exercise much direct influence over the desire to emigrate, beyond spreading knowledge as to the real conditions of life in America for which home life is often ignorantly bartered', his understanding of emigration as the symptom of a national wasting disease looked to the popular press as the cure.[6]

Accordingly, the fiction published in *The Irish Homestead* between 1900 and 1904 uniformly insisted that emigration was not a road to self-fulfilment, adventure, or even Eveline Hill's 'Escape!' (*D* 33). Rather, it ruptured the natural bonds of lovers, families, community and nation.[7] If Joyce followed Russell's advice and scanned back issues of the paper for likely stories to reinterpret, then one typical emigration story which might have appealed to his well-documented delight in coincidence was Father Jeremiah O'Donovan's 'The Awakening of Brian Joyce'.[8] It is set in Galway, home to 'generations of the Joyces', on the eve of Brian Joyce's departure

---

[4] *The Irish Homestead*, 20 October 1900; 8 November 1902.
[5] Horace Plunkett, *Ireland in the New Century* (London: J. Murray, 1904), 41.   [6] *Ibid.*, 40.
[7] Examples include George Morris, 'Monica's Twin Sister', *The Irish Homestead*, 6 February 1904, 114, where parental insistence that the hero take a dowered bride rather than the penniless Monica forces the desperate lovers to contemplate 'clearing off to the land of Stars and Stripes, aye, and sink or swim'. The lead story of the 1904 'Celtic Christmas' supplement, 'An American Visitor' similarly tells of a past emigrant who regrets ever leaving Ireland, a theme repeated by Seumas McManus' poem in the same issue, 'The Disillusioned', where another repentant emigrant rues the day he saw 'a glittering world beyond' the old country, and pleads 'With ye I'll find forgetfulness of a world so void and vain / Oh mountains, mountains of my youth, fling wide your arms again' ('A Celtic Christmas', *The Irish Homestead*, December 1904). America was repeatedly constructed as a 'glittering', but ultimately 'void and vain' locus of disappointment and heartbreak.
[8] Jeremiah O'Donovan, 'The Awakening of Brian Joyce', in 'A Celtic Christmas', *The Irish Homestead*, December 1901, 14–16. O'Donovan's life story ironically shadows his commitment to the prevention of emigration through propaganda. He met Plunkett in 1899, and was described in a pen-portrait in *The Irish Homestead*, 20 January 1900 as 'one of the best exponents of the co-operative movement, not only in its idealist, but in its practical aspect'. His skill as a propagandist made him a regular contributor of articles and short stories to *The Irish Homestead* between 1898 and 1903, but in 1904, O'Donovan left the priesthood after a dispute with the church over his political activities, and emigrated to England, where he changed his name to Gerald, married, and found work as a journalist. During the First World War, his 'energy and enthusiasm' led to his appointment as Head of British Propaganda in Italy under the Ministry of Information, where the novelist and travel writer Rose Macaulay was his secretary. They began a clandestine relationship, which continued until his death in 1942. See John Ryan, 'Gerald O'Donovan: Poet, Novelist and Irish Revivalist', *The Journal of the Galway Archaeological and Historical Society* 48 (1996), 1–48 for a fine account of O'Donovan's life.

for America. Brian's farewell party is marred by the tears of his girlfriend Nora, who laments

The fever for roaming is in your blood. The people are in Ireland all for America now. I'm not the first girl America put a heavy cross on.[9]

That night, Brian's sleep is disturbed by a dream vision of Kathleen Ni Houlihan, who appears 'to the sound of harps' and asks 'Are you, like the others, going to leave me?'[10] Chastened, O'Donovan's Joyce stays in Ireland to marry Nora, explaining 'I've learnt my duty now to God and to you and to Ireland, and I'll do it.'[11] 'The Awakening of Brian Joyce', 'simple, rural and livemaking', is a typical *Homestead* emigration story. Firstly, America threatens to lure the protagonist away from his true love and a whole-some, sober and industrious rural community with (hollow) promises of material gain. Secondly, O'Donovan gestures towards the national cultural inheritance the hero is on the verge of renouncing through smattering the dialogue with Gaelic, and through the Kathleen Ni Houlihan figure. Finally, the protagonist is brought to the realisation that emigration is a betrayal of Ireland, and must therefore lead to misery.

This, then, was the kind of 'simple, rural' emigration narrative Russell urged Joyce to emulate, where the refusal to board the steamer in the closing paragraph signals not paralysis but national awakening. Instead, Joyce's story queries the conventions of *Homestead* emigration fiction: lovers are parted, not reconciled, by Eveline's decision to stay at home; the story is set not amid the pretty cottages and wholesome peasantry of rural Galway, but amid the urban landscape of 'little brown houses', 'new red houses' and at that familiar stranger in the city, the 'man out of the last house' who daily passes her home (*D* 29). Even Joyce's use of Gaelic challenges the use of smatterings of the language in the *Homestead* to encourage those 'believers in the language movement' studying in Gaelic League classes: 'Derevaun Seraun!' (*D* 33) is Gaelic corrupted into a nonsense withholding its meaning from heroine and reader alike.[12] However, 'Eveline' most significantly differs from 'Brian Joyce' in the gender of its would-be émigré. Predictably, whilst *The Irish Homestead* considered male emigration to be a betrayal of Ireland, it took female emigration still more seriously. It had good reason to do so, since, as Hasia Diner and Janet Nolan both note, single literate young women like Eveline Hill composed the majority of emigrants leaving Ireland

[9] O'Donovan, 'Awakening', 15.   [10] *Ibid.*, 16.   [11] *Ibid*.
[12] For a summary of possible interpretations of 'Derevaun Seraun', see John Wyse Jackson and Bernard McGinley, eds., *James Joyce's Dubliners: An Annotated Edition* (London: Sinclair Stevenson, 1993), 31.

between 1885 and 1910, an anomaly in the history of European emigration patterns.[13] Such women were slamming the door on the 'home country' which *The Irish Homestead* and affiliated nationalist groups promoted as an Irishwoman's proper place. Their behaviour unleashed a widespread moral panic about these unchaperoned, independent and adventurous women, and the sexual dangers which could await them.

   The gender of would-be emigrants supplied a potent dimension to the Irish emigration anxieties outlined above, as nationalist critics borrowed from social purity rhetoric to predict what John Verschoyle described as 'the moral murder of countless virtuous Irish maidens'.[14] Nationalist concerns about the sexual vulnerability of female emigrants were exemplified in Agnes O'Farelly's 1900 lecture to the Gaelic League:

Oh, those poor little brown-haired Irish girls – they don't know yet what is before them. No wonder the wisest pinch and scrape for a few years so that they may go home and settle down. But they are not all wise.[15]

This glimpse of nebulous peril was enlarged upon by Father O'Donovan, a Gaelic League colleague of O'Farelly's:

What of the girls? Ask those who know the slums of Chicago, of New York, of Boston. I shall throw no mud at an Irish girl, even when she has fallen. Poor, misguided, trusting girls, innocent even in their guilt, was there no-one to tell them of the whirlpool into which they were being cast adrift?[16]

O'Donovan responded to his own call to propaganda in *The Irish Homestead* later that year, where his story 'Rose Brolley' offers a guided tour of the 'whirlpool' of loose living awaiting the Irish girl abroad. Rose, a nineteen-year-old Galway girl, throws over 'an honest man's love and a little cottage by the sea' for the temptations of 'balls, parties and big wages and theatres and fine clothes' described to her in letters from her friend Nell, recently settled in New York.[17] Telling her disappointed suitor 'I would make a bad wife to you with the longing for excitement that is in my blood', Rose joins Nell to seek pleasure in Lower East Side dance halls:

[13] Hasia Diner, *Erin's Daughters in America: Irish Immigrant Women in the Nineteenth Century* (Baltimore: Johns Hopkins University Press, 1983), xvi; Janet Nolan, *Ourselves Alone: Women's Emigration from Ireland 1885–1920* (Kentucky: University Press of Kentucky, 1989), 49.
[14] John Verschoyle, 'The Condition of Kerry', *Living Age*, 171 (1886), 552–3.
[15] Agnes O'Farrelly, 'The Reign of Humbug', *Gaelic League Pamphlets* 10 (Dublin: Gaelic League, 1900), 11.
[16] Jeremiah O'Donovan, 'An O'Growney Memorial Lecture', *Gaelic League Pamphlets* 26 (Dublin: Gaelic League, 1900), 15.
[17] Jeremiah O'Donovan, 'Rose Brolley', *The Irish Homestead*, December 1902, 21.

The men were drunk and the women were encouraging them. Rose was shocked by their coarse talk. The natural refinement of the Irish peasantry clung to her and her heart sickened at the vulgarity which surrounded her.[18]

Soon, Rose succumbs to a mystery illness, and her story closes with her exemplary death in the care of the Sisters of Mercy, lamenting in a letter to her slighted Galway lover

I was young and foolish and led away by love of excitement. It is hollow and disappointing life is here. The only happy days I have spent are the few with the Sisters, waiting to die.[19]

Jeremiah O'Donovan forcefully constructs 'home', meaning both the 'little cottage by the sea', and Ireland, as his heroine's proper place, calling upon the *Homestead*'s readers' understanding of the 'natural refinement' of Irish womanhood to emphasise her displacement. He draws upon a contemporary nationalist insistence upon the innate moral purity of the Irish, a synthesis of national pride and sexual chastity contained in Arthur Griffith's boast that 'all of us know that Irish women are the most virtuous women in the world'.[20] In this context, O'Donovan diagnoses Rose's desire to leave her homeland as the symptom of 'a longing for excitement' that is, like a congenital and contagious disease, 'in my blood'. O'Donovan's insistence that Rose's emigration is a fatal act of un-Irish sexual impropriety is underscored by her deathbed association with the Sisters of Mercy, well known throughout Ireland as the supervisors of Magdalen Asylums for penitent fallen women.[21]

If this is the kind of story George Russell expected Joyce to reproduce for his £1, then what startles is the meticulousness of the pastiche. Joyce's naïve nineteen year old, like Rose Brolley, is enchanted by the tall tales she hears about 'abroad', in this case not the accounts of balls, parties and frocks offered by an emigrant girlfriend, but, perhaps more sinisterly, the 'stories of the terrible Patagonians' (*D* 32) and fantasies of the 'home waiting for her' (*D* 31) in Buenos Ayres supplied by her mysterious lover Frank. Eveline even shares Rose's 'longing for excitement' that O'Donovan presents as almost a fatal disease 'in my blood': she enjoys Frank's attentions because 'First of all it had been an excitement for her to have a fellow'

---

[18] *Ibid*., 22.   [19] *Ibid*.
[20] Quoted in Margaret Ward, 'Conflicting Interests: The British and Irish Suffrage Movements', *Feminist Review* 50 (1995), 133.
[21] For an account of the Sisters of Mercy's rescue work with magdalen asylums, see Maria Luddy, *Women and Philanthropy in Nineteenth Century Ireland* (Cambridge: Cambridge University Press, 1995), 110–15.

Table 1. *Emigration from Ireland to America and to Argentina 1886–1904[a]*

	Total emigration	To America	To Argentina
1886	63,416	50,723	41
1887	82,923	69,798	44
1888	78,684	66,906	123
1889	70,477	59,723	1,651
1890	61,313	52,685	65
1891	59,623	52,273	27
1892	50,867	46,550	30
1893	48,147	45,243	12
1894	35,895	33,096	20
1895	48,703	45,298	24
1896	38,995	35,216	7
1897	32,535	28,760	3
1898	32,241	27,855	31
1899	41,232	35,433	18
1900	45,288	37,765	16
1901	39,870	31,942	1
1902	40,190	33,683	0
1903	40,653	33,501	0
1904	37,415	30,580	0

[a] Table compiled from *Parliamentary Papers*, 'Emigration: III: Statistical Table: Ireland', 1886–1904. For Irish emigration patterns to Argentina, see Patrick McKenna, 'Irish Emigration to Argentina: A Different Model', in Andy Bielenberg, ed., *The Irish Diaspora* (London: Longman, 2000), 195–212.

(*D* 32) and, above all, 'she wanted to live' (*D* 33). Frank, with his tan, his fascinating stories, his theatre tickets, his song about the lass that loved the sailor, and, above all, his prepaid passage to Buenos Ayres offers Eveline the kind of 'excitement' which proved fatal to Rose Brolley and which *The Irish Homestead*, discerning the 'exit' buried in 'excitement', described as 'a dangerous thirst for sensation more easily slaked abroad'.[22] However, the most significant difference between 'Eveline' and 'Brian Joyce', 'Rose Brolley' and the host of other anti-emigration stories to be found in *The Irish Homestead* between 1900 and 1904 is Eveline's intended destination. North, not South America is the ubiquitous temptation in *The Irish Homestead* throughout this period and Argentina is never mentioned. A glance at Irish emigration statistics shows why (see table 1). During the two decades

[22] 'Recreation in Rural Ireland', *The Irish Homestead*, 20 October 1900, 14.

preceding Frank's return to Dublin, the rate of migration to Argentina from
Ireland had steadily diminished, surging suddenly in 1889, then dwindling
away to zero. Behind these statistics lies Argentina's reputation in Ireland
as the locus of tall tales, betrayals and disappointments.

At the turn of the century, Argentina was host to a thriving Irish colony
of about 30,000 people, as the Irish journalist William Bulfin noted:

Over the richest sheepruns in the province of Buenos Ayres you may gallop during
every hour of the longest day in summer without crossing a single rood of land
that is not owned by some son of the Emerald Isle.[23]

However, few more Irish were joining them. They were deterred by a migration crisis in 1889, when, as a British parliamentary report noted, 'an excep-
tionally high number of 1,651 (1,497 who went by the same ship *Dresden*)'
had left Ireland for Buenos Ayres.[24] These emigrants were given free steamer
passages through Dublin agents on commission from the Argentinean government: they were promised free employment bureau services and temporary accommodation on their arrival, but when on 12 February 1889 the
Dresden docked, it became clear the authorities were ill-prepared.[25] The
reception hostel was severely overcrowded, as one eye-witness reported:

There were 3,000 people there, all mixed together regardless of sex or nationality.
The Irish having come last, many hundreds were sleeping in the courtyard.[26]

Furthermore, the new recruits were ill-suited for the kind of work on offer.
As George Jenner, the British *Charge D'Affaires* in Buenos Ayres complained
to the Foreign Office

the subordinate agents employed in Ireland have proved utterly corrupt and worthless, and have allowed the propaganda to fall into the hands of a class of persons
most unfitted for emigration to this country, including prostitutes and beggars.[27]

When the Irish expatriate community learned that a further 12,000 Irish
were preparing to escape bad harvests in Ireland and sail for Argentina, they
protested that the Dublin agent 'has been scattering falsehoods broadcast

[23] William Bulfin, *Tales of the Pampas* (London: Overseas Library, 1900), 205. William Bulfin was
    an Irish settler in Buenos Ayres, who wrote from the 1870s until the 1890s about the lives of the
    Irish migrants under the name 'Che Buono', and much of his writing appeared in both *The Weekly
    Freeman* and *The Southern Cross* around that period. He was better known for his popular *Rambles
    In Eirinn*, which contains an account of meeting Joyce and Oliver StJohn Gogarty at the Martello
    Tower in Sandycove. Joyce commented scathingly on his contributions to Arthur Griffith's *Sinn
    Féin* in several letters to Stanislaus (*L* II: 191, 209).
[24] 'Emigration: (III: Statistical Tables): Ireland', *Parliamentary Paper* 79 (1890), 761.
[25] Paedar Kirby, *Ireland and Latin America: Links and Lessons* (Blackrock: Trocaire, 1992), 88.
[26] 'Emigration from Ireland to Argentina', *Parliamentary Paper* 76 (1889), 243.   [27] *Ibid.*, 240.

throughout Ireland', and petitioned the Catholic Archbishop of Dublin to 'use his influence to stop all emigration to this country'.[28] Irish Home Rule MPs urged the Foreign Secretary to 'issue a warning to poor Irish people to abstain from emigrating to Argentina' and when Tim Healy MP discovered in June 1889 that 3,500 people had, on the promise of free passages, sold up their property and travelled to Queenstown to board a steamer that never arrived, he protested 'It is a monstrous thing that a foreign government trying to recruit its population here should be allowed to bring ruin on thousands of people.'[29] Further distribution of assisted passages was swiftly prohibited, and customs officers in all Irish ports were obliged to report 'any large body of Irish emigrants travelling to the Argentinean Republic'.[30] Argentina swiftly became perceived as an unscrupulous foreign power intent upon exploiting Irish hardship. As the emigration statistics clearly show, its reputation persisted into the next century.

In this context, then, Joyce's use of Argentina in his *Irish Homestead* emigration story seems suspicious in its apparent conformity to Horace Plunkett's request that such fiction should remind readers of the dangers of abroad 'for which home life in Ireland is often so ignorantly bartered'. Firstly, Argentina must have enjoyed a contemporary reputation in Ireland as the locus of disappointment, exploitation and betrayal, a reputation which would surely signal to *Homestead* readers that Eveline is wise to remain on shore. Secondly, this reputation compromises Frank's claims to have 'fallen on his feet in Buenos Ayres' (*D* 32), since just as his tales of the terrible Patagonians are suspect because the Patagonians became extinct many years before his birth, so too his narrative of success in Argentina seems to call upon a distant, half-remembered story of Irish enterprise abroad, rather than its present reality. No wonder Mr Hill articulates his distrust of Frank in terms which insist upon the dangers of participating in Frank's propaganda: rather than warn Eveline not to have anything to do with him, he forbids her 'to have anything to say to him' (*D* 32), a nuance which betrays his fear of his daughter's vulnerability to her lover's persuasive and seductive discourse. These details appear to confirm Joyce's docile accommodation of George Russell's brief that he 'cater to the common understanding' and reproduce the *Homestead* editorial line on emigration. However, Joyce subverts that brief through smuggling into the Irish nationalist journal of self-reliance a pastiche of a second anti-emigration campaign, this time

[28] *Buenos Ayres Standard*, 17 April 1889.
[29] *Hansard*, 26 March 1889, col. 841; 'Emigration from Ireland to Argentina', *Parliamentary Paper* 76 (1889): 300.
[30] 'Emigration from Ireland to Argentina', *Parliamentary Paper* 76 (1889), 275, 280.

orchestrated by social purists in Britain and the United States. This act of cultural hijack is particularly suggestive since, by 1904, the traditional seduction and betrayal story, which shadows Hugh Kenner's reading of 'Eveline', had a very contemporary twist. For over a decade, social purists had been disseminating their own narrative of female emigration and sexual danger, a narrative produced in England, exported to Ireland, and centred upon Buenos Ayres.

II

On New Year's Day, 1880, Alfred Dyer, an evangelical writer of purity tracts against 'self-abuse' and the editor of the purity journal *The Sentinel*, broke a sensational story in the British press. Dyer had rescued four young British women from a state-registered brothel in Brussels, where they had been imprisoned for some months. The first was Ellen Newland, a nineteen-year-old former maidservant from Brighton, and her experiences were exemplary. She had been courted by a man 'of respectable exterior' she had met in the street, who 'walked out' with her and treated her to supper and the theatre. After a time, her suitor offered marriage if she would leave the country with him. The couple travelled as far as Calais, where Ellen was abducted by her fiancé's accomplice and taken to Brussels. Speaking no French, she was gynaecologically examined, registered as a prostitute and sold to a *maison tolérée*.[31] For Dyer, Ellen's case indicated a cross-channel traffic in young English girls, lured abroad to what he termed 'the confinement and horrors of a licensed hell'.[32] His account of her rescue, *The European Slave Traffic in English Girls* ran to six editions in nine months. Dyer had produced a paradigmatic narrative of sexual betrayal and disgrace which would capture the public imagination for four decades. 'White slavery' was a moral panic that answered a question which many social purists were unwilling to face: what could induce a woman to enter prostitution? To organisations like the National Vigilance Association, the proliferation of prostitutes and brothels at the turn of the century could best be explained by a melodrama of coercion which alleged that every year thousands of virginal young women were decoyed from their homes, captured and sold into prostitution by unscrupulous procurers. Crucially, white slavery was an international phenomenon. Whilst some women were undoubtedly tricked into brothels in their own country, many, social purists alleged, were

---

[31] Alfred Dyer, *The European Slave Traffic in English, Irish and Scottish Girls: A Narrative of Facts* (London: Dyer Brothers, 1881), 25–32.
[32] *Ibid.*, 32.

lured abroad under false promises of marriage or employment, and, once away from home, were forced into 'regulated houses', or legalised brothels in countries that tolerated prostitution. Such countries, it was theorised, demanded a constant flow of fresh recruits to replace those worn down by disease. Furthermore, the white women of England, Ireland and America were particularly alluring to 'foreign' men who craved racial difference. Emigration paranoia would take on a wholly new complexion.

White slave panic persisted well into the twentieth century, fuelled by the campaigns of social purity leagues who were determined to alert naïve young women to the dangers of emigration. In 1897, members of the National Vigilance Association and the Travellers' Aid Society began a twenty-year attempt to patrol the ports and railway stations of all major UK cities, including Liverpool and Dublin.[33] They placed 'Friendly Warnings' at all British and Irish ports, and aboard all passenger steamers entering or leaving them, which read 'There is risk to young women when travelling alone from one country to another' and advised women foolhardy enough to travel unchaperoned to contact the stewardess who would direct them to social purity agents at their destinations.[34] In Dublin, 'very large posters' displaying this warning had been placed in all train stations and Ladies Waiting Rooms since 1888.[35] By 1910, the National Vigilance Association was able to boast 'Over the last thirteen years, no fewer than 38,000 cases have been dealt with either at railway stations or ports.'[36] Such direct action was not the only weapon in social purity's war against the traffickers. White slavery spawned an exotic literary genre of its own, as in both the USA and the United Kingdom, reformers competed with one another to issue moralising and frequently sensational tracts, pamphlets and books. Often Gothic in tone and luridly illustrated, these writings were enticingly

---

[33] Details of railway and port work of the National Vigilance Association's 'International Guild of Service for Women' gathered from 'Correspondence Respecting the International Conference on the White Slave Traffic', *Parliamentary Paper* 137(1907), 907 and *The Vigilance Record*, 2 April 1903, 35. The National Vigilance Association was imitating the Travellers Aid Society who, since the mid 1880s, had been distributing their distinctive pink handbills warning young women of the dangers of travel, meeting women off trains and steamers, and putting up posters in Ladies' Waiting Rooms. The Travellers' Aid Society was active in Dublin from 1886, and was financially supported by large annual contributions from brewery magnate Arthur Guinness (*Travellers' Aid Society Annual Report* (1890), 18). Information gathered from Travellers' Aid Society minutes and annual reports, held in 1/TAS Box 201, The Fawcett Archive, London Guildhall University. In 1887, the Dublin branch of the society reported 'We have joined the Vigilance Association in placing large placards in Dublin stations' (*Annual Report* (1887), 14).

[34] National Vigilance Association, *Sixteenth Annual Report* (1901), 19.

[35] *The Vigilance Record*, March 1888, 15.

[36] Anon., *The White Slave Traffic* (London: C. Arthur Pearson, 1910), 23.

titled – *In the Grip of White Slavery, The Horrors of the White Slave Trade, The House of Bondage, The Girl Who Disappeared* – and traced startlingly uniform melodramas of innocent country girls, villainous suitors from overseas, false promises of marriage, and, eventually, the chloroformed cloth, hypodermic syringe or drugged drink that led to certain 'ruin' in an overseas 'house of shame'. By 1912, films such as *The Traffic in Souls* and *The Inside of the White Slave Traffic* were attracting flourishing audiences. These cultural articulations of widespread anxiety had two specific functions, firstly to warn young women and their parents of a danger conceived as hidden and secret, and secondly to garner popular support for legislative action. In the United States, social purity agitation led to the 1910 Mann Act, which prohibited the transportation of women across state lines 'for the purposes of prostitution or debauchery or for any other immoral purpose'.[37] In the United Kingdom, white slavery agitation began in 1880, when Alfred Dyer's 'Belgian Scandal' precipitated a House of Lords Select Committee into the international traffic in women. A second wave of the crusade began in 1899, when the National Vigilance Association formed the British National Committee for the Suppression of the White Slave Traffic, hosted the first International Congress on the Suppression of the White Slave Trade and helped to introduce the first of several White Slavery bills into the House of Commons. Progress was slow, despite the support of the Women's Social and Political Union, which demanded the vote 'to stop the White Slave Traffic', and a 'Pass-the-Bill Committee'. The bill was finally passed in 1912 as the second Criminal Law Amendment Act, amid a flurry of apocryphal stories, street demonstrations and mass petitions.[38]

One might speculate that Joyce was keenly alert to this cultural unease when writing 'Eveline' since, in the midst of a decade turbulent with white slavery rumours, he, like Frank, was persuading his girlfriend to leave the country with him.[39] His alertness is confirmed in the ways 'Eveline' closely shadows the genre of apocryphal melodrama which so proliferated throughout the decade of its publication. White slave panic coincided with a transitional era when many women were eager to participate in the new urban occupations requiring young female labour – namely telephonists,

[37] Mark Thomas Connelly, *The Response to Prostitution in the Progressive Era* (Chapel Hill: University of North Carolina Press, 1980), 128.
[38] Alan Hunt, *Governing Morals: A Social History of Moral Regulation* (Cambridge: Cambridge University Press, 1999), 179.
[39] Brenda Maddox outlines the courage of Nora Barnacle's decision to emigrate with Joyce, *Nora* (London: Minerva, 1988), 65.

stenographers and shop assistants.[40] As one white slavery tract put it, 'within the last twenty years, great social changes mean that today's womanhood is entering more strenuously than ever the battle of life'.[41] Eveline is one of these women, working as a salesgirl in one of the new department stores which swiftly became notorious as locales of sexual danger for their poorly paid and morally unsupervised female employees. The opening chapter of one tract, 'The Shopgirl and the Trafficker', spelt out this danger, describing how shopgirls, 'living in' and subsisting on 'a weekly wage of perhaps not more than ten shillings a week' were frequently driven 'to find money in other ways'.[42] Those 'who struggle heroically' against the temptation of clandestine prostitution nonetheless for want of money spend their leisure time in the streets, where

Nothing is more natural than that a chance acquaintance should be struck up. A theatre or dinner is proposed, then by slow and certain degrees she is drawn into the inevitable vortex which invariably ends in the same thing – the career of the unfortunate. The procurer has no need to travel far to find his prey – undoubtedly, large numbers of his victims are drawn from the ranks of the shopgirl class.[43]

Furthermore, Eveline is not only a member of this most precarious of professions, she shares with the heroine of white slave tracts an estrangement from home and family. Her home is a cheerless place: her mother is dead, her father a bully, and her longing for 'escape' overwhelming.[44] White slave narratives like _The Girl Who Disappeared_ frequently emphasised precisely the kind of estrangement Eveline feels: protagonists are 'giddy' or 'stage-struck', resistant to parental authority, dissatisfied with life at home and, like Rose Brolley, desirous of 'excitement' elsewhere.[45]

Significantly, the white slaves of purity tracts not only share Eveline's dangerous discontent, but also her ambiguously sentimental attachment to

---

[40] This anxiety over working women is particularly evident in one National Vigilance Association publication, _The Dangers of False Prudery_ (London: National Vigilance Association, 1910), which contained chapters headed 'The Domestic Servant', 'The Factory Girl', 'The Perils of the Business Girl'.

[41] Anon., _The White Slave Traffic_, 10.

[42] Anon. ['By the Author of _The White Slave Traffic_'], _In the Grip Of the White Slave Trader_ (London: C. Arthur Pearson, 1910), 16.

[43] _Ibid._, 21.

[44] Interestingly, a 1938 League of Nations survey into the causes of prostitution discovered a high correlation between the loss of a parent and entrance into prostitution. See Edward Bristow, _Prostitution and Prejudice: The Jewish Fight Against White Slavery 1880–1939_ (Oxford: Clarendon Press, 1982), 27.

[45] See _The White Slave Traffic_, 15; Clifford G. Roe, _The Girl Who Disappeared_ (Chicago: Bureau of Moral Education, 1914), 11–15. As Mark Connelly suggests, this emphasis on dissatisfied daughters fleeing home 'might have been a manifestation of a larger social problem that urban social workers dealt with on a daily basis: runaways from unpleasant home conditions' (Connelly, _The Response to Prostitution_, 125).

memories of home. These sentimental recollections are poignantly manifest once the heroine has taken the 'fatal step' and is imprisoned within her 'life of shame':

She saw a vision of home... the face of her loving father and the kindly hand of her tender mother... she saw those other things that went to make for happiness in childhood; there was the sitting room in the old homestead; she saw the big log burning in the fireplace and her brothers and sisters playing near the fire.[46]

Before she even leaves, Eveline is plagued by a strange anticipatory nostalgia, as she muses 'Perhaps she would never see again those familiar objects from which she had never dreamed of being divided' (D 30), remembers an innocent childhood spent playing in the back field with her siblings and 'The children of the avenue' (D 29), and even recalls her father reading a ghost story, making toast over an open fire and wearing her mother's bonnet on a picnic 'to make the children laugh' (D 32). These are precisely the kind of mawkish happy memories which added pathos to white slavery tracts: it is as if Eveline, looking back to a lost time when 'they seemed to have been rather happy then' (D 29), imagines for herself the future of nostalgia and regret so frequently delineated in contemporary narratives of Girls Who Disappeared.

These similarities between 'Eveline' and white slave cautionary tales are intensified through the shady persona of Frank: 'over to the old country just for a holiday' (D 32), Frank closely matches the stereotype of the itinerant international procurer, 'bully' or 'cadet', charming the gullible with tall tales and rash promises. Procurers in social purity propaganda were almost always 'of foreign parentage, probably a Jew, a Frenchman, an Italian, or perhaps a Greek'; mysterious visitors from another country armed with compelling narratives of abroad.[47] Frank's uncertain national identity and his 'face of bronze' (D 31) mark him out as dangerously 'other', like the street organist supplying that 'melancholy air of Italy' (D 33) which haunts Eveline's mother's deathbed. Furthermore, his mode of courtship is suspicious. Rather than attempt to gain Mr Hill's good will and thus secure a formal engagement, Frank has helped to deepen the rift between his fiancée and her irascible father, participating in a quarrel which means 'after that she had to meet her lover secretly' (D 32). He meets Eveline in the street, and woos her through his attentiveness, endearments, seats in an 'unaccustomed part of the theatre' and 'tales of distant countries' (D 31–2). These were precisely the seductive methods of procurement gathered from

[46] Roe, *The Great War on White Slavery*, 27–8.   [47] *Ibid.*, 202.

the testimonies of 'white slaves' and rehearsed over and over again in vice society reports, newsletters and publications. 'If the girl is one of the "love-sick" kind, they pretend they are in love with her and promise to marry her' claimed one procurer to a social investigator, 'The whole idea is to get the girl's confidence and the fellow will say anything to do this.'[48] This courtship ploy was even illustrated in photo-stories of moustache-twirling rogues luring innocents to their doom. The extent to which Frank's courtship uncannily suggests that of the villain in white slave tracts is probably most strikingly demonstrated in an extract from *The White Slave Market* (1912), a book Joyce owned and annotated:

Some pimps take months and months to gain proper control over their victims... For a long time, one fiend incarnate contented himself with merely 'walking out' with the girl, taking her to cheap picture shows, buying her little presents, meeting her as she came home from work and doing everything that would take her mind off his villainy. Once he had taught her to trust him, to love him, he ruined her and ruthlessly 'dumped' her into the inferno at Buenos Ayres.[49]

Eveline's job, domestic discontent, sentimental recollections of 'home', the circumstances of her meeting Frank, the manner of their courtship, his dubious promise of marriage and plans for emigration all bring Joyce's short story unmistakeably into collision with the white slave cautionary tale. One detail of Joyce's story, however, as we have said, pushes the similarities beyond coincidence, and that is Eveline's intended emigration destination.

By the turn of the century, the phrase 'going to Buenos Ayres' had become a slang euphemism for 'taking up a life of prostitution, especially by way of a procurer's offices'.[50] As the anonymous author of *In The Grip of the White Slave Trader* insisted, this was no mere figure of speech:

On all sides it is admitted that the hotbed of this abominable trade in human flesh is the Argentine. Buenos Ayres is the grave of many of England's daughter's hopes, the ultimate port of missing women, the destination of the ignorant and innocent English girl who, full of buoyant enthusiasm, leaves her home to enter unawares

[48] Maude Miner, *The Slavery of Prostitution* (New York: Macmillan, 1916), 96.
[49] Olive Christian McKirdy, *The White Slave Market* (London: Stanley Paul, 1912), 276; Joyce made notes from McKirdy, particularly of the slang terms surrounding the white slave traffic, which he transferred to *Finnegans Wake*, mainly pp. 351–2. See James Joyce, *The Index Manuscript: Finnegans Wake Holograph Workbook VI. B. 46*, transcribed, annotated and with an introduction by Danis Rose (Colchester: A Wake Newslitter Press, 1978), 121–4. *The White Slave Market*, like many similar books on the subject, summarises the received wisdom on the traffic built up over the past three decades, and although Joyce obviously read it many years after composing 'Eveline', I would argue that his use of MacKirdy as a source for *Finnegans Wake* reprises a long-standing fascination with the white slave narrative most strikingly manifest in 'Eveline'.
[50] Eric Partridge, *A Dictionary of Slang and Unconventional English* (London: Routledge, 1938), 101.

the most vile servitude the mind of man ever created. Buenos Ayres – the name incessantly rings in my ears – what hideous irony of nomenclature is Buenos Ayres – 'Pure air!' – the port of missing women and shattered hopes![51]

Buenos Ayres' international reputation had been sustained for several decades in Britain, since the National Vigilance Association had in 1889 published the first of many revelations of 'the business details of an arrangement for taking girls to Buenos Ayres for immoral purposes'.[52] Social purity conventions repeatedly identified the city as the main destination of procured women. At the first International Conference on the White Slave Trade in 1899, Millicent Fawcett asserted that 'there were at least 3,000 European women imprisoned and enslaved in the "tolerated houses" of Buenos Ayres'.[53] Preventative and rescue work was shared between a variety of organisations, from the British Immigration Society, set up in the Argentine capital to 'transmit accurate information to Britain and Ireland concerning Argentina for the protection of women' to the Argentine League for the Protection of Young Women, which liaised closely with the National Vigilance Association in order to 'combat the unworthy traffic which seems unhappily to have taken deep root in this country'.[54] In 1907, Frederick Bullock, the Chief Constable of Scotland Yard, surrendered to purity pressure and requested powers 'to prevent passengers starting from London to South America should suspicion exist as to their character when they are escorting young women'.[55] The chairman of the National Vigilance Association, William Coote, provided a retrospective assessment of the decade's work in 1910, asserting 'From statistics and other information in our possession, we know that in Buenos Ayres a constant demand existed for the victims of the traffickers, and a large price was paid for them.'[56] By the time Frank offers to take Eveline there, Buenos Ayres' reputation as 'the worst of all centres of immoral commerce in women' was fixed.[57]

---

[51] Anon., *In the Grip of the White Slave Trader*, 77.

[52] The National Vigilance Association, *Fourth Annual Report* (1889), 26.

[53] Millicent Fawcett, *The White Slave Trade: Its Causes and the Best Means of Preventing It* (London: National Vigilance Association, 1899), 2.

[54] These organisations met women off boats and attempted to provide them with hostel accommodation and offers of respectable employment. See *The Vigilance Record*, February 1890, 10; *The Vigilance Record*, October 1902, 71.

[55] 'Correspondence Respecting the International Conference on the White Slave Traffic', *Parliamentary Paper* 137 (1907), 11.

[56] William Coote, *A Vision and its Fulfilment* (London: National Vigilance Association, 1902), 122.

[57] *The Vigilance Record*, October 1902, 71.

Figures 1–3 Three images from Clifford G. Roe, *The Horrors of the White Slave Trade: The Mighty Crusade To Protect the Purity of our Homes* (London, New York: n.p., 1912), pp. 28, 31, 32.

THE FIRST MEETING.
The white slave trader, skilled in the arts and wiles of flattery, accosting a young girl on the street.

Figure 1

THE SECOND MEETING—SHE KNOWS NOT THE DANGEROUS TRAP BEING SET FOR HER.
The smooth tongued villain tells of his affection and undying love for her. He paints a beautiful picture of how happy they will be. She is enraptured and promises to meet him and go to dinner with him.

Figure 2

THE THIRD STEP—DRUGGED AND LED TO HER RUIN.
Having taken the drugged potion she is now incapable of self-
control and is easily led to her ruin. Awaking she will find herself an
inmate of a house of shame.

Figure 3

III

What is the significance of Joyce's creative reinvigoration of one of social
purity's most potent cautionary tales? To address this question, we must
first return to *The Irish Homestead*, the organ of the Irish co-operative
movement, closely affiliated to Horace Plunkett's project of promoting national self-sufficiency by improving agricultural and dairy practices and
thereby 'brightening rural life'. As we have seen, it demanded that its
fiction writers contributed to that end by boosting Irish national pride,
and, in particular, discouraging that emigration which was perceived to be

depleting the country of its brightest and best. At first glance, Joyce's manipulation of white slave panic in 'Eveline' might seem to conform to that demand, since it, like 'The Awakening of Brian Joyce' and 'Rose Brolley', insinuates a terrible fate for those foolhardy enough to leave their native land. However, Joyce's conformity is distinctly tongue in cheek, since in the first decade of the twentieth century, social purity movements like the National Vigilance Association were bitterly resented in nationalist Ireland as compromising that very self-sufficiency *The Irish Homestead* hoped to instil. The only social purity association active in Ireland at the time was the Dublin White Cross Vigilance Association, a satellite group of the main British National Vigilance Association, self-defined as a 'band of earnest, thoughtful young men who love Ireland and Irish chastity' and boasting, by 1891, fourteen branches and 530 members.[58] Commandeering nationalist notions of indigenous Irish chastity, they understood social purity work to be

of national as well as international importance, as there is grave danger of Ireland losing her proud reputation for purity if the immoral tendencies which are at work amongst other countries are allowed to spread among our people.[59]

However, the Dublin White Cross Vigilance Association occupied an uncomfortable position within the Ireland they sought to protect, since their politics were distinctly Unionist and their Protestantism evangelical. The organisation preserved an only limited sense of separate identity from the parent organisation in London, as the name's emphasis upon 'Dublin' rather than 'Ireland' suggests. Reports from 'our Dublin branch' were listed in *The Vigilance Record* alongside those from Southampton, Liverpool and Hull, thus implicitly locating Dublin as one of Britain's provincial towns, rather than Ireland's capital. The group's complicity with British administration in Ireland was compounded by its choice of president, the Earl of Aberdeen, simultaneously viceregent of Ireland. Furthermore, the group was supported by two subsequent Church of Ireland Archbishops of Dublin, and its rules required each member to be recommended 'by the minister of whose congregation he is an accustomed member', and each meeting to begin with 'united prayer and devotional exercises'.[60] Such statutes did little to smooth

---

[58] *Ibid.*, April 1891, 7.
[59] *Ibid.*, May 1893, 36. The Dublin White Cross Vigilance Association's foundress, social purist Ellice Hopkins, concurred, stating 'the purity which is often quoted is evidently a matter of race', although she went on to criticise what she perceived as Irish Roman Catholic apathy towards social purity work and argued that Irish sexual conduct was due to racial character rather than 'the influence of the priest', *The Purity Movement* (London: Hatchards, 1885), 16.
[60] *The Vigilance Record*, April 1891, 18.

over the sectarian tensions witnessed in 1904 by the anti-Catholic commentator Michael McCarthy:

The Dublin White Cross Vigilance Association are the sort of people who are stoned [by Catholic nationalists] in Phoenix Park on a Sunday, whom, forsooth, their stoners are taught to look on as worshippers of an apostate monk and a degenerate nun who lived together in a life of fornication.[61]

The distrust was mutual and strikingly underlined in *The Vigilance Record*'s report on the *Dresden* crisis, where concern for the Irish immigrants was displaced by concern for 'white slaves' in Argentina, and the hapless immigrants were accordingly described as 'the whiskey-loving scum of Queenstown and Cork'.[62]

These were the vigilantes circulating white slavery propaganda in Ireland, patrolling Irish ports and railway stations in search of white slaves, and distributing posters and flybills of their 'Friendly Warnings to Young Women Travelling Abroad'. Their presence was an uneasy one in Catholic nationalist Dublin, and, so too, was the presence of one of their best-known propagandas within the Irish journal of national renewal and self-sufficiency, *The Irish Homestead*. White slave panic was clearly an ideological import; and Joyce, by using it as the submerged intertext in 'Eveline', performs a disconcerting act of cultural and creative 'emigration'. In smuggling this rival, Anglocentric anti-emigration narrative into the pages of the *Homestead*, Joyce critiques the didactic purpose Plunkett's paper assigned to its fiction by highlighting the suggestive and compromising overlap between ideologically divergent propagandas. If Joyce responded to Russell's suggestion that he 'play to the common understanding' by corrupting the staple fictions of *The Irish Homestead* into something far more complicated and challenging, then the corruption buried within 'Eveline' is that the story masquerades as a simple anti-emigration propaganda along 'Rose Brolley' lines, whilst simultaneously interrogating the drive to 'stop emigration' through the propaganda it supposedly embodies.

IV

'Eveline's' archly unpatriotic use of a British anti-emigration propaganda may have been one reason why, after three stories, Joyce was quietly dismissed from *The Irish Homestead* fiction pages on the grounds that too many of its readers had complained (*L* 1: 98). However, Joyce's subversion

[61] Michael McCarthy, *Priests and People in Ireland* (London: Hodder and Stoughton, 1908), 293.
[62] *The Vigilance Record*, February 1890, 10.

of the *Homestead*'s demand that its fiction writers inculcate a self-sufficient brand of national identity was surely compounded by the way 'Eveline' customises the nuances of the white slave cautionary tale to hint most strongly that emigration is a more attractive alternative than staying at home and that the sexual danger of her elopement should, perhaps, be risked. Indeed, it is significant that only Kenner reads against the story's rhythms of paralysis to emphasise the untrustworthiness of Frank and the desirability of Eveline's remaining on shore. Other readers more commonly concur with Richard Ellmann:

> These stories challenged the work of Joyce's compatriots. Yeats' *The Countess Cathleen* had extolled the virtue of self-sacrifice; 'Eveline' evokes the counter-virtue of self-realisation. When Joyce's character is held by Ireland, she reduces herself to a 'helpless animal' as if surrendering the very qualities that had made her human.[63]

Ellmann's reading compels because 'Eveline' certainly does manipulate ideas of fatal hesitancy, entrapment and moral cowardice to suggest that its heroine, through a catatonic failure of nerve, condemns herself to that paralysis *Dubliners* so meticulously delineates. Her wretched life as the housekeeper to a violent, hard-drinking father who confiscates her meagre wages and then refuses to hand them back for her to spend on family 'provisions' (*D* 31), and as an assistant at the stores, where her bullying supervisor Miss Gavan 'always had an edge on her, especially whenever there were people listening' (*D* 32), together suggest that 'home' is the real locus of Eveline's exploitation. Furthermore, whilst Eveline's character, occupation, home life, courtship and emigration plans each precisely reflect the various components of the white slave genre outlined above, her potential fate is forever occluded since the story halts at the North Wall, and thus frustrates both the 'happy ever after' ending Eveline clearly hopes for, and the melodrama of betrayal and degradation identified as her likely fate in contemporary social purity propaganda. The open-ended nature of the story's structure ensures that both Eveline and Joyce's readers will never know whether she has missed the chance of a lifetime or had a lucky escape. It is within this radical instability and uncertainty that Joyce's subversion chiefly resides.

To understand Joyce's intertextual use of the white slave narrative fully we must excavate a little further behind contemporary social purity propaganda to determine, firstly, what ideological configurations often underpinned the

---

[63] Ellmann, *James Joyce*, 164.

crusade, and, secondly, how those configurations were interpreted and challenged by Joyce's contemporaries. Two statements particularly exemplify the reactionary agenda often perceived to lurk behind white slave paranoia. One pamphlet asserted

There are hundreds of wretched parents who do not know if their daughters are alive or dead, for they have suddenly vanished. Well, we can tell them where they have been brought, and what has become of them. They are in Buenos Ayres. This trade is a very lucrative one, as the men in South America are of a very amorous disposition, and the fair merchandise soon finds buyers.[64]

In June 1913, Chief Constable Frederick Bullock added in a private memorandum

In such cases it has become fashionable to attack the stigma of the white slave traffic, but is it not reasonable to suspect also that modern desire for independence and liberty of action which has become so characteristic of women? It is not only the man who is to blame for the deplorable consequences which follow in the search for a free uncontrollable life.[65]

These statements are both loaded with a telling set of assumptions. The first displays a crude yet potent cocktail of racial and sexual anxieties to figure the white slave as a symbol of sullied national honour, a piece of 'fair merchandise' to be rescued from the vile appetites of foreign men, the symbol of national contamination. The second expresses a deep suspicion of those 'great social changes [which] mean that today's womanhood is entering more strenuously than ever the battle of life' that another white slave pamphlet warned of, betraying, in a year dominated by militant suffrage agitation, a conservative nostalgia for a lost world where women required 'protection', not political, social and economic liberation.[66] This paranoid underbelly of the white slave crusade engaged a number of dissidents, suspicious of its repressive implications. Doubt as to the existence of an international white slavery conspiracy was certainly encouraged by an exaggeration of the panic, both by entrepreneurs profiting from sensational novelettes and films, and by reformers amplifying the danger for political purposes. As one purist blithely explained, 'Apathy is more of a crime than exaggeration when dealing with this subject.'[67] Scepticism was most devastatingly voiced

---

[64] Anon., *The White Slave Traffic*, 18.
[65] Memorandum 'White Slave Traffic', 12 June 1913, quoted in Bristow, *Prostitution*, 43.
[66] Anon., *The White Slave Traffic*, 10.
[67] Ruth Rosen, *The Lost Sisterhood* (London: Johns Hopkins University Press, 1982), 114.

by Teresa Billington-Greig, a dissident feminist, suffragette recusant and vocal critic of the National Vigilance Association. In the wake of the Criminal Law Amendment (White Slave) Act of 1912, she challenged over fifty social purists and all British and Irish Chief Constables to supply evidence of 'any fully proved cases of attempted trapping' and found that not one could produce a single case of white slavery since 1895.[68] Her research, exposing instead what she described as 'an epidemic of terrible rumours, a campaign of sedulously cultivated sexual hysterics' was published in *The English Review* to great controversy, yet her impatience with white slavery hysteria had long been shared by a significant minority of radical feminists and intellectuals.[69]

As Ruth Rosen notes, to ascertain whether or not white slavery actually existed is both an extremely difficult and highly controversial task for any historian to attempt, and it is not a question best explored here.[70] However, a glimpse of the relationship white slavery scare stories bore to reality is provided by Donna Guy, who notes how the circumstances of prostitution in that hotbed of vice, Buenos Ayres was 'less glamorous and more depressing than that reflected in most white slavery stories'.[71] Since 1875, prostitution in Argentina had been a state-registered legal enterprise, and the city accordingly gained an underworld reputation for tolerance, prosperity, and most importantly a surplus of young single male pioneers, which made it a comparatively attractive place to work as a prostitute. A 1912 survey showed that most European prostitutes had sold sex before registering in Argentina, suggesting that 'cheap steamship fares and imbalanced sex ratios made it easier and more attractive for them to emigrate... they saw immigration to a new land or even a new continent as the key to survival'.[72] The theory that prostitutes in Europe saw Buenos Ayres as an attractive alternative to their lives in their home countries, a city where prostitution was tolerated, clients more plentiful and wages higher, is intriguingly borne out by George Jenner's complaint during the 1889 *Dresden* Irish immigration crisis that free passages had been supplied to 'a class of persons most unfitted for emigration to this country, including prostitutes and beggars'. Guy's research reflects the contemporary testimonies of sceptics like Billington-Greig, who were instinctively distrustful of the

[68] Teresa Billington-Greig, 'The Truth about White Slavery', *The English Review*, June 1913, 431.
[69] Lucy Bland, *Banishing the Beast: English Feminism and Sexual Morality 1885–1914* (London: Penguin, 1995), 297–302; Rosen, *The Lost Sisterhood*, 115–16.
[70] *Ibid.*, 112–14.
[71] Donna Guy, *Sex and Danger in Buenos Aires: Prostitution, Family and Nation in Argentina* (London: University of Nebraska Press, 1991), 7.
[72] *Ibid.*, 73, 77.

way social purists' melodrama of innocent virgins kidnapped and enslaved both elided the social and economic realities of prostitution, and, in an age of increasing feminist militancy, constructed women as 'impotent and imbecile weaklings'.[73] As Guy shows, and as some Edwardian social commentators seemed to recognise, the story of prostitution was frequently a more prosaic narrative of poor women making highly circumscribed and often coercive economic choices between one type of work and another, or between prostitution at home or abroad.

Some indication that Joyce both relished the white slave melodrama of sexual coercion and was similarly sceptical of its ideological purpose is retrospectively provided in *Finnegans Wake*. Lecturing his sister Issy on proper conduct, Shaun warns her against

Autist Algy, the pulcherman and would-do performer, *oleas* Mr Smuth, stated by the vice crusaders to be well known to all the dallytaunties in and near the ciudad of Buellas Arias, taking you to the playguehouse to see the *Smirching of Venus*. (*FW* 434: 35–435: 3)

Algy is a 'pulcherman', a trader in female pulchritude under a corruption of that most common of British aliases, Mr Smith. He is an aspiring 'performer', contemporary slang for 'whoremonger', well known to both 'vice crusaders' and 'dallytaunties', a perversion of 'dilettantes' which compresses the dalliance and the taunting of the soliciting prostitute.[74] Like Frank, he takes girls to the 'playguehouse', where the theatre is neatly collapsed into the brothel. The pun 'Buellas Arias' mediates the city through 'puella' and 'aria', retrieving 'songs about girls' from its name. To Joyce, Buenos Ayres was clearly a city synonymous with the sexual betrayal of women, and the ill wind of its notoriety blows across 'Eveline'. However, Joyce's filtering of the city's name through 'puella aria' or fiction of the feminine also implies his perception of the scandal of Buenos Ayres as the kind of imprisoning ideological construct his censorious, vice-crusading Shaun the Postman might well deploy.

In this context, 'Eveline' can clearly be seen to articulate those misgivings about the effects of white slavery propaganda on its bewildered young consumers that contemporary social purity dissidents like Teresa

---

[73] Billington-Greig, 'The Truth about White Slavery', 443.
[74] Definition of 'performer' as slang for 'whoremonger' taken from Roland McHugh, *Annotations to Finnegans Wake* (London: Johns Hopkins University Press, 1991), 435. Compare Joyce's expression 'vice crusaders' with the colourful rhetoric of William Coote, secretary of the National Vigilance Association: 'Our readers will naturally be anxious to know the results of our legal crusade against vice in all its hydra-headed form', *The Romance of Philanthropy* (London: National Vigilance Association, 1916), 113.

Billington-Greig attempted to highlight. For Joyce places his critique of such propaganda at the heart of 'Eveline' by creating a heroine whose paralysis within the city whose soul he set out to betray is imposed by her vulnerability to the persuasive fictions of others. Initial hints that she is a heroine overdetermined by other narratives are contained in Eveline Hill's two eponymous pornographic namesakes, the heroine of a mid-Victorian classic of the genre, *Eveline, or the Adventures of a Lady of Fortune who was Never Found Out*, and John Cleland's *Fanny Hill*, whilst the name of her lover might also allude to the Victorian flagellant novella *Frank and I*. Furthermore, within the text Eveline is obviously constrained by the conflicting fictions of Frank's 'lass that loved a sailor' and her father's version of the sailor with the girl in every port. Intriguingly, Eveline's capacity to imagine herself the heroine of other people's fictions is deeply implicated in her fantasy of marriage to Frank. 'He would give her life' (*D* 33), she thinks, the 'life' of a lass who loves a sailor that her lover's stories promise. Eveline's fantasy of entrance into the kind of contemporary women's magazine fiction R. B. Kershner has compellingly analysed most poignantly appears when she speculates upon the reaction of an implied readership to the page-turning gesture of elopement she contemplates:

What would they say of her in the Stores when they found out that she had run away with a fellow? Say she was a fool, perhaps; and her place would be filled up by advertisement. (*D* 30)

Although only the disapproval of her formidable superior Miss Gavan is explicitly contemplated, the hesitation on 'perhaps', marked off by comma and semi-colon into a phrase of its own, hints at a host of alternative, elided responses. Eveline's fear that she will be replaced by 'advertisement' neatly alludes to the way her story had been relentlessly circulated and promoted by contemporary vigilance activists.

It is, therefore, poignantly appropriate that a heroine so susceptible to transference into other stories – advertisements, pornographic novels, lover's fantasies, father's warnings, magazine romances – should be so easily incorporated into one of the most notorious and well-publicised morality tales circulating around young women at the time. As if to underline this susceptibility, Eveline sits for most of her story with the evidence and symbol of her literacy, her two white letters of farewell, gleaming indistinct in her lap. Young, single, female, literate and above all vulnerable to a teeming variety of fictions of her destiny, Eveline is the propagandist's sitting target. She is trapped by the alternative fictions which compete to predict her future – the happy ever after ending promised by Frank and the women's magazine romances which perhaps inspire him, the vision of loss and disappointment offered in stories like 'Rose Brolley', the Gothic melodrama of disgrace propagated by social purity campaigners. At the North Wall, it would seem, the most potent and emotive of those fictions wins out, as Eveline heeds the warnings relentlessly saturating her culture through leaflets, tracts, posters and public meetings. Her mute anguish, her 'silent, fervent prayer' (*D* 34), her white face set 'passive, like a helpless animal' (*D* 34) together articulate the conditions of aphasia that such warnings have imposed upon her. She has no voice, and although her body might eloquently internalise her terror through her nausea, it can communicate nothing to Frank: 'Her eyes gave him no sign of love or farewell or recognition' (*D* 34). Tellingly, her paralysis places Frank beyond recognition: she cannot prioritise the different intertextual identities which frame his character to discern who he is. Frank may well be 'saying something about the passage over and over again' (*D* 34), but Eveline attends to other, more deeply embedded repetitions. In her desperation to privilege one form of propaganda over its rivals and thus navigate her 'maze of distress', Eveline 'prayed to God to direct her, to show her what was her duty' (*D* 33). What Eveline craves is the kind of monolithic vision common to *Homestead* emigration narratives such as 'The Awakening of Brian Joyce', where a quasi-divine apparition appears to teach the protagonist 'his duty to God and to Ireland', but she is permitted no such certainty. Instead, the closest approximation to a vision Eveline is granted is her glimpse of the steamer that is to carry her to Buenos Ayres as 'the black mass' (*D* 33); as the pun suggests, something vague, sinister, unholy, symbolically containing her impending sacrifice, a *trompe l'œil* of an emigration ship predetermined by cautionary tales.

Eveline's submission to white slave panic is not figured as a rescue or an escape, since Joyce halts the narrative at the North Wall, the point at which the social purity hypothesis would be ascertained or dismissed, thereby endlessly deferring the moment of 'proof' and replacing it with perpetual uncertainty. If, as Kenner asserts, Eveline will spend the rest of her life 'regretting her great refusal', then the true tragedy of her story is that her regret will take the form of endless rehearsal of the conclusion to her story her quayside catatonia suspends. For Eveline, a woman whose inertia stems from her susceptibility to didactic stories, is bullied as surely by social purity propaganda as by her father or Miss Gavan into choosing to experience city life from behind the glass of 'home', in an atmosphere so saturated with propaganda that she must breathe it in along with the odour of dusty cretonne. The word 'home' pulses relentlessly through 'Eveline', culminating in Eveline's deathbed promise to her mother to 'keep the home together as long as she could' (*D* 33). 'Home' is countered with 'house', both words appearing six times each in a five page story, and the tension between the two loosely synonymous terms articulates the difference between a physical and an ideological space. 'Home', for Eveline, offers not the placid 'safety' suggested in white slavery tracts, but instead signals an oppressive and overwhelming force she is powerless to resist. It is a force Joyce surely recognised in both the *Homestead* emigration stories, and that suggestively similar genre, the white slavery cautionary tale. For here, on the very brink of his creative career, he covertly resists the very first constraint placed upon his writing – Russell's demand that he 'cater to the common understanding for once in a way' and produce something designed to 'not shock the readers'. 'Eveline' simultaneously suggests something shocking and sensational – white slavery – and attacks the very didactic manipulations of readers that he was expected to produce. Joyce's most eloquent subversion of Russell's plea that he 'cater to the common understanding' takes the form of holding aloft 'my nicely-polished looking glass' (*L* 1: 64) to reflect back to *The Irish Homestead* readers a mirror-image of a fellow reader of emigration propaganda. Eveline, a vulnerable, bewildered and credulous adolescent, is a prototype of the imperilled innocent *The Irish Homestead* and social purity activists were each trying to protect. For Joyce, such 'protection' easily mutates into paralysis.

CHAPTER 3

'True manliness': policing masculinity in A Portrait of the Artist as a Young Man

The suggestion that *A Portrait of the Artist as a Young Man* continues Joyce's assault upon a Protestant, evangelical social purity movement seems, at first glance, counterintuitive. For, as many critics have noted, the regulation of sexuality in Joyce's first novel is a self-evidently Catholic affair, as the adolescent Stephen Dedalus finds his sexual development subject to the continual strictures of the agents of his church.[1] The priest-schoolmasters at Clongowes school, determined to beat the sin of 'smugging' (*P* 42) out of their charges; Father Arnall's hell-fire invective against 'that lewd habit, that impure habit' (*P* 123); Stephen's penitent confession of 'sins of impurity' (*P* 144): each episode insists upon Catholicism's inescapable dominance over Stephen's erotic imagination. However, these Catholic proscriptions are complemented by a contemporary social purity discourse of 'true manliness', which disseminated the specific construction of masculinity to which Stephen is in thrall. Such a collision between rivals is, of course, ironic since, as we have seen in the previous chapter, social purity was widely resented in Ireland as a proselytising agency determined to usurp Catholic moral authority. In this context, Joyce's insistence upon a suggestive overlap between Catholic and social purist ideologies of 'true manliness' is deeply subversive, since *A Portrait* pointedly observes how diligently two ostensibly polarised discourses mutually reinforce each other to intensify Stephen's experience of paralysis.

An early indication of this pattern of subversion is evident in Joyce's 1906 letter to his brother Stanislaus, written with the twin indignities in mind of his failed negotiations with Grant Richards, and Oliver StJohn Gogarty's outpourings on the sexual misdemeanours of 'Ugly England':

---

[1] See especially Mary Lowe-Evans, 'Sex and Confession in the Joyce Canon: Some Historical Parallels' *Journal of Modern Literature* 16: 4 (Spring 1990), 565–70; Patrick McCarthy, 'The Jeweleyed Harlots of His Imagination: Prostitution and Artistic Vision in Joyce', *Eire-Ireland* 17: 4 (1982), 91–109.

they are still at the 'venereal excess' cry in *Sinn Féin*. Why does nobody com-
pile statistics of 'venereal excess' from Dublin hospitals. <u>What</u> is 'venereal excess'?
Perhaps Mr Skeffington-Sheehy could write something on the subject, being, as
J.J.B. puts it, 'a *pure* man'. 'Infant Jesus meek and mild, Pity me a little child.
Make me humble as thou art, And with thy love inflame my heart'. Anyway
my opinion is that if I put down a bucket into my own soul's well, sexual department, I draw up Griffith's and Ibsen's and Skeffington's and Bernard Vaughan's and
St Aloysius' and Shelley's and Renan's water along with my own. And I am going
to do that in my novel (inter alia) and plank the bucket down before the shades
and the substances above mentioned to see how they like it: and if they don't like
it I can't help them. I am nauseated by their lying drivel about pure men and pure
women and spiritual love and love forever: blatant lying in the face of the truth.
(*L* II: 191–2)

Significantly, Joyce's plans for 'my novel', group together Catholic, Irish
nationalist and social purity sexual ideologues. Firstly, Joyce's disgust is precipitated by Gogarty's shameless borrowing of purity rhetoric for an Irish
nationalist purpose in Arthur Griffith's newspaper *Sinn Féin*. Secondly,
Father Bernard Vaughan, notorious for his sermons and essays on morality, is here thrown into uneasy alliance with Joyce's pacifist feminist friend
Francis Sheehy-Skeffington, whose commitment to social purity included
the rigorous practice of exercises designed to suppress the libido, and a professional friendship with the founder of the National Vigilance Association,
W. T. Stead.[2] Both national and religious allegiances are, Joyce suggests,
eroded by the campaign for sexual purity, as Joyce holds Vaughan, Sheehy-
Skeffington and Griffith, rather than the sexual radicals Ibsen or Shelley,
responsible for the 'blatant lying in the face of the truth' he threatens to
expose. The kind of sexual repression Joyce inveighs against here transcends
boundaries of nation and faith, in an early echo of his later claim to Carlo
Linati that the explicitness of his writing mobilised 'a great movement...
initiated by Puritans, English Imperialists, Irish Republicans, Catholics –
what an alliance! I ought to be given the Nobel prize for peace!' (*L* I: 147).
Joyce's theory that the policing of sexuality offered common ground for otherwise ideologically opposed organisations would be eloquently expanded
in the novel he promised.

---

[2] Margaret Ward outlines the extent of Sheehy-Skeffington's commitment to social purity: 'In his diary
before marriage he confided his resolution to be "pure", embarking on a rigorous series of exercises,
meticulously ticking off each occasion he performed the requisite number, an act in part bound up
with the enforced suppression of sexual desire', *Hanna Sheehy-Skeffington: A Life* (Cork: Attic Press,
1997), 31. For Sheehy-Skeffington's friendship with Stead, who 'first directed my attention to the
importance of the woman-question', see Leah Levenson, *With Wooden Sword: A Portrait of Francis
Sheehy-Skeffington* (Dublin: Gill and Macmillan, 1983), 135–6.

That novel was *A Portrait of the Artist as a Young Man*, then germinating as *Stephen Hero*. There, Stephen's friend Madden repeats Griffith's and Gogarty's insistence upon Irish national purity – 'The Irish are noted for at least one virtue all the world over... – they are chaste' (*SH* 59), only to be rebuked by his more worldly companion's 'my countrymen have not yet advanced as far as the machinery of Parisian harlotry because... they can do it by hand' (*SH* 60). Yet, Madden's Catholic nationalism and Stephen's satiric retort are foreshadowed by their friend McCann's commitment to a contemporary ideology of disciplined and continent masculinity propagated and popularised by the social purity leagues. McCann, a fictional version of Francis Sheehy-Skeffington, is ridiculed for his 'insistence on a righteous life and his condemnation of licence as a sin against the future' (*SH* 56), for Stephen goads him into misreading Ibsen ('*Ghosts* teaches self-restraint' – *SH* 57), mocks his 'moral snap of the jaws' (*SH* 56) and 'delighted to riddle these theories with agile bullets' (*SH* 54). Madden the devout patriot and Sheehy-Skeffington the social purity enthusiast are thus lumped together as allies and vanquished, as Stephen wins arguments and, unmoved, finds his 'chastity' a 'great inconvenience' to be 'quietly abandoned' (*SH* 40). However, in *A Portrait of an Artist as a Young Man*, Stephen's chastity is not abandoned with such ease and, similarly, propagandas of male sexual purity are not so glibly dismissed. The impact of the Catholic church on Stephen's developing sexuality in the later novel has been too often discussed to require further elucidation here. However, the complementary branch of sexual regulation emanating from organisations like the National Vigilance Association and imposed on British and Irish adolescents alike is yet to be uncovered. As we shall see, the social purity vision of masculinity articulated by McCann is more subtly and insidiously diffused throughout *A Portrait*. There, Joyce presents the young Stephen as an intimidated and overwhelmed victim of contemporary attempts to promote 'true manliness', attempts reinforcing and often elaborating upon the injunctions of the Catholic church.

I

'True manliness' was a gender identity emphasising the virtues of sexual self-control in a language redolent of medieval chivalry. It derived from the social purity campaign to eradicate the 'double standard' by raising male sexual behaviour to the threshold demanded of women, and involved an ideological transference of surveillance from women to men. This transference was first incited by Josephine Butler's Ladies' National Association's campaign against the Contagious Diseases Acts in the 1870s. For these early purity-feminists, the Contagious Diseases Acts' insistence upon the gynae-cological inspection of 'known prostitutes' represented an institutional and cultural insistence upon scrutinising women, whilst turning a blind eye to the sexual misdemeanours of men.[3] Surveillance, they theorised, should instead be turned upon elite men controlling a corrupt public sphere in preference to the women economically coerced into the sex industry, a shift of focus summarised as 'setting a floodlight on men's doings'.[4] Although the Ladies' National Association's attempts to liberate prostitute women from state surveillance were to be disregarded by subsequent mainstream purity organisations, this call to scrutinise men for sexual misdeeds was enthusiastically adopted. The surveillance of masculinity took two distinct and interconnected forms. One was the pursuit and relentless exposure of those men in public life, particularly politicians, who were compromised in courtroom sex scandals. As Ellice Hopkins, the founder of the purity pledge association for boys and young men, the White Cross League, put it, 'How can we entrust the nation to a libertine who habitually violates the obliga-tions of his own manhood?'[5] The second was a more general, grass-roots initiative directed towards the rising generation of schoolboys and ado-lescents, which specifically insisted that masturbation was a 'weakening', 'demoralising' and even fatal practice leaving visible stigmata of degenera-tion on the male body. Both purity discourses of 'true manliness' find their way into the first four chapters of *A Portrait*, where they are unmistakeably intertwined.

Stephen's vulnerability to the first aspect of this purity campaign is un-forgettably dramatised during 'his first Christmas dinner' (*P* 30) away from the nursery. This initiation into adult masculinity is dominated by a quar-rel over Ireland's most obvious casualty of social purity's collaboration with the Irish Catholic Church in the drive to police male sexuality. The Irish Parliamentary party leader Charles Stewart Parnell's relationship with a colleague's wife, Katherine O'Shea, had long been an open secret within political circles.[6] However, popular moral indignation was only released

[3] Judith R. Walkowitz, *Prostitution and Victorian Society: Women, Class and the State* (Cambridge: Cambridge University Press, 1980), 129–31.
[4] Judith R. Walkowitz, *City of Dreadful Delight: Narratives of Sexual Danger in Late-Victorian London* (London: Virago, 1998), 90.
[5] Ellice Hopkins, *Power of Womanhood, or, Mothers and Sons* (London: White Cross Society, 1899), 160.
[6] Edward Hamilton branded the affair a 'notorious and recognised fact' four years before divorce proceedings were instigated, Herbert Gladstone claimed that Commons gossip had peaked as early as 1885, and Tim Healy's confidante Harold Frederic had given an interview to the *New York Times*

once the scandal had been exposed in the divorce courts in December 1889, as Leopold Bloom remembers:

witnesses swearing to have witnessed him on such and such a particular date in the act of scrambling out of an upstairs apartment with the assistance of a ladder in night apparel, having gained admittance in the same fashion, a fact the weeklies, addicted to the lubric a little, simply coined shoals of money out of. (*U* 16: 1375–9)

This best-known and entirely fabricated detail of the divorce trial came to summarise Parnell's disgrace. Cartoons proliferated, bearded dolls sliding up and down toy ladders were hawked in the street, and Tim Healy raged 'the sunburst and the harp are to be replaced by the sign of the fire escape'.[7] The fire escape theatricalised Parnell's sexuality, transforming him into the cad of Victorian melodrama, and, as Joyce notes in his 1912 essay 'Home Rule Comes of Age', this notoriety was briskly exploited by social purists:

Only in 1891 did [the Irish] give proof of their altruism when they sold Parnell, their master, to the pharisaical conscience of the English non-conformists, without exacting the thirty pieces of silver. (*OCPW* 144)

Joyce's allusion to the 'pharisaical conscience of the English non-conformists' rephrases one synonym for evangelical social purists, 'the non-conformist conscience'.[8] The Christmas dinner scene of *A Portrait* expands upon this insight, as there Joyce dramatises how English social purists and the Irish Catholic Church hierarchy worked together to expel a conspicuous sexual transgressor from political office.

The Christmas confrontation over Parnell is anticipated in Stephen's hallucinatory dream in the Clongowes infirmary. Stephen and his friend Athy have been reading newspaper reports of the divorce trial and its aftermath, and, as the elder boy notes, 'Now it is all about politics in the papers' (*P* 25). When Stephen falls asleep against a background murmur of gossip, 'Someone had put coal on and he heard voices. They were talking', he imaginatively transforms these 'voices' into the waves carrying Parnell's hearse to Ireland, 'talking among themselves as they rose and fell' (*P* 27). Stephen's

in October 1888 alluding to Katherine O'Shea as Parnell's 'ruinous infatuation'. Hamilton and Gladstone quoted in Frank Callanan, *T. M. Healy* (Cork: Cork University Press, 1995), 243; Frederic in *New York Times*, 26 October 1888.
[7] Callanan, *T. M. Healy*, 319–47. For the wonderful Parnell Escaping Doll, see Jules Abels, *The Parnell Tragedy* (London: Bodley Head, 1966), 321.
[8] For Laura Chant, editor of the purity journal *The Vigilance Record*, the nation needed 'the calm steady voice of righteous public opinion . . . the non-conformist conscience, as some call it'. Quoted in Lucy Bland, *Banishing the Beast: English Feminism and Sexual Morality 1885–1914* (London: Penguin, 1995), 110.

dream emphasises Parnell as an object of mass scrutiny: his funeral cortege is awaited by 'a multitude of people gathered by the waters' edge to see the ship that was entering their harbour' (*P* 27). Even in death, he remains defined as spectacle: 'He is dead. We saw him lying upon the catafalque' (*P* 27). Stephen has clearly internalised an impression of Parnell as obsessively and invasively scrutinised and exposed, and such an impression was aggressively emphasised by social purists. Three days after the divorce ruling, the editor of *The Methodist Times*, the Revd Hugh Price-Hughes set a tone he was later to regret when he addressed a capacity crowd at St James' Hall on a platform with the wronged husband Willie O'Shea and W. T. Stead.[9] He proclaimed Parnell 'the acknowledged enemy of God and social purity', and controversially added

If the Irish deliberately select as their representative an adulterer of Mr Parnell's type, they are as incapable of self-government as their bitterest foes have asserted. So obscene a race as in those circumstances they would prove themselves to be are obviously unfit for anything other than a military despotism.[10]

The emphasis here is, crucially, upon what has been publicly broadcast, as Price-Hughes' pointed 'deliberately select' states. Even hostile commentators repeated the point about a conflict of reputations: *The Freeman's Journal* staunchly condemned his 'shameful libel on the purest race in the world', whilst Stead similarly protested 'The Irish are the least open to so foul a reproach: their women are pre-eminent for being at once beautiful and passionate and pure.'[11] Accordingly, social purists pressed Catholic Ireland to vindicate its reputation by rejecting Parnell: Stead wrote privately to the Catholic Archbishop of Dublin, William Walsh whilst the divorce trial progressed, suggesting that Parnell should endear himself to his electorate by 'publicly confessing his sin'.[12] The Standing Committee of Irish Bishops responded to the challenge with 'Surely Catholic Ireland, so eminently conspicuous for its virtue and the purity of its social life, will not accept a leader so dishonoured?'[13] When Parnell refused to counter public disgrace by public contrition, Stead vowed to 'go most reluctantly on the warpath', and in his broadside *The Discrowned King of Ireland*, discounted rumours

---

[9] For an excellent account of Hugh Price-Hughes' involvement in Parnell's fall, and the conflict between his commitments to Home Rule and social purity, see Christopher Oldstone-Moore, 'Hugh Price Hughes and the Nonconformist Conscience', *Eire-Ireland* 30: 4 (1996), 122–35.

[10] Speech reprinted in *The Methodist Times*, 20 November 1890.

[11] *Freeman's Journal*, 21 November 1889; W. T. Stead, *The Discrowned King of Ireland* (London: Review of Reviews, 1891), 2.

[12] Letter from Stead to Walsh, dated 15 February 1889, quoted in F. S. L. Lyons, *Charles Stewart Parnell* (London: Fontana, 1991), 465.

[13] *Ibid.*, 461.

of Willie O'Shea's long-standing tolerance of his wife's relationship with Parnell with

Just as it is true that public action cannot be taken up on private scandal, so it is true that public judgement cannot be stayed by private scandal. The public must act upon public grounds.[14]

It was a telling moral equivocation.

This emphasis upon the 'public', 'acknowledged' or 'conspicuous' status of Parnell's transgression dominates the Dedalus family Christmas dinner. Querying English social purists' interference in what they construe as an Irish matter, Simon Dedalus asks 'Were we to desert him at the bidding of the English people' (*P* 32) and insists with his friend John Casey that public figures be judged on firmly public issues, exemplified as 'catholic emancipation' and 'the fenian movement' (*P* 38). Stephen's devoutly Catholic aunt Dante, however, follows Price-Hughes and Stead, borrowing their rhetoric: 'It is a question of public morality'(*P* 31), 'He was a public sinner' (*P* 32), '*Woe be to the man by whom the scandal cometh!*' (*P* 32). Dante conjures up a Parnell overexposed in divorce court and newspapers, the version of Parnell which haunted Stephen in Clongowes infirmary and which preoccupied social purists. Through Dante, Joyce imports social purity ideology into the Christmas dinner scene, and through Casey and Dedalus, he documents its devastating, divisive effects. Casey's 'story about a very famous spit' (*P* 34) directly responds to Dante's ventriloquism of social purity discourse by transferring that ventriloquism to a very different persona. Casey's old woman, 'a drunken old harridan she was surely' (*P* 36) may ironically refer to the Shan Van Vocht archetype, but also caricatures the kind of 'mob' a self-consciously populist social purity campaign attempted to influence through its use of mass rallies and affiliations to W. T. Stead's sensationalist 'new journalism'.[15] She is violent, intemperate and vindictive, but most damningly she seems to take a prurient delight in laying claim to that scrutiny of the private lives of public men which social purists insisted upon. Frank Callanan has rigorously documented how anti-Parnell invective relied upon the ceaseless reiteration of divorce-court snippets to produce a compelling iconography of disgrace. The old woman follows this very strategy, bawling the representative soundbites of Parnell's notoriety – '*Priest-hunter! The Paris Funds! Mr Fox! Kitty O'Shea*' (*P* 36).[16] Casey's wroth

[14] *Ibid.*, 465; Stead, *Discrowned King of Ireland*, 10.
[15] For an account of social purity's affiliations with the 'new journalism', exemplified by the sensational publication of W. T. Stead's 'Maiden Tribute' articles in *The Pall Mall Gazette* of 1885, see Walkowitz, *City*, 102–7.
[16] Callanan, *T. M. Healy*, 319–47.

is triggered by this prurience: 'she called that lady a name that I won't sully this Christmas board nor your ears, ma'am, nor my own lips by repeating' (*P* 36). His coy evasion of the word 'whore' and charge of coarse impropriety in invading the private sphere of Parnell's adultery repeats a common accusation levelled at social purists, since what social purists perceived as challenging 'that modest silence that has landed England in child-harlotry' might also be interpreted as prurient muckraking.[17]

Casey's form of revenge allegorically challenges social purity's claim to inspect and publicise sexual irregularity. His 'famous spit' (*P* 34) both blinds and silences, simultaneously assaulting his victim's capacity to see and to disseminate what she has seen:

He clapped his hand to his eye and gave a hoarse scream of pain.
– *O Jesus, Mary and Joseph!* says she. *I'm blinded! I'm blinded and drownded!*
He stopped in a fit of coughing and laughter, repeating:
– *I'm blinded entirely.* (*P* 37)

The thinly disguised parallel between the old woman and Dante becomes strikingly explicit when Dante stares across the table and Casey 'scrap[es] the air from before his eyes with one hand as though he were tearing aside a cobweb' (*P* 39), in a gesture so resonant of assault that Uncle Charles and Simon Dedalus try to hold him back. His gesture viscerally clears a path for his own gaze whilst 'tearing aside' the almost ectoplasmic manifestation of hers, and, restrained, he stares across the table out of 'dark flaming eyes' (*P* 39). As the old woman is shamed by Casey's spit and his impersonation of her, so too this confrontation turns all eyes from Parnell to Dante, who rises, 'shoved her chair violently aside', upsets her napkin ring and slams out of the door, 'her cheeks flushed and quivering with rage' (*P* 39). Casey turns the tables on those he considers representative of the ideology which proclaimed the right to scrutinise Parnell. His assault transforms spectators into spectacle, as those inspecting and publicising Parnell are themselves watched and publicly ridiculed.

Casey's revenge-fantasy has particularly terrifying implications for Stephen, who has been positioned as the assumed audience to the Parnell controversy. Uncle Charles attempts to remonstrate with his nephew by drawing attention to Stephen, listening and watching: 'Simon! Simon!... The boy' (*P* 32), and the other adults in turn appeal to him to remember 'the language he heard against God and religion and priests in his own

---

[17] For contemporary challenges to purity attempts to break the 'conspiracy of silence', see Frank Mort, *Dangerous Sexualities: Medico-Moral Politics in England since 1830* (London: Routledge and Kegan Paul, 1987), 89–91.

home' and 'the language with which the priests and the priests' pawns broke Parnell's heart and hounded him into his grave' (*P* 34). These references to Stephen as onlooker ironically make him conspicuous: no wonder that, dressed for mass, paraded in Eton jacket and called upon to say Grace, he is suffused with an uneasy sense of being on display. His sense that, like Parnell, he is being watched is manifest through his preoccupation with eyes and glances: Mr Casey has 'sleepy eyes' (*P* 28), his father 'put up his eyeglass' (*P* 29) to look down upon him when he laughs at a joke meant for adults, Eileen covers his eyes with her 'long white hands' (*P* 36), a memory suggestive in turn of Dante's threat to 'pull out his eyes' (*P* 8). As the conflict mounts, Stephen attempts to secede from this world of interchanging glances by looking away. When Dante leaves, the narrative cinematically tracks his averted gaze, following 'her napkin-ring which rolled slowly along the carpet and came to rest against the foot of an easy-chair' (*P* 39). Only then does Stephen dare look up and risk catching anybody's eye, when he sees 'his father's eyes were full of tears' (*P* 40). Stephen's custody of his gaze is a self-defensive measure, as by looking away he attempts to become what he wistfully recalls in *Ulysses*; 'I am the boy / That can enjoy / Invisibility' (*U* 1: 260–2). His obsession with eyes and glances, with looking and with avoiding being looked at, implies that he has internalised the example of Parnell. When he returns to Clongowes, the lesson is still more immediately personalised. There, Stephen too is subjected to an intrusive and punitive regime of inspection, with sexual dissidence as the target of institutional surveillance. Instead of taking the position of onlooker at Parnell's disgrace, Stephen finds himself the target of social purity's regime of scrutinising and policing male sexuality.

II

When, in *Stephen Hero*, Stephen Daedalus shocks Madden by asserting that masturbation is general all over Ireland, he draws upon a cautionary tale familiar to them both: 'Ask Father Pat and ask Dr Thisbody and ask Dr Thatbody. I was at school and you were at school – and that's enough about it' (*SH* 60). Stephen refers to the second strand of the purity campaign to 'demand purity and righteousness in men', a crusade against adolescent masturbation which, like the agitation against 'corrupt public men', attempted to redefine masculinity.[18] Schools were the main locus of a medico-moral campaign to eradicate the double standard by educating

---

[18] Sheila Jeffries, *The Spinster and her Enemies* (London: Pandora Press, 1985), 13, 18.

young men for chastity, and, as Edward Bristow notes, the purity leagues enjoyed a virtual monopoly on sex education, being the only organisations willing to break a 'conspiracy of silence' over sex.[19] What formal written instruction about sexual development Irish schoolboys like Stephen and Madden would have received would most probably have been mediated through the mass of popular pamphlets and tracts disseminated both officially and furtively through British and Irish boys' schools of all denominations by groups such as the White Cross League and the Alliance of Honour. Penny purity pamphlets supplied in bulk to concerned schoolmasters, and warnings of the dangers of 'a forbidden pleasure within your reach, forcing itself on your notice' were distributed on a vast scale and thoroughly infiltrated popular culture.[20] For instance, Henry Varley's *Lecture to Men Only* (1882) sold 90,000 copies in three years, Alfred Dyer's *Plain Words to Young Men on An Avoided Subject* and *Safeguards Against Immorality* were each selling 150,000 copies during the 1890s, whilst Ellice Hopkins' seminal *True Manliness* ran to a million by 1909.[21] As Lesley Hall notes, the amount of such literature produced and the scale of its dissemination indicates that the masturbation crusade was a late-Victorian and Edwardian preoccupation, rising in the 1880s, peaking at around 1900 and sustained until the First World War.[22] Elite adolescent males, educated together in residential schools and marked out as future leaders, were the targets of this zeal.[23] The prevalence of masturbation anxiety during Joyce's own adolescence and young manhood leaves its traces not only on *Stephen Hero*, but more intriguingly on *A Portrait*, where Stephen Dedalus, a middle-class schoolboy preoccupied with his own developing sexual identity, is a sitting target for these populist propagandas of 'true manliness'. As Stephen attempts to come to terms with his puberty, the implication that masculinity is perilously conspicuous, foregrounded by the Parnell scandal, becomes overwhelmingly personal.

When Stephen returns to Clongowes after the Christmas holiday, still traumatised by the Parnell quarrel, he learns that 'five fellows out of the higher line' have been 'caught with Simon Moonan and Tusker Boyle in the square one night' (*P* 42) by the silent, stealthy nocturnal patrol

---

[19] Edward Bristow, *Vice and Vigilance: Purity Movements in Britain since 1700* (Dublin: Gill and Macmillan, 1977), 126.

[20] Ellice Hopkins, *True Manliness* (London: White Cross Society, 1885), 1.

[21] Circulation figures from Bristow, *Vice and Vigilance*, 131, 138; Lesley Hall, 'Forbidden by God, Despised by Men: Masturbation, Medical Warnings, Moral Panic and Manhood in Great Britain, 1850–1950', in *Forbidden History*, ed. John C. Fout (Chicago: Chicago University Press, 1991), 298.

[22] *Ibid.*

[23] Alan Hunt, 'The Great Masturbation Panic and the Discourses of Moral Regulation in Nineteenth- and Early Twentieth-Century Britain', *Journal of the History of Sexuality* 8: 4 (1998), 575–615; Beisel, *Imperilled Innocents*, 54–6; Bristow, *Vice and Vigilance*, 125–53.

of an all-seeing master. Stephen's schoolmates are initially unsure of the nature of their transgression, but Athy eventually reveals all, through the mysterious word 'smugging' (*P* 42). Stephen wonders 'What did that mean about the smugging in the square?' (*P* 42), and the term is still resistant to a precise definition.[24] I would read 'smugging' as masturbation, the privileged target of Edwardian anxieties over schoolboy sexuality.[25] Social purists were preoccupied with the moral dangers of school life, and the boarding-school especially 'lent itself readily to the imagery of contagion and corruption that were such established themes in social purity discourses'.[26] To combat 'that immorality, used in a special sense, which I need not define', headmasters of the principal public schools formed a prestigious Schoolmasters Committee of the Church of England Purity Society in 1883.[27] Individual members endeavoured to gather information on the subject which would both justify and assist their project: for instance, Clement Dukes, the physician at Rugby school, won an award from the London Statistical Society for a prize essay claiming that between 90 and 95 per cent of boys at public schools engaged in masturbation.[28] Such was the panic induced by this kind of revelation that schoolmasters in the vanguard of the crusade almost unanimously agreed that 'the snake or serpent which creeps into many a school' could be vanquished by a combination of strategies J. M. Wilson, head of Clifton College and author of the pioneering *Immorality in Public Schools* (1883) summarised as 'incessant watchfulness'.[29]

[24] Don Gifford cites the *English Dialect Dictionary*'s interpretation 'to toy amorously in secret' to offer 'the practice of schoolboy homosexuality', *Joyce Annotated: Notes for 'Dubliners' and 'A Portrait of the Artist as a Young Man'* (Berkeley: University of California Press, 1982), 151, Chester Anderson concurs, 'a mild form of homosexual petting' ('Baby Tuckoo: Joyce's Features of Infancy', in *Approaches to Joyce's 'Portrait': Ten Essays*, ed. Thomas Staley and Bernard Benstock (Pittsburgh: University of Pittsburgh Press, 1976), 155), whilst James Carens suggests 'something a bit more intense than petting has been going on', '*A Portrait of the Artist as a Young Man': A Companion To Joyce Studies* (Westport, CT: Greenwood, 1984), 317. Both the secrecy and the group nature of 'smugging' in *A Portrait* indicate to me that masturbation is most probably meant.

[25] As Alan Hunt convincingly argues, whilst homophobia was an important aspect of masturbation panic, it was not its ultimate focus. For instance, many pamphlets suggested that mutual masturbation is dangerous because it allows older boys to introduce younger boys into habits of sexual incontinence which would lead them eventually to heterosexual impurity, rather than because the younger boys would be initiated into homosexuality. See Hunt, 'Great Masturbation Panic', 589, 605–7. Lesley Hall concurs, suggesting that 'rather surprisingly, the fears were not of creating a permanent homosexual or "inverted" tendency ... but that mutual experimentation would lead to solitary self-abuse'. See Hall, 'Forbidden by God', 301.

[26] Hunt, 'Great Masturbation Panic', 585.

[27] J. M. Wilson, in the *Journal of Education* (supplement), 1 November 1883, 255; Bristow, *Vice and Vigilance*, 134.

[28] Clement Dukes, *The Preservation of Health as it is Affected by Personal Habits* (1883), cited in Bristow, *Vice and Vigilance*, 134.

[29] Revd G. Everard, *A Strange Companion* (London: White Cross Society, 1884), 5; J. M. Wilson, *Sins of the Flesh: A Sermon Preached in Clifton College Chapel* (London: Social Purity Alliance, 1883), 255.

Accordingly, sleeping with one's hands under the bedclothes was a caning offence, toilet cubicles were commonly kept doorless and masters crept through darkened dormitories in stockinged feet.[30] Inspecting Irish grammar schools in 1881, J. P. Mahaffy was shocked to find one school in Tipperary which had not instigated this regime: dormitories had cubicles to allow privacy for the boys' prayers, but as Mahaffy noted, 'there are other things promoted by privacy besides prayers, and in England, where morality is not so good and the boys not so innocent as they are in Ireland, the cubicle system is out of favour'.[31] Such espionage techniques were augmented with mixed success by attempts to recruit schoolboy informants. The code of schoolboy honour against 'peach[ing] on a fellow' (*P* 9) was in conflict with advice to schoolmasters to 'discourage active confidences about a boy's surroundings except in regard to the all-important question of purity'.[32] Masturbation anxiety reached such heights by the turn of the century that, as one Old Wellingtonian recalled, 'expulsion from a public school was generally attributed to sexual depravity, and any boy so disgraced would find universities and professions barred to him'.[33] The associations between masturbation and public schools were thus of such a weight as to make Athy's reference to 'smugging' an unmistakeable allusion to the solitary vice. The paranoid climate of surveillance which overwhelmed most Edwardian residential boys' schools is markedly in evidence at Clongowes.

For Stephen's schoolmates, surreptitiously discussing smugging in the playground, the legacy of 'incessant watchfulness' is clear. 'Wells looked round to see if anyone was coming' before advancing his explanation of the older boys' disgrace 'secretly' (*P* 41), and Athy 'lowered his voice' and 'paused for a moment' (*P* 43) before disclosing all. Athy's naming of 'smugging' intensifies the atmosphere of nervous self-consciousness amongst the boys. Stephen looks 'at the faces of the fellows' to search for some clue about 'What did that mean about the smugging in the square', but finds 'they were all looking across the playground' (*P* 42). His more sophisticated schoolfellows

[30] Alisdare Hickson, *The Poisoned Bowl: Sex and the Public School* (London: Duckworth, 1996), 47, 50, 67.
[31] Report of Revd J. P. Mahaffy, FTCD, Inspector of Grammar Schools, in Appendix A, *Report from the Commissioners of Endowed Schools (Ireland)*, vol. xxxv (Dublin: Thom. and Co., 1881), 242. Mahaffey, Classics Professor at Trinity College, Dublin, is better known for another view on educational reform: 'James Joyce is a living argument in favour of my contention that it was a mistake to establish a separate university for the aborigines of this island – for the corner-boys who spit into the Liffey', Richard Ellmann, *James Joyce* (Oxford: Oxford University Press, 1983), 58.
[32] Edward Lyttelton, *The Causes and Prevention of Immorality in Schools* (London: Social Purity Alliance, 1887), 39.
[33] Hickson, *Poisoned Bowl*, 52.

are clearly alert to the cultural paranoia surrounding 'smugging', and instinctively deploy counter-surveillance measures to protect themselves from authority's espionage. They dramatise what Eton headmaster Edward Lyttelton predicted: 'I admit many boys improve, but some only appear to do so – they learn wariness and decorum more easily than virtue.'[34] Joyce strikingly allegorises this connection between 'smugging' and 'incessant watchfulness' by entangling Stephen's disorientation over a scandal he does not understand with his disorientation resulting from the loss of his glasses. Stephen is acutely aware of his myopia in an atmosphere where sharpness of sight is constituted as an essential mode of defence. His thoughts alternate between curiosity over 'smugging' and anxiety over his own imperfect sight; the 'fellows' seem 'smaller', the blackboard is legible 'only by closing his right eye tight and staring out of the left eye' (*P* 46). The interconnecting nature of these anxieties are suggested in the way Joyce counterpoints references to hands and eyes. A highly sensuous, suggestive preoccupation with 'Lady Boyle ... always at his nails, paring them' (*P* 43), Eileen's 'long thin cool white hands' (*P* 43), Athy's 'knuckly inky hands', (*P* 45) or Mr Gleeson's 'clean white wrists and fattish white hands' (*P* 45) is balanced with memories of how 'he had shut his eyes and opened his mouth' (*P* 47) to receive his first communion, or curiosity over Father Arnall: 'his face was black-looking and his eyes were staring' (*P* 47). As Father Dolan beats Fleming, this narrative oscillation between eyes and hands moves into direct speech: 'An idler of course. I can see it in your eye...A born idler. I can see it in the corner of his eye', 'Hold out!', 'Other hand!' (*P* 49). It is recapitulated during Stephen's beating, when his thoughts veer between his tear-filled eyes and trembling hand so repeatedly that within one page the words 'hand', 'hands', 'palm' 'fingers' and 'arm' appear eighteen times and 'eyes' and 'tears' ten times (*P* 51). The insistent association between eyes and hands metonymically stands for the dense cultural connections between institutional surveillance and schoolboy masturbation.

Father Dolan prefaces both beatings by insisting that his victims' transgressions are somehow inscribed on their bodies; 'I can see it in your eye', 'I see schemer in your face' (*P* 49, 50). Each boy is punished in front of his classmates, and Stephen's horrified, fascinated response to the sight of Fleming 'squeezing his hands under his armpits, his face contorted with pain' (*P* 49) demonstrates how the beating is meant to transform offenders into cautionary spectacle.[35] As Cecil Thunder later complains, Stephen's

---

34 Lyttelton, *Causes and Prevention*, 23.
35 See Colleen Lamos, 'James Joyce and the English Vice', in *Novel: A Forum on Fiction* 29: 1 (1995), 23 for a fuller discussion of the theatricality of *A Portrait's* pandying scenes.

punishment is larded with spectacular flourishes: 'I saw him lift the pandy-bat over his shoulder and he's not allowed to do that' (*P* 53). This forces the victim to be agonisingly aware of his body as a sight, and Stephen, imagining his hands 'beaten and swollen with pain [...] as if they were not his own but someone else's' (*P* 51), and trying to stop his shameful tears before his classmates, is particularly susceptible to such a lesson. Even after the 'pandying' has finished and he walks alone to Father Conmee's study to complain, Stephen imagines himself under scrutiny from 'the portraits of the saints and great men of the order' who he senses 'were looking down on him silently as he passed' (*P* 56). Stephen internalises the paranoid consciousness of potential surveillance which social purists endeavoured to inculcate. Through this emphatic connection of masturbation with a consciousness of being watched, Joyce allegorically hints at a morality crusade which urged schoolmasters to 'maintain such a degree of watchfulness over the boys so as to enable you to detect any private irregularities'.[36] *A Portrait* reflects how social purists attempted to hotwire the secret, furtive pleasures of autoeroticism to the terror of espionage, discovery and retribution.

III

As Stephen progresses through adolescence, his uneasy conception of self as spectacle, demonstrated through the Parnell controversy and abruptly rendered personal at Clongowes, is directed inwards and thereby intensified. His journey with his father to Cork supplies a moment of epiphany which explicates anxieties only dimly apprehended earlier. Stanislaus Joyce's *Dublin Diary* suggests that a private joke lay behind Joyce's decision to site this epiphany within the Queen's College lecture theatre, for Stanislaus transcribed a bawdy pastiche of a popular song favoured by Joyce and his medical student friends, which claimed the Cork medical school as the locus of one Dr Dooley's 'great discovery / Whilst a student at the Queen's' that 'It's masturbation / That kills the nation', a maxim he 'preaches round the town'.[37] If Queen's College, Cork was for Joyce the apocryphal home of medico-moral masturbation panic, it is fitting that here Stephen comes face to face with the sudden annunciation of his own stagnant, thwarted and sterile sexuality: 'the word Foetus cut several times in the dark stained wood' (*P* 90). He imagines the scene of the word's inscription:

[36] Joseph Howe, *Excessive Venery, Masturbation and Continence: The Etiology, Pathology and Treatment of the Diseases resulting from Venereal Excesses* (London and New York: E. B. Treat, 1883), 25.
[37] Song quoted in full in Stanislaus Joyce, *The Complete Dublin Diary* (Ithaca: Cornell University Press, 1975), 65. Joyce later pastiched the song again, as 'Dooleysprudence' (*Poems* 120).

A broad-shouldered student with a moustache was cutting in the letters with a jack-knife, seriously. Other students stood or sat near him laughing at his handiwork. One jogged his elbow. The big student turned on him, frowning. He was dressed in loose grey clothes and had tan boots. (*P* 90)

This 'big', 'broad-shouldered' student carries echoes of one of the Clongowes smugglers, 'big Corrigan', whose 'broad shoulders and big hanging black head' fascinate the younger Stephen enough to recall how he looked in the bath, 'with skin the same colour as the turf-coloured bogwater' (*P* 54). The vision reprises that scene of furtive male transgression earlier discovered in the school lavatories, with a penknife substituted for a penis as the object of collective voyeurism.

The counterpoint between Stephen's 'Foetus' vision and Clongowes is anticipated by the confusion between 'smugging' and graffiti made earlier, when, baffled, he wonders 'But why in the square?', and wrongly deduces 'because it was a place where some fellows wrote things for cod' (*P* 43–4). This fantasy of collective inscription induces panic that his sexuality is legible to all. The word 'capered before his eyes as he walked back across the quadrangle' (*P* 90): in his imagination it is written everywhere, unbearably publicising his secret shame. Stephen is shocked 'to find in the outer world a trace of what he had deemed till then a brutish and individual malady of his own mind' (*P* 90). His distress involves both horror that his sin is not original, and paranoia that it is thereby universally known. Accordingly, he begins to consider his own 'bodily weakness' as 'mad and filthy orgies' (*P* 91), reconfiguring masturbation not as a solitary but a collective practice. His horror is displaced onto his psychosomatic alienation from forms of public writing comparable to graffiti in their solicitation of a mass audience: he closes his eyes in an attempt to escape the capering vision of 'Foetus' only to open them and find 'He could scarcely interpret the letters of the signboards of the shops' (*P* 92). Stephen's alienation from shop signs displaces his fear that his sexuality will be similarly inscribed in the public sphere: 'Nothing moved him or spoke to him from the real world unless he heard in it an echo of the infuriated cries within him' (*P* 92). His terror that his debased, solipsistic sexuality is 'echoed' or broadcast throughout the 'real world' prompts him to compare himself explicitly to Parnell. Remembering Clongowes, Stephen muses 'Parnell had died . . . He had not died but he had faded out like a film in the sun' (*P* 93). Joyce's image captures the quick of Stephen's distress: he fears the condition of overexposure metonymically figured by a light-sensitive film negative left to bleach in sunlight.

Stephen's anxiety over his conspicuous sexual debility is manifest when he tries to 'to realize the enormities which he brooded on' (*P* 99) in Dublin's brothel quarter. There, his 'cry for an iniquitous abandonment' is 'but the echo of an obscene scrawl which he had read on the oozing wall of a urinal' (*P* 100). As Clair Wills has noted, Stephen's prowls through Monto in search of 'sin with another of his kind' (*P* 100) strikingly 'lack the anonymity required for state-of-the-art *flânerie*', since he is petrified that he may be seen by somebody who knows him.[38] Instead of moving through Monto with the *flâneur's* potent, detached invisibility, watching the prostitutes flaunt themselves and selecting from them at leisure, Stephen approaches the 'maze of narrow and dirty streets' with painful circumspection, 'peering into the gloom of lanes and doorways, listening eagerly for any sound' until 'a trembling seized him and his eyes grew dim' (*P* 100). Unsurprisingly, it is the prostitute who takes over the traditionally masculine role of scopic aggressor in this transaction, 'gaz[ing] into his face', transmitting 'the meaning of her movements' in 'her frank uplifted eyes' and prompting Stephen to 'close his eyes, surrendering himself to her, body and mind' (*P* 101).

Stephen's predisposition to imagine himself watched by others is yet more pronounced in chapter 3, where his anxieties about his body explicitly reproduce contemporary purity discourses of 'true manliness'. Purity pamphlets urged adolescent schoolboys to recognise the stigmata of masturbation in a host of commonplace adolescent ailments, since the threat outlined above of 'incessant watchfulness' in schools was obviously not able to eradicate alone a vice by its nature solitary and secret. Instead, boys had to be actively recruited for chastity and encouraged to inspect *themselves* for tell-tale signs. Tracts insisted that the stigmata of masturbation was legible on the body, drawing upon established theories of 'spermatic economy' which argued that 'the vigour of the nervous system is mainly dependent on the seed'.[39] Advice relied heavily upon the threat that the adolescent's secret sin might become visible to others through an array of somatic 'symptoms'. The therapeutic practice of the purity crusade was thus to instruct the sufferer in scrupulous self-observation.

Masturbation propaganda was in this respect a branch of the late-Victorian enthusiasm for 'self-help', since resisting 'the commonest form of impurity which taints the moral nature' was a process of acquiring 'the ability to overcome abnormal desires' through 'power of suggestion, right

---

[38] Clair Wills, 'Joyce, Prostitution and the Colonial City', in *The South Atlantic Quarterly* 95: 1 (Winter 1996), 89.

[39] Ellice Hopkins, *Who Holds the Rope?* (London: White Cross Society, 1886), 6.

living and inspirational occupation'.[40] J. M. Wilson presented his students with a stark choice: 'It has to be settled whether you are your own master or slave; whether your body shall be kept under and you will be strong enough to rule it.'[41] For Ellice Hopkins, the boy was 'an intelligent being mounted on a spirited horse' which he had to tame.[42] Boys were enjoined both to resist temptation and to excise existing signs of degeneration through a host of disciplinary strategies. A concentration upon rigorous regimes of somatic discipline and inspection attempted to produce an acute self-consciousness in the reader, since purity advice urged boys to consider their bodies treacherous spectacles offering highly visible evidence of solitary vice:

The devil, with his counterfeit modesty, has taught us to call it the secret sin. In reality, it is the very opposite of secret. The pale, bloodless face, the sunken eyes, the soft, flabby flesh, the slovenly gait, soon give it away.

The outward signs of debasement are all too obvious: the frame is stunted, the complexion sallow, pasty or covered in acne, the eye sunken or heavy.

To detect the secret sensualist is not at all difficult: the bloodless countenance, sunken eyes with darkened shadows beneath, lack of vigour, palpitations of the heart give him away.[43]

Detecting the secret sensualist in *A Portrait* is all too easy, since Stephen's 'sincorrupted flesh' (*P* 137) lacks the 'vigour of rude male health' and he fears that 'no life or youth stirred in him' (*P* 96). Warnings against such generalised emasculating enervation was a vital part of the armoury of threats: self-abuse threatened to 'stunt your growth, soften your muscles, and in fact wreck your health prematurely', turning the sufferer into 'an enfeebled unmanned man'.[44]

These theories have clearly persuaded Stephen, for his solitary indulgence is 'the luxury that was wasting him', 'the wasting fires of lust' (*P* 99): 'At his first violent sin he had felt a wave of vitality pass out of him and had feared to find his body or his soul maimed by the excess' (*P* 103). Furthermore, his fears echo the specific details of masturbation paranoia: he is 'listless and dishonoured, gazing out of darkened eyes, helpless, perturbed' (*P* 112), and as he waits to enter the confessional prays 'with his darkened eyes' (*P* 143). His disturbed self-image is evident not only in direct and familiar

---

[40] Hopkins, *Power of Womanhood*, 54; Benjamin Jeffries and J. L. Nichols, *Light on Dark Corners* (New York: 1895), 173.

[41] Wilson, *Sins of The Flesh*, 5.   [42] Hopkins, *True Manliness*, 3.

[43] Reader Harris, *An Address to Men Only* (London: n.p. 1899), 6; F Arthur Sibly, *Private Knowledge for Boys* (Gloucester: Stonehouse Press, 1912), 5.

[44] Edward Kirk, *A Talk With Boys About Themselves* (London: n.p., 1905), 35. Kirk's 'Sex Series', a collection of 'Papers on Health' enjoyed a circulation well over 100,000 by 1905 (Bristow, *Vice and Vigilance*, 138).

connections between short sight and the solitary vice ('one of the most patent signs of this habit in our youth today is the almost universal use of eyeglasses and spectacles') but in the ubiquitous references to the 'sunken eyes' of the onanist cited above.[45] His willingness to trace on his body the culturally designated stigmata of 'that one sin' (*P* 142) is particularly notable in his view of his penis:

What a horrible thing! Who made it to be like that, a bestial part of the body able to understand bestially and desire bestially? Was that then he or an inhuman thing moved by a lower soul? His soul sickened at the thought of a torpid snaky life feeding itself out of the tender marrow of his life and fattening upon the slime of lust. (*P* 140)

Stephen's phallophobia reproduces the melodramatic Edenic imagery common to the genre. Strikingly, Ellice Hopkins urged boys to take drastic measures: 'imitate an Australian sawyer who, when bitten in the little finger by a deadly serpent, chopped it off, saving his life. That secret act of impurity, chop it off and cast it from thee.'[46] In his willingness to construct himself an abject spectacle of debility, weak of body, sunken of eye, lacking 'manly vigour', 'wasted' by lust, sapped by the 'torpid snaky life' of his disobedient penis, Stephen internalises the system of surveillance imposed at Clongowes, scrutinising his body for the commonplace complaints which make the effects of masturbation 'plainly discernible in the boy's appearance'.[47]

Significantly, Stephen's policy of 'mortification of the senses' inflects purity's emphasis upon the self-regulation of the wayward body through Catholic ritual. Stephen senses that 'From the evil seed of lust all other deadly sins had sprung forth' (*P* 106), and his understanding of the interconnectedness of his sins seems to derive from both the Catholic tradition and the purity crusade. His decision to overhaul his conduct through an ascetic regime of prayer, diet and cold baths painstakingly follows popular purity advice to young men to place sexual continence within a generalised regime of abstinence. Diet was particularly understood as an arena for the exercise of self-control, and rich foods were avoided as they inflamed the passions. Dr Robert Bullen, the secretary of the Social Purity Alliance was

---

[45] James Barker, *A Secret Book for Men* (Brighton: n.p., 1888), 7.
[46] Ellice Hopkins, *Wild Oats and Acorns* (London: White Cross League, 1883), 10. Other enthusiasts compared masturbation to 'the viper secreting the deadly poison of a lustful passion', anon., *The Garment of Purity* (London: King, Sell and Routon, 1896), 17, or 'the snake or serpent which creeps into many a school', Everard, *A Strange Companion*, 5.
[47] Henry Varley, *Private Address to Boys and Youths on an Important Subject*, (London: Christian Commonwealth, 1884), 8.

one of many who urged young men to limit their consumption of meat and instead to eat plain, cereal-based foods such as wholemeal bread and oatmeal porridge.[48] In America, the zeal for cereals led social purists John Harvey Kellogg and Sylvester Graham to invent cornflakes and Graham's crackers, the former insisting that 'the exorbitant sexuality of civilised people is not natural' but 'due to the incitements of an abnormally stimulating diet'.[49] This dietary strain is evident in *A Portrait*. Finding 'he had sunk to the state of a beast that licks his chaps after meat' (*P* 111), Stephen renounces the pleasure he has taken in 'stew for dinner, turnips and carrots and bruised potatoes and fat mutton pieces', which induced memories of 'the squalid quarter of the brothels' and the prostitutes' 'soft perfumed flesh' (*P* 102). Instead, 'he practised strict habits at table, observed to the letter all the fasts of the church and sought by distraction to divert his mind from the savours of different foods' (*P* 151).

Purity literature's perennial recommendation of cold baths is also evident when 'he left parts of his neck and face undried so that the air might sting them' (*P* 154) resonating with advice such as 'use a rough bath towel and rub the flesh until the surface of the skin is red', or Robert Baden-Powell's injunction to boy scouts to 'bathe the racial organ in cold water daily'.[50] Stephen is especially vigilant at bedtime, 'never consciously chang[ing] his position in bed' (*P* 151), echoing purity advice to sleep in well-ventilated rooms, never on one's back and with hands firmly outside the bedclothes.[51] Even the supposedly innocent activity of walking with one's hands in one's trouser pockets was suspected to 'create those physical sensations that ought of all things to be kept in abeyance': at Harrow in 1895, all boys' pockets were sewn up.[52] Accordingly, Stephen 'carried his arms stiffly at his sides like a runner and never in his pockets', unless they are gainfully employed: 'he carried his beads loose in his trouser pockets that he might tell them as he walked the streets' (*P* 148). Stephen's policy of 'mortification of the

---

[48] Robert Bullen, *Our Duty as Teachers with Reference to Social Purity Work, An Address* (London: n.p., 1886), 16.

[49] Kellogg quoted in Alan Hunt, *Governing Morals: A Social History of Moral Regulation* (Cambridge: Cambridge University Press, 1999), 126. Both Graham and Kellogg wrote various tracts warning youths against the temptations of the flesh. Kellogg published *Plain Truths about Boyhood, Youth and Manhood* in 1890, and his *Social Purity* ran to 175, 000 copies by 1895 (circulation details from frontispiece of *Social Purity*, North Fitzroy, Victoria, Aus.: Echo Publishing Co., 1895). Graham wrote *A Lecture to Young Men on Chastity* (London: 1854).

[50] Barker, *Secret Book for Men*, 34; Baden-Powell quoted in Bristow, *Vice and Vigilance*, 140.

[51] See Varley, *Private Address*, 27. Maurice Hime was a fresh-air fiend, insisting on open windows and 'hardish mattresses' in his dormitories, *Schoolboys' Special Immorality* (London: White Cross League, 1901), 52.

[52] *Ibid.*, Hunt, 'Great Masturbation Panic', 602; John Chandos, *Boys Together: English Public Schools 1800–1864* (London: Yale University Press, 1984), 338.

PRIVATE.

Rules for those who desire to lead a pure life.

CARE OF THE MIND.

When sexual thoughts occur to the mind, banish them *instantly*. Every moment that such thoughts remain in the mind they increase their hold on it. The least tolerance or encouragement of such thoughts is therefore fatal to real chastity.

The best way to *avoid* evil thoughts is to keep the mind always occupied with innocent ones. For this and for other reasons you should cultivate all innocent tastes. Take an interest in sports, in books, in science, Nature, music, social questions, and the like. A hobby, too, is an excellent thing. The more innocent enjoyment you have, the less will you be tempted to evil.

The best way to *banish* evil thoughts when they do occur is to turn the mind on to some other subject. During the day seek companionship, or read a book, or begin to do something that interests you. At night, in bed, take two or three very deep breaths, and then think about anything which interests but which does not excite you. If you are sleepy, breathe moderately, slowly and deeply, and count the numbers as you breathe. As you count, sleep will come.

The earnest expression of your desire for a clean heart—either in the form of prayer to God, or in the form of an emphatic statement to yourself—will help you much. Speak aloud if you are alone—quietly but intensely. This exercise is of *special* value when you are dropping off to sleep.

Absolutely avoid exchanging glances with or admiring the good looks of servants or other girls below you in social position. While such admiration need not necessarily have any conscious impurity about it, it dangerously strengthens the instinct of sex in you. With most girls in your own social position, the higher elements of love shut out the least stirring of sex consciousness. Even here, however, you need be on your guard.

Absolutely avoid everything which can put impure thoughts into your mind: for example—

Paragraphs of a certain kind in newspapers;
Smut written on walls and fences;
Animals engaged in sexual acts;
Pictures of naked bodies—if you are conscious that any sexual excitement mingles with the pure sense of beauty.

CARE OF THE BODY.

In order to make these rules easy to obey, much care of the body is needful. It must not be indulged, but made the ready servant of the will. Obedience to the following rules will not only give you great help in avoiding impurity, but will much strengthen your general health—

Absolutely avoid wine and—during youth at least—tobacco.

Eat only moderately—*specially in the evening*—of stimulating foods, such as shell-fish, meat, eggs, fish and cheese.

Take plenty of exercise: tire yourself if you like, but do not overtire yourself.

Visit a W.C. at a regular time daily. Always visit a urinal or use a chamber shortly before going to bed.

In bed carefully avoid making yourself needlessly warm. As long as you do not feel chill, the lighter your clothing the better. A mattress is much better than a bed, and a moderately hard mattress is better than a soft one. Keep your window open. Do not sleep on your back. Do not lie in bed after you awake.

Keep the private parts clean, cool, and free from irritation. When you have the opportunity, it is desirable to wash not merely the outside of the private parts with soap and water, but to draw back the loose foreskin and wash it and the underlying parts. If you suffer from irritation or inflammation keep a penny tin of boric acid powder and dust the interior of the foreskin with it when you visit the W.C.

In cleansing the private parts and at all other times, avoid needlessly handling them.

Figure 4 An image from F. Arthur Sibly, *Private Knowledge for Boys* (Gloucester: Stonehouse Press, 1912), 14.

senses' thus closely follows popular purity advice, much as his fears about what he looks like to others, with his pallor, sunken eyes, lack of vigour and anti-social disposition reflect with startling literalness the fantasies of degeneration masturbation propaganda attempted to induce. Social purity propaganda works in tandem with the strictures of Stephen's church, coinciding with and intensifying Catholicism's condemnation of 'sins of impurity' (*P* 144).

This convergence of Catholic and social purity sexual discourse is underlined when Stephen, stunned by one of Father Arnall's sermons, imagines himself watched by none other than 'the Blessed Virgin':

The eyes were not offended which she turned upon him nor reproachful. She placed their hands together, hand in hand, and said, speaking to their hearts:

– Take hands now, Stephen and Emma. It is a beautiful evening now in heaven. You have erred but you are always my children. (*P* 116)

Stephen's fantasy of a forgiving Mary overseeing his sins draws not only upon Catholic theology but also upon a continually reiterated social purity strategy of persuasion. White Cross League recruits promised 'To treat all women with respect and endeavour to protect them from wrong and degradation', and as part of this campaign to inculcate chivalry, purity tracts repeatedly urged boys to imagine precisely the kind of pure woman's gaze Stephen is so willing to conjure up.[53] Tracts frequently urged boys to imagine an idealised female figure – mother, sister or sweetheart – looking on in sorrow whenever they were tempted to masturbate or indulge in erotic fantasy. One typically urged 'set before the boy a noble ideal of womanhood, to be kept as a sacred thing within him to preserve him from self-disrespect', whilst the White Cross League attempted to recruit 'knights of purity' through this kind of 'appeal to the real chivalrous feeling that exists in the hearts of young men towards girlhood, maidenhood, womanhood'.[54] Its founder, Ellice Hopkins, summarised this strategy of emotional blackmail, counselling other women purity workers to 'make your womanhood a sort of external conscience to boys. You can appeal to them never to say or to do things which they would be ashamed for you to know.'[55] Such women were secular versions of Stephen's Blessed Virgin, their gaze an 'external conscience' intended to mobilise a boy's 'higher instincts'.

[53] Bristow, *Vice and Vigilance*, 100, 103.
[54] Eustace Miles, *A Boy's Control and Self-Expression* (Cambridge: E. P. Dutton and Company, 1904), 79. Alfred Dyer, *Plain Words to Young Men upon an Avoided Subject* (London: Dyer Brothers and Co., 1886), 10. Dyer was a founding member of the White Cross League.
[55] Ellice Hopkins, *Village Morality* (London: White Cross League, 1883), 13.

Social purity's secularisation of Mariolatry is suggested when Stephen substitutes the more accessible Emma Mary, for precisely the kind of asexual sweetheart-figure purists hoped would mobilise chivalry 'in the hearts of young men towards girlhood, maidenhood, womanhood':

God was too great and stern and the Blessed Virgin too pure and holy. But he imagined that he stood near Emma in a wide land and, humbly and in tears, bent and kissed the elbow of her sleeve. (*P* 116)

Appropriately, Stephen finds his vision of Emma looking on reproachfully during 'his hours sinning in thought and deed' provokes the kind of veneration and remorse purists like Ellice Hopkins hoped to inspire: 'Was that boyish love? Was that chivalry? Was that poetry? The sordid details of his orgies stank under his very nostrils' (*P* 116). Stephen's histrionic conscience and White Cross elevation of 'boyish love' and 'chivalry' is, however, laden with subversion. For dramas of sexual surveillance in the Joyce canon are rarely so simply divorced from underground visual pleasures and associated so wholeheartedly with punishment as this reading of Stephen abject before the censorious stare of purity has outlined.

A Portrait is no exception, for Stephen's disposition to imagine his sexuality watched by others is crucially compromised by the way Joyce slyly blends moral panic with submerged sexual excitement:

The image of Emma appeared before him, and under her eyes the flood of shame rushed forth anew from his heart. If she knew to what his mind had subjected her or how his brute-like lust had torn and trampled upon her innocence! (*P* 115–6)

The flavour of Joyce's burlesque is evident in the way the passage stages a suggestive counterpoint between Emma's pure gaze of rebuke and the 'shameless or bashful wantonness' of the 'harlots with gleaming jeweleyes' who look out from 'the soot-coated packet of pictures which he had hidden in the flue of the fireplace' (*P* 115–6). Stephen's fearful remorse is juxtaposed with disavowed pleasure, since being watched by women as he masturbates clearly has its consolations. The women in the photographs give the illusion of looking on, being present and complicit in 'the sordid details of his orgies' (*P* 116). Their conspiratorial gaze is reminiscent of the prostitute's 'frank uplifted eyes' (*P* 101), a gaze that made Stephen swoon into erotic surrender. Stephen's exhibitionist desire to have women watching as he 'sins' is displaced into the 'foul long letters' describing his sexual fantasies and 'written in the joy of guilty confession', which he scatters under cover of night among the grass in the corner of a field or beneath some hingeless door in some niche in the hedges where a girl might come upon them as she walked by and read them secretly. (*P* 116)

Emma's, and indeed the Virgin Mary's, pure gaze of reproach is irretrievably sullied in the context of these exhibitionist fantasies of sexually charged female espionage. It is queried also by Emma's earlier incarnations in Stephen's fantasy life; their first meeting at the children's party where 'amid the music and the laughter her glance travelled to his corner, flattering, taunting, searching, exciting his heart' (*P* 69), the Whitsuntide play where from the audience 'her dark eyes had invited and unnerved him' (*P* 83), the Emma 'by day demure and innocent' but by night 'her face transfigured by a lecherous cunning, her eyes bright with brutish joy' (*P* 99). Stephen's purity-inspired vision of Emma looking on in sorrowful reflection as he masturbates is compromised by this weakness for the titillating female gaze. For Stephen, pleasure is subversively implicated within the strategies of self-control he attempts to deploy.

This hint of a submerged complicity between strategies of sexual surveillance and the illicit pleasures such strategies attempted to discipline is elaborated in Stephen's experience of that most potent and long-established of institutions for the surveillance of sex, confession. His impulse 'Confess! Confess!' (*P* 139) and his abashed visit to the priest is informed by a similar 'joy of guilty confession' to that afforded by his 'foul long letters', since Joyce implies through a series of cumulatively unmistakeable innuendos that his protagonist gains both sacred and profane release. Sharing the contemporary paranoia about masturbation as the most fatal sin for youth, Stephen's priest asks a series of questions – 'Anything else, my child?', 'With yourself, my child' (*P* 144) – designed to elicit his secret, and then, curiously gliding over Stephen's confession of fornication with prostitutes, homes in on 'that wretched habit' which 'dishonour[s] your body' (*P* 145), surely masturbation. For Stephen, confession involves a highly suggestive release of stored-up tensions:

His sins trickled from his lips, one by one, trickled in shameful drops from his soul, festering and oozing like a sore, a squalid stream of vice. The last sins oozed forth, sluggish, filthy. There was no more to tell. He bowed his head, overcome. (*P* 144)

Confession becomes self-induced ejaculation, the innuendo rendered blatant through the imagery of sin as a viscous liquid 'trickl[ing] in shameful drops' (*P* 144), the novel's most explicit reference to the vice Stephen attempts to control.

Stephen's subsequent ritualised 'resolute piety' further outlines how self-discipline substitutes and tropes for masturbation. He carries his rosary beads 'loose in his trousers' pockets that he might tell them as he walked the streets' (*P* 148), a visual pun Joyce later dramatised in 'Nausicaa', where a man fiddling with something in his pockets is unambiguous. His prayers are 'ejaculations' (*P* 147), a pun implicit when Stephen's impulse to confess becomes compulsive and habitual, taking on a masturbatory rhythm of 'confess and repent and be absolved, confess and repent again and be absolved again, fruitlessly' (*P* 153). These suggestions that confession, in its self-absorption, is a displaced form of self-stimulation are supported by other moments where Stephen hotwires his piety to his desire; for instance when he considers 'the attitude of rapture in sacred art' with 'parted lips and eyes as of one about to swoon' (*P* 150), an image resonant of sexual surrender, or feels the Eucharist supplies similarly erotically charged 'dissolving moments of virginal self-surrender' (*P* 152). Joyce posits an intimate, symbiotic relationship between self-restraint and eroticism, a relationship made most explicit when Stephen seems to stimulate himself through the techniques of mental self-control recommended by social purists:

This idea of surrender had a perilous attraction for his mind now that he felt his soul beset once again by the insistent voices of the flesh which began to murmur to him again during his prayers and meditations. It gave him an intense sense of power to know that he could, by a single act of consent, in a moment of thought, undo all that he had done. He seemed to feel a flood slowly advancing towards his naked feet and to be waiting for the first faint timid noiseless wavelet to touch his fevered skin. Then, almost at the instant of that touch, almost at the verge of sinful consent, he found himself standing far away from the flood on a dry shore, saved by a sudden act of the will or a sudden ejaculation. (*P* 152)

If delay, deferral and displacement are the most potent of aphrodisiacs, then Stephen's 'perilous attraction' is easily understood. Self-restraint becomes a form of autoeroticism, the means of deliberately prolonging sensation through inciting, savouring and then 'almost at the verge of sinful consent', deflecting desire. Joyce's suggestion that sexuality and its control are in intimate collaboration is expanded when Stephen is invited to join the priesthood and realises that collaboration with claustrophobic horror.

    The director of studies introduces his invitation with a 'disingenuous' discussion about priestly dress, or 'jupes', which Stephen senses 'had been spoken lightly with design' (*P* 155). The word lures Stephen into an erotic reverie incorporating 'the names of articles of dress worn by women', 'the brittle texture of a woman's stocking' beneath his 'trembling fingers' which 'brought always to his mind a delicate and sinful perfume' (*P* 155). Through this daydream, Stephen intuits the nature of the 'secret knowledge and secret power' (*P* 159) he is being offered:

He would know the sins, the sinful longings and sinful thoughts and sinful acts, of others, hearing them murmured into his ears in the confessional under the shame of a darkened chapel by the lips of women and of girls; but rendered immune mysteriously at his ordination by the imposition of hands. (*P* 159)

The masturbatory innuendo here will later be made more explicit by Leopold Bloom, who describes confession as a 'Great weapon in their hands' (*U* 5: 426), but here Stephen recognises in the invitation a concealed attempt to enfold him within a regime where sexual desire is deflected into the paralytic pleasures of surveillance. Stephen is urged to turn the techniques of self-scrutiny his 'resolute piety' has perfected outwards and to police the sexuality of others as he has policed his own. However, his fantasies of presiding over the seductive confessions of 'women and girls' are abruptly derailed by another, more troubling vision. 'Masked memories' of Clongowes interrupt, 'the echoes of certain expressions used in Clongowes sounded in remote caves of his mind' (*P* 157). The 'certain expression' supplying 'distant echoes' at this epiphanic moment is surely 'smugging', and the spectre of the 'smugging' incident prompts a viscerally somatic revulsion:

At once from every part of his being unrest began to irradiate. A feverish quickening of his pulses followed, and a din of meaningless words drove his reasoned thoughts hither and thither confusedly. His lungs dilated and sank as if he were inhaling a warm moist unsustaining air and he smelt again the moist warm air which hung in the bath in Clongowes above the sluggish turf-coloured water. (*P* 161)

This odour, redolent of the spectacle of 'big Corrigan' in the bath discoloured by 'turf-coloured water', combines with 'the troubling odour of the long corridors of Clongowes' (*P* 161) to remind Stephen of the connection between the scrutiny he is tempted to impose on others, and the overwhelming atmosphere of 'incessant watching' which characterised Clongowes. An instinct 'subtle and hostile... armed him against acquiescence' (*P* 164), an instinct to resist incorporation within a self-perpetuating culture of mutual surveillance.

A Portrait thus dramatises how the existing strictures on sexuality imposed by the Catholic church on Irish schoolboys like Stephen are compounded and intensified by social purity discourse. The Stephen who will later define himself as 'a servant of two masters... an English and an Italian' (*U* 1: 638) finds his adolescent sexuality thoroughly mastered not only by

Catholicism, but, crucially, also by an English organisation closely affiliated to the state regulation of sexuality. For, if sexuality in general belongs
to the private sphere, then masturbation, the 'solitary vice', is the most
private sexual act of all. Stephen's sexuality is thus doubly proscribed from
both England and Rome, as the intimate zone of his body and its most
secret acts is infiltrated by both Irish Catholic and English evangelical purity propaganda. As we have seen, these parallel and mutually reinforcing
moral discourses impose a paralysis which turns inwards to feed off itself.
Through Stephen's penitent habits of punitive self-government, inflected
through religious zeal, Joyce demarcates the covert pleasures implicit in
social purity's attempts to moralise masculinity. His scrupulous rituals are
described in an innuendo-laden language emphasising not merely the dor-
mant salaciousness behind Stephen's efforts to 'amend his life', but also the
extent to which his suppressed sexual energies are re-routed and stimulated
through disciplinary practices. Joyce traces the process of his corruption
into a faked virtue which only thinly disguises a fetishistic, obsessive mode
of sexuality. This portrait of developing masculinity thus dissolves the distinction between sexual proscription and sexual dissidence which social purity's organised war on the double standard attempted to uphold. Instead,
A Portrait argues for the integral nature of eroticism and contemporary
modes of its suppression, demonstrating an underlying continuity between
self-pollution and self-policing.

v

Once again, Joyce's complex intertextual assault upon social purity directly
engages with the circumstances of his publication. As we have seen, *A
Portrait's* serialisation in *The Egoist* and subsequent publication through
the literary press of the same name was hindered by the objections of a
succession of printers to Joyce's sexual explicitness. Passages such as that
describing the red-light district at the end of chapter 2, or the 'signs of
adolescence that made repellent the pitiable nakedness' of Stephen's bathing
schoolfellows, were accordingly omitted from the serial version, and the
novel was published only when printed sheets could be imported from the
USA.[56] These difficulties, and the determination of *The Egoist's* editors to
surmount them, offer an intriguing context to *A Portrait's* subversions of
social purity rhetoric. For *The Egoist* articulated an ideological hostility

[56] Jane Lidderdale and Mary Nicholson, *Dear Miss Weaver: Harriet Shaw Weaver 1896–1961* (London:
Faber and Faber, 1970), 99–100.

towards the sexual politics of social purity which closely coincides with the hostility manifest throughout Joyce's novel. Joyce's earliest readers read *A Portrait* alongside *The Egoist*'s radical theories about sexuality and its policing, and by following their example, we might see how Joyce offers a specifically Irish Catholic perspective upon an international avant-garde intellectual debate.

The Egoist began life in 1912 as *The Freewoman*, a radical feminist journal which, in the words of contributor Rebecca West, 'mentioned sex loudly and clearly and repeatedly and in the worst possible taste'.[57] As Lisa Tickner notes, it thereby

offered a challenge to the social purity position which continued to dominate the Edwardian women's movement. This challenge ... represented in some respects the most 'modern' position on female sexuality.[58]

Whilst the Women's Social and Political Union was demanding the vote to 'Stop the White Slave Traffic' and campaigning with the National Vigilance Association for the draconian Criminal Law Amendment (White Slavery) Act of 1912, *The Freewoman* was choreographing ideological collisions between sex-radicals and social purists, and thereby creating an open circle of debate over sexuality. To the determined anti-suffrage leader Mrs Humphrey Ward, the journal's 'speculations and contentions with regard to the relations between the sexes' represented the 'dark and dangerous side of the women's movement'.[59] It was boycotted on these grounds by the purity-influenced distributor W. H. Smith and succumbed to bankruptcy in less than a year.[60] Resurrected as *The New Freewoman* in June 1913, the discussion of sexuality and feminism continued until December 1913, when editors Dora Marsden and Harriet Shaw Weaver conceded to a suggestion made by literary editor Ezra Pound and other male contributors that 'the present title of the paper causes it to be confounded with organs devoted solely to the advocacy of an unimportant reform in an obsolete political institution', namely, women's suffrage.[61] Alongside the change of

---

[57] Rebecca West, 'The Freewoman', *Time and Tide*, 16 July 1926, 649.

[58] Lisa Tickner, *The Spectacle of Women: Imagery of the Suffrage Campaign* (London: Chatto and Windus, 1989), 223.

[59] Ward in letter to *The Times*, quoted in Bruce Clarke, *Dora Marsden And Early Modernism: Gender, Individualism, Science* (Ann Arbor: University of Michigan Press, 1996), 219.

[60] W. H. Smith claimed the boycott was 'due to the nature of certain articles which render the paper unsuitable to be exposed on the bookstall for general sale'. Quoted in Gillian Hanscombe and Virginia Smyers, *Writing for their Lives: Modernist Women 1910–1940* (London: Women's Press, 1987), 165.

[61] *New Freewoman*, 23 December 1913.

title to the gender-neutral *The Egoist*, designed to signal its appeal 'to virile readers only', Pound aimed to 'fire the sex-problem' from the journal's
pages.[62] These twin transitions have led recent historians of Modernism
to argue that the title change in January 1914 was a 'symbolic moment'
marking the displacement of radical sexual polemic in favour of literary debate and experimentation.[63] Critical focus upon Pound's own perception
of a contest between radical feminism and high Modernism has, however,
obscured the extent to which his attempt to silence 'the sex problem' was
unsuccessful.

Pound's project foundered amid a stream of articles and letters in
The Egoist resolutely continuing to discuss sexuality. *The Freewoman* and
The New Freewoman had carried articles on contraception and abortion,
marriage as prostitution, 'Uranianism' or homosexuality, the 'Chastity of
continence' and 'Free unions'.[64] Specifically, the journal relentlessly crit-
icised social purists, protesting that the 1912 Criminal Law Amendment
Act was 'vicious, not curative, but punitive' and singling out the National
Vigilance Association for particular censure:

It is a shocking thing that social ills such as prostitution and white slavery should
be played with by a load of persecuting faddists. The prostitute is there chiefly
because until women have a decent alternative in the way of earning their bread
they must become prostitutes or starve. The National Vigilance Association do
nothing to investigate the low remuneration paid to women ... Mr Coote's strange
organisation aims to conceal as much as is possible of this terrible canker.[65]

The Personal Rights Association, a feminist libertarian organisation fiercely
opposed to the coercive policies of the National Vigilance Association, used

[62] 'Virile readers' described in advertisement for *The Egoist* carried inside the front cover of *The
Little Review* June 1918. 'Do you want to edit *The Egoist*? Present editrix writes me this A.M.
that she is willing to quit ... Of course one would fire Carter and Ricketts and the sex problem',
Ezra Pound to Amy Lowell, 23 February 1914, Pound, *The Letters of Ezra Pound 1907–1941*, ed.
D. D. Paige (London: Faber and Faber, 1962), 70–1.

[63] For Rachael Blau DuPlessis, the title change signals 'a symbolic moment', marking 'the equivocal
relationship of "high" Modernisms to feminisms and gender issues', *The Pink Guitar: Writing as
Feminist Practice* (London: Routledge, 1990), 44; for K. K. Ruthven, 'a paradigmatic instance of the
subordination of women by a male-dominated Modernism', 'Ezra's Appropriations', *Times Literary
Supplement*, 20–6 November 1987, 1300. *A Portrait's* debut has therefore commonly been interpreted
as a crucial contribution towards an ideological shift from the journal's early feminist affiliations
towards an emphasis upon male literary Modernism, especially since Joyce's introduction there as
'an author of known and notable talents' and the first instalment of *A Portrait* took place within
The Egoist's first three numbers.

[64] Andrew Thacker, 'Dora Marsden and *The Egoist*: "Our War is With Words"', in *English Literature
in Transition* 36: 2 (1993), 188.

[65] C. N. Norman, 'Champions of Morality', *The Freewoman*, 6 June 1912; 'An Alternative Bill', *The
Freewoman*, 20 June 1912; letter from 'Fatum', *The Freewoman*, 20 June 1912.

The Freewoman to publicise the case of Jessie Brown, a Glasgow virgin falsely arrested for soliciting and forcibly gynaecologically examined.[66] In 'Private Life and Public Morality', another contributor attacked social purists for driving MPs cited in divorce cases out of office, an agitation resulting from 'that hideous philosophy of Mrs Grundy, born in that Victorian age of sham'.[67] *The Egoist* continued this war on social purity unabated in articles critiquing 'Modern Writers on Chastity', attacking Anthony Comstock for his attempts to prosecute birth control pioneer Margaret Sanger, debating the 'meddlesome oldmaidish laws' on statutory rape and obscenity introduced by social purity groups in the USA., and petitioning against the barring of Theodore Dreiser's novels by the New York Society for the Suppression of Vice.[68] A closer look at the underlying argument of several of these articles demonstrates how Joyce's resistance to Pound's attempts to 'fire the sex problem' from *The Egoist* went further than his insistence on commemorating the journal under its former title as 'that New Free Woman with novel inside' (*FW* 145: 28).

The Egoist journals reveal a growing oppositional voice against social purists, partly fuelled by an affiliated enthusiasm for alternative and, at the time, avant-garde theories of sexuality heavily influenced by the new science of 'sexology'.[69] That contentious topic, masturbation, was widely discussed. Writing in an early issue of *The Freewoman*, 'A Mother of Sons' began cautiously, complaining of a relative 'entirely ruined' by 'the practices taught to him by his schoolfellows', and recommending the sex advice literature of one of the more moderate social purists, Eton head Edward Lyttelton.[70] However, her ostensibly liberal call for more 'sex education' of the type pastiched in *A Portrait* was undercut by other contributors who queried whether masturbation was harmful at all. 'A New Subscriber', later revealed as the sexologist Stella Browne, attempted to distinguish between 'Chastity and Continence' by asking

[66] Letter from J. H. Levy, Secretary of the Personal Rights' Association, *New Freewoman*, 15 June 1913, 32. Elsewhere, writers complained that 'sentimentality lies thick on militant suffragism', objecting to a cautionary tale released to the press by Sylvia Pankhurst about a working-class girl who 'found it hard to keep straight' and had vanished from her lodgings, presumably into the arms of white slave traders: 'Perhaps she had married or gone into domestic service, but they always see the black side, these purity people, having the shiver of the reader in view', *New Freewoman*, 15 August 1913, 98.
[67] William Foss, 'Private Life and Public Morality', *New Freewoman*, 15 July 1913, 55.
[68] Ezra Pound, 'The Dreiser Protest', *The Egoist*, October 1916, 159.
[69] As Lucy Bland notes, men and women contributors 'seem to have read as much sexology as they were able to get their hands on', and often offered to lend their copies of Havelock Ellis, Iwan Bloch and August Forel to other readers. Bland, *Banishing the Beast*, 278–80.
[70] Letter from 'A Mother of Sons', *The Freewoman*, 28 March 1912, 376.

How many single women have entirely refrained from these practices? I distinctly repudiate passing any moral judgement on these various forms of onanism, whose danger to health and sanity have been much overrated. My point is that they constitute sexual indulgence just as surely as normal sexual relations.[71]

From here, the debate splintered into two distinct and contradictory arguments. The first, exemplified in a July 1912 article on 'Self-Abuse and Insanity', asserted that masturbation had no ill effects on general mental and physical health. The second stigmatised masturbation by insisting that purists were all closet onanists themselves, either literally, or, most perversely, stimulating themselves imaginatively by attempting to monitor the sexual behaviour of others:

Cultivated pure people are obsessed by their own lewdness. Through its suppression, sexual desire grows in its intensity. Frequently, more or less ill-advised marriages result. With others, various forms of auto-eroticism are initiated, and by frequent repetition become habitual at first and then obsessive as well as inhibitive to normal temptation or gratification. Such perverts often become purist leaders and proclaim the vileness of normal sexuality as a means of self-justification and as a means of warding off suspicion.[72]

This notion that social purists were, if not literal, at least figurative onanists, titillating themselves over and over again through a stagnant preoccupation with the vice they affected to deplore, became frequently reiterated:

During the negotiations for the Criminal Law Amendment Act, women and womanlike men have wallowed in righteousness. There has been an orgy of virtuous feeling, highly pleasurable, no doubt, to all those who shared in it.[73]

Masturbation became freighted with metaphoric significance, a sexual act troping for social purists' enervated, paralytic and covert sexuality.

To turn to the issue of *The Egoist* featuring the 'smugging' episode of *A Portrait* is to recognise immediately how closely Joyce's satire upon the anti-masturbation campaign shares the ideological flavour of the journal's wider struggle against the vice crusaders. Alongside Joyce's contribution runs editor Dora Marsden's acerbic review of that year's keynote text of purity feminism, Christabel Pankhurst's *The Great Scourge and How to End it*. Pankhurst's polemic synthesised two already enmeshed suffragette

[71] 'A New Subscriber', 'The Chastity of Continence', *The Freewoman*, 22 February 1912, 345.
[72] Theodore Schroeder, 'Concerning Free Love', *New Freewoman*, 15 June 1913, 14–15.
[73] Dora Marsden, 'Views and Comments', *New Freewoman*, 15 August 1913, 83. Such statements concurred with Stella Browne's provocative insistence that purity zealots committed 'autoeroticism' deriving from the 'imaginative and psychic agitation in all its various forms' which attended their work ('A New Subscriber', 'The Chastity of Continence', *The Freewoman*, 22 February 1912, 4).

objectives; firstly the acquisition of the vote, and secondly the abolition of 'male vice', since her 'great scourge' was venereal disease and her proposed cure 'Votes for Women and Chastity for Men'.[74] For Marsden, the surveillance strategies and discourses of sexual prohibition employed by purity feminists like Pankhurst deflected desire into a hothouse of dangerous obsession. 'The "unnatural" practices Miss Pankhust refers to' in her allusion to a Piccadilly brothel specialising in flagellation 'are due to quite identical psychological vagaries with those which cause women suffragists to concentrate on virginity.'[75] Expanding this comparison between brothel client and purity crusader, Marsden argued

The vicious amuse themselves by imagining and thereafter 'touching' [Pankhurst's euphemism for sexual contact]; the 'pure' prolong the excitement by imagining and thereafter refraining. Fundamentally, there is nothing to choose between them: but in the sequel, owing to this difference of treatment, the 'vicious' put the image to the test of experience and for the time being destroy it: the 'pure' suppress it and turn it inward where it grows into an atmosphere of permanent obsession.[76]

Marsden's paradox-theory that 'there is a slight difference of degree, none in kind' between 'the rake' and 'the pure', since the 'pure' find stimulation 'first by concentration and then by a refusal which is in itself a further stimulation' was a particularly explicit statement of the position on social purity her journals had helped to define.[77]

Significantly, Marsden's onslaught upon 'the dull heats of virginity' finds direct illustration in Stephen Dedalus' struggles with his sexuality.[78] As Stephen represses his 'mad and filthy orgies' (*P* 91) in favour of 'resolute piety' and sexual abstinence, he dramatises what contributors to *The Egoist* only theorised. Stephen finds, as Marsden predicts, that the rituals of sexual surveillance and fetishised abstinence which Joyce lifts from purity advice literature soon corrupt into an introspective, autoerotic and paralytic sexuality. Marsden's understanding that purity involves 'prolonging the excitement by imagining and thereafter refraining', that it is in effect an exacerbated and obsessive form of self-stimulation is also asserted by Joyce, who pictures Stephen overwhelmed by the 'perilous attraction to his mind' of 'the idea of surrender' (*P* 152).[79] Stephen's deliberate provocation

---

[74] 'Votes for Women and Chastity for Men' became the Women's Social and Political Union's new campaigning slogan. Some suffragettes wore this banner and distributed pamphlets and badges urging men to 'wear the white flower of a blameless life', a strategy clearly borrowed from the White Cross leagues and demonstrating the totality of the crossover between mainstream feminism and the purity crusade. See Tickner, *Spectacle of Women*, 24.
[75] Dora Marsden, 'The Chastity of Women', *The Egoist*, 2 February 1914, 45.
[76] *Ibid.*, 46.   [77] *Ibid.*   [78] *Ibid.*, 47.   [79] *Ibid.*, 46.

and repudiation of 'the insistent voices of the flesh' is imagined as a process of waiting for 'the first faint timid noiseless wavelet to touch his fevered skin', a pattern of anticipation, arousal and sudden deferral 'almost at the verge of sinful consent' (*P* 152). As Joyce implies through puns on prayers as 'sudden ejaculation', confession as 'virginal self-surrender' or 'the channel for the escape of scrupulous and unrepented imperfections' (*P* 152), purity's admonitions are a particularly potent form of aphrodisiac.

It is therefore unsurprising that Dora Marsden should have so swiftly commissioned *A Portrait of the Artist as a Young Man* for serialisation in *The Egoist*.[80] Joyce was not merely introduced through his open letter 'A Curious History' as a victim of that interminable and paralytic purity censorship with which her readers were familiar. More importantly, the kind of propaganda the purity leagues were disseminating to such crippling effect is woven into the fabric of the novel. For Joyce's portrait of a young man struggling through puberty in a climate of fear orchestrated initially by the Irish Catholic church but terrifyingly popularised by the White Cross Leagues and Vigilance Associations of Edwardian Britain deploys the language and texture of a vast literature of sexual anxiety with an accuracy which surely appealed to *The Egoist*'s self-consciously radical readership. Through entwining two parallel aspects of the purity crusade to reshape masculinity – the campaign against 'corrupt public men' integral to Parnell's downfall, the affiliated drive against adolescent masturbation – Joyce dramatises the deflection of desire firstly into self-policing and then into the surveillance of others. Stephen's longing to listen to 'the sinful longings and sinful thoughts and sinful acts of others' (*P* 159) filters through his devout Catholicism the very reading of the policing of sexuality articulated by the Modernist dissidents who formed *The Egoist*'s intellectual coterie. For *A Portrait* elaborates upon precisely the subversive theories about social purity and sexuality which flourished elsewhere in the journal, as Joyce adopts and refashions their dominant trope. Masturbation, as we have seen, was the form of sexuality repeatedly ascribed to the 'cultivated pure people obsessed by their own lewdness' who *The Egoist* so uncompromisingly deplored. *A Portrait* expands upon that trope to underscore a disconcerting continuity between purity and prurience.

---

[80] Lidderdale and Nicholson, *Dear Miss Weaver*, 74. Marsden did not remain so fervent an admirer of Joyce. Writing to Weaver in April 1918, she called *A Portrait* 'a tip-top novel' but complained 'I have just re-read episode three of *Ulysses*. My dear editor, go down on your knees and thank your stars for possessing *one* writer of metaphysics who is CLEAR! That's ME! Joyce is – my word! He's appalling.' Unpublished letter 10 April 1918, cited in Thacker, 'Dora Marsden', 190.

A Portrait of the Artist as a Young Man thus offers a specifically Irish Catholic incursion into an international intellectual debate. For Joyce's analysis of masculinity in the process of its construction not only supplies a highly localised portrait of a young man struggling to fly by the nets of his national, religious and sexual identity; it furthermore directly participates in contemporary avant-garde and transatlantic debates over censorship and the regulation of sexuality. Joyce's anticipation and provocation of the vice crusaders is thus in his first novel particularly intimately entwined with the conditions of its publication. For *A Portrait* is more than simply a cause célèbre in the debate with social purists about art, sexuality and censorship that *The Egoist* maintained. Rather, Joyce's depiction of anxious, self-regarding adolescence simultaneously embodies the kind of high Modernist text such a debate attempted to protect, and encodes the wider terms and rhetorical strategies of that debate within its creative experiment.

CHAPTER 4

Typhoid turnips and crooked cucumbers: theosophical purity in 'Scylla and Charybdis'

> I got hold of the first two volumes of *The Secret Doctrine* and read steadily through it, so many pages a day, in the most favourable conditions for such study... Though I understood so little yet, the bigness, strangeness, newness of the subject matter, the virility of the style, the curiosity it awoke in me, held my interest without flagging.[1]

Gretta Cousins' memoirs give a disconcerting account of her honeymoon. She confesses how she found 'bigness, strangeness, newness' and even 'virility' from Helena Petrovna Blavatsky's best-selling introduction to theosophy, *The Secret Doctrine*, rather than from a more conventional source. As though anticipating readerly raised eyebrows at this substitution of that most fashionable of Edwardian religious faiths for more usual nuptial pleasures, Gretta explained how 'providential' it was that spiritual matters preoccupied her during a time of crisis. She grew 'white and thin' during her first year of marriage, not, as friends suspected, on account of her vegetarianism, but rather due to 'problems of adjustment to the revelation that marriage had brought me as to the physical basis of sex':

> Every child I looked at called to my mind the shocking circumstance that brought about its existence. My new knowledge, though I was lovingly safeguarded from it, made me ashamed of humanity, and ashamed for it. I found myself looking on men and women as degraded by this demand of nature. Something in me revolted then, and has ever since protested against certain of the techniques of nature concerned with sex. Nor will I, and many men and women of like nature, including my husband, be sanctified, purified and redeemed, life after life, until the evolution of form has substituted some more artistic way of continuance of the race.[2]

Gretta Cousins, a talented pianist, and her husband James, a poet and playwright active in the Irish Literary Revival, were friends of Joyce, and

---

[1] Gretta and James Cousins, *We Two Together* (Madras: Ganesh, 1950), 104–5.   [2] *Ibid.*, 109.

he lodged with them from time to time during the summer of 1904.[3] Unable to stomach the couple's proselytising of theosophy, celibacy and vegetarianism for long, Joyce eventually fled, grumbling to Stanislaus of indigestion resulting from 'a typhoid turnip'.[4] His discontent with the couple was, however, grounded in more than the menu. Gretta's revulsion from 'certain of the techniques of nature concerned with sex' exemplified a theosophical somataphobia directly drawn from social purity discourse. In 'Scylla and Charybdis', the former timid adolescent of *A Portrait of the Artist as a Young Man*, once painfully preoccupied with his own sexual 'degeneracy', confronts those theosophical mystics of the Celtic Revival who shared Gretta's ostentatious revulsion from a 'degrading demand of nature'. Through Stephen Dedalus' encounter with a captive audience of Dublin theosophists in the National Library, Joyce accomplishes a deeply subversive assault upon perhaps the most influential strand of social purity ideology in Ireland. In a chapter groaning with sexual innuendo and excess, Joyce discloses the faultlines permeating theosophical chastity through a network of intertextual references which recover a buried and latent sexual disorder.

I

Theosophy was intimately associated with contemporary social purity campaigns to impose a single moral standard of sexual continence. Converts were implored to 'obtain the power to control their desires', and so resist the surrender of 'the divine nature to the animal nature'.[5] Celibacy was recommended as having 'superior advantages for meditation and study', whilst 'marital continence' permitted 'the union of the male spirit with the female soul', and disciples or 'chelas' were urged to live in quasi-monastic communes.[6] Helena Blavatsky shared her home with several prominent theosophists, and conspicuously led by example, responding to allegations of bigamy and illegitimate children with the characteristically bizarre claim

I could never have connection with any man because I am lacking something and that place is filled up with some crooked cucumber.[7]

---

[3] To Gretta, Joyce was 'a favourite of mine though he was reputed to be a "bad boy". I delighted in his lovely tenor voice especially when I accompanied some of his Irish songs with nobody but ourselves to hear in our little drawing room', *ibid.*, 106.

[4] Richard Ellmann, *James Joyce* (Oxford: Oxford University Press, 1983), 162.

[5] The Theosophist, *Five Years of theosophy: mystical, philosophical, theosophical, historical and scientific essays selected from 'The Theosophist'* (London: Reeves and Turner, 1885), 141.

[6] *Ibid.*, 143. As Annie Besant explained, 'Purity is one of the divine properties which are wanted in discipleship', *The Path of Discipleship* (London: Theosophical Publishing Society, 1896), 67.

[7] Commune-dwellers included Isabel Cooper-Oakley, Charles Webster Leadbeater, Blavatsky's second in command, Colonel Olcott, and her eventual successor, Annie Besant. See Sylvia Cranston, *HPB:*

Her successor, Annie Besant, was only admitted into the movement on recanting her notorious teachings on contraception. She destroyed unsold copies of *The Law of Population*, writing *Theosophy and the Law of Population* in replacement, which advocated complete abstinence, since 'the sexual instinct that man has in common with the brute is the most fruitful source of human misery'.[8] Predictably, many theosophists were also dedicated social purity campaigners. For Charlotte Despard, Josephine Butler introduced 'the close connection between the women's movement and the spiritual awakening which marked the closing decades of the last century'.[9] Blavatsky's companion Isabel Cooper-Oakley was a prominent member of the Social Purity Alliance, and National Vigilance Association founder W. T. Stead was another celebrity convert.[10] Unsurprisingly, the Theosophical Society frequently published material which more commonly issued from social purity presses. Two theosophy pamphlets marketed as 'of special interest to women' were Lucy Re-Bartlett's *Sex and Sanctity*, which recommended less of the former and more of the latter, and Edith Ward's *The Vital Question: An Address on Social Purity*, a millennial polemic against 'marital incontinence'.[11] By 1900, theosophy was clearly identified as the spiritual wing of the social purity movement.

This intimate alliance between theosophy and social purity is particularly significant in Ireland, where as we have seen the Dublin White Cross Vigilance Association was mistrusted by many Catholic nationalists for its

---

The Extraordinary Life and Influence of Helena Blavatsky (New York: G. P. Putnam's Sons, 1993), 32. 'Crooked cucumber' quote from Mary K. Neff, *Personal Memoirs of H. P. Blavatsky* (Illinois: Wharton, 1971), 188.

[8] Annie Besant, *Theosophy and the Law of Population*, appendixed to Sripati Chandrasekhar, *A Dirty, Filthy Book: The Writings of Charles Knowlton and Annie Besant*, (Berkeley: University of California Press, 1981), 211. Chandrasekhar provides a thorough account of the pressures placed on Besant to recant her views on contraception by Blavatsky and others in the London Theosophical Society.

[9] Charlotte Despard, *Theosophy and the Women's Movement* (London: Theosophical Publishing Society, 1913), 1.

[10] Diana Burfield, .'Theosophy and Feminism: Some Explorations in Nineteenth Century Biography', in *Women's Religious Experience*, ed. Pat Holden (London: Croom Helm, 1983), 43–4. Stead commissioned Annie Besant to review *The Secret Doctrine* for *The Review of Reviews*, an experience which led to her conversion. He championed *The Secret Doctrine* in his journal when many other publications were hostile. See Peter Washington, *Madame Blavatsky's Baboon* (London: Secker and Warburg, 1993), 93. After his death on the Titanic, mediums received messages reassuring believers he was carrying on his 'labour to save helpless women and children' from beyond the grave. See *Has W. T. Stead Returned? A Symposium*, ed. James Coates (London: L. N. Fowler, 1913), 7.

[11] Both pamphlets were published by the Theosophical Society and promoted alongside *Vegetarian Savories: A Practical Book of Recipes* as 'of special interest to women' on the flyleaf of Despard's *Theosophy and the Women's Movement*. Also recommended was Laurence Housman's essay 'The Moving Spirit in Womanhood', in *Theosophical Ideals* (London: Theosophical Publishing House, 1914), which discussed prostitution, white slavery, 'social motherhood', the age of consent and other contemporary social purity concerns.

enthusiastic Unionism and evangelical Protestantism. Theosophy, however, was an alternative and less objectionable conduit for social purity ideology into an Ireland sympathetic to its sexual politics, yet suspicious of its political affiliations. To John Eglinton, the Irish Literary Revival was precipitated by 'the ferment caused in the minds of a group of young men by the activities of the theosophy Movement in Dublin', and, according to him, W. B. Yeats once declared 'theosophy has done more for Irish literature in three years than Trinity College in its three centuries'.[12] Founded by Yeats and George Russell in 1886, the Dublin Hermetist Society included Revivalist poets James Cousins and Susan Mitchell, the journalist Charles Johnstone, the publisher George Roberts and Harry Norman, editor of *The Irish Homestead*.[13] Many were Joyce's friends or mentors, and, as his brother Stanislaus tells us, 'he did indeed toy with theosophy as a kind of interim religion', reading 'with serious intent expository works on theosophy by Madame Blavatsky, Col Olcott, Annie Besant and [Charles Webster] Leadbeater'.[14] Joyce's Trieste library contains three of theosophy's key texts, Henry Olcott's *A Buddhist Catechism*, which he signed 'J A Joyce, May 7, 1901', and Annie Besant's *Une Introduction à la Theosophie* and *The Path of Discipleship*.[15] Consequently, as Ralph Jenkins notes, Joyce's knowledge of theosophical doctrine is greater than is often assumed.[16]

If Joyce was briefly intrigued and swiftly disillusioned by the hermetists, then one of the reasons for his disillusion must have been the earnestness with which 'the sex question' was pondered:

In those early days we unmarried ones all hoped to become Chelas and expected to remain celibate, and were rather shocked to hear of Charles Johnstone's marriage, even to a niece of Madame Blavatsky! The urges of sex, natural to youngsters in their twenties, were hardly ever spoken of, except in the disguise of 'Karma', and were sternly suppressed.[17]

George Russell found conversion a welcome escape from 'desires of body and heart with which we so soon learn to taint our youth'.[18] The predictable serpent was only vanquished when 'I became aware of a mysterious life

---

[12] John Eglinton, *A Memoir of A. E.* (London: Macmillan, 1937), 11; *Irish Literary Portraits* (London: Macmillan, 1935), 43.
[13] Pierre Leslie Pielou, 'The Growth of the Theosophy Movement in Ireland' (1927), 6. Unpublished pamphlet held in the National Library of Ireland, Dublin, Pamphlets P. 1919. Mary E. Bryson, 'Metaphors for Freedom: Theosophy in the Irish Literary Revival', *Canadian Journal of Irish Studies* 3: 1 (June 1977), 1.
[14] Stanislaus Joyce, *My Brother's Keeper*, ed. Richard Ellmann (London: Faber and Faber, 1958), 140.
[15] Richard Ellmann, *The Consciousness of Joyce* (New York: Oxford University Press, 1977), 101, 122.
[16] Ralph Jenkins, 'Theosphy in Scylla and Charybdis', in *Modern Fiction Studies* 15: 1 (1969), 36.
[17] Eglinton, *A Memoir of AE*, 17.   [18] *Ibid.*, 12.

quickening within my life, carrying with it unsated desires, base and august, and as I divined it, myriads of memories and secret wisdom'.[19] The monthly journal of the hermetists, *The Irish Theosophist* was similarly voluble on 'the sex question'. Despite his embarrassing descent into marriage, Charles Johnstone used its pages to inveigh repeatedly against 'man's animal part', elaborating in one three-page essay the many ways in which 'Lust is but a disappointment, to be overcome.'[20] Russell concurred, arguing that theosophy's most valuable lesson was that 'the lower part of man, the body and its attachments, be conquered and purified'.[21] As an unsigned article on 'The Sex Problem' in 1894 pondered, 'Why cannot love be noble?' since 'the soul is sexless and passionless'.[22] These individual reminiscences imply how theosophy was the acceptable face of social purity in Ireland. Its success there was inextricably bound up with its puritan sexual politics.

'Aeolus' notes theosophy's close links with the Dublin literary establishment when J. J. O'Molloy asks Stephen

What do you think really of that hermetic crowd, the opal hush poets: A. E. the mastermystic? That Blavatsky woman started it. She was a nice old bag of tricks. A. E. has been telling some yankee interviewer that you came to him in the small hours of the morning to ask him about planes of consciousness. Magennis thinks you must have been pulling A. E.'s leg. (*U* 7: 783–7)

In 'Scylla and Charybdis', Stephen finally responds to O'Molloy's question, as he seizes the opportunity to deliver his elaborate reading of Shakespeare to a captive audience of Dublin theosophists. Stephen's Shakespeare theory has long been discredited as contradictory, irrelevant, historically inaccurate, a mere theatrical façade and of little literary value, readings all preempted by Stephen's own declaration that he does not believe in it himself (*U* 9: 1067).[23] Desmond McCarthy offers one way out of the puzzle, noting how trying to discern Shakespeare's personality from the paucity of

---

[19] *Ibid.*, 13.

[20] Charles Johnstone, 'Fear and Valour', *The Irish Theosophist* 4: 11 (15 August 1896), 206.

[21] A. E., 'How Theosophy Affects One's View of Life: A Paper read before the Dublin Lodge', *The Irish Theosophist* 2: 12 (15 September 1894), 172.

[22] 'The Sex Problem', *The Irish Theosophist* 3: 7 (15 April 1894), 92. The article contains extracts from a special study of theosophy and sex by Jerome Anderson, who posited a nirvana where gender and desire are both transcended: 'The Higher Ego is sexless... the differentiation which would correspond to sex upon this plane is unknown. We must recognise in Woman not the weak passive vessel created as an avenue to a Sensuous Paradise, but a soul', 92.

[23] Frank Budgen dismissed it as 'contradictory' (*James Joyce and the Making of Ulysses*, Bloomington: Indiana University Press, 1960, 117); Robert Adams adds it is a 'theatrical façade' (*Surface and Symbol: The Consistency of James Joyce's Ulysses* (New York: Oxford University Press, 1962, 124); Robert Kellogg describes it as 'outlandish' and 'besides the point' ('Scylla and Charybdis' in *James Joyce's Ulysses: Critical Essays*, ed. Clive Hart and David Hayman, Berkeley: University of California Press, 1974, 151).

information about him which remains is 'like looking at a very dark glazed picture in the National Portrait Gallery: at first you see nothing, then you begin to recognise features, then you realise that they are your own'.[24] Rather than reflecting himself, however, the darkened glass of Stephen's portrait ostentatiously holds the mirror up to his listeners. As Len Platt notes, Stephen's remark 'Khaki Hamlets don't hesitate to shoot' (*U* 9: 133), and his reference to Swinburne's infamous defence of the British concentration camps during the Boer War together introduce this allegorising drive, as Stephen's Shakespeare is soiled by an imperial complicity his Ascendancy listeners defensively disavow.[25] The allegory is abruptly personalised with 'Elizabethan London lay as far from Stratford as corrupt Paris lies from virgin Dublin' (*U* 9: 149–50). Tellingly, the 'Local colour' Stephen provides to 'Make [his listeners] accomplices' (*U* 9: 158) takes the form of a highly sexualised backdrop; Sir Walter Raleigh's 'pair of fancy stays', the excessive amount of underlinen hoarded by the 'gombeenwoman Eliza Tudor', 'the punks of the bankside, a penny a time', 'the holy office the ostler does for the stallion' (*U* 9: 629, 630, 640, 664). Such jibes are a political provocation comparable to 'Khaki Hamlets don't hesitate to shoot', since again Stephen uses the supposedly safe domain of literary criticism to mask a more loaded critique of the contemporary. 'Virgin Dublin' provocatively invites his listeners to ponder their own sexual identity, and read his remarks on Shakespeare as disconcertingly personal.

II

'Virgin Dublin' seems to be on Stephen's mind from 'Scylla's' inception, since he intersperses his conversation with Russell and Eglinton on Yeats, 'the mystic mind' and 'The shining seven' (*U* 9: 27–8) with an internal monologue upon the complexities of theosophical doctrine. 'Formless spiritual', Stephen muses, 'Father, Word and Holy Breath. Allfather, the heavenly man. Hiesos Kristos, magician of the beautiful', but his thoughts soon shift from paternity to fraternity:

Dunlop, Judge, the noblest Roman of them all, A. E., Arval, the Name Ineffable, in heaven hight: K. H., their master, whose identity is no secret to adepts. Brothers of the great white lodge always watching to see if they can help. The Christ with the bridesister, moisture of light, born of an ensouled virgin, repentant sophia,

---

[24] Desmond McCarthy quoted in Samuel Schoenbaum, *Shakespeare's Lives* (Oxford: Clarendon Press, 1970), viii.

[25] Len Platt, 'The Voice of Esau: Culture and Nationalism in "Scylla and Charybdis"', *James Joyce Quarterly* 29: 4 (1992), 740–3.

departed to the plane of buddhi. The life esoteric is not for ordinary person. O. P. must work off bad karma first. Mrs Cooper Oakley once glimpsed our very illustrious sister H. P. B.'s elemental.

O, fie! Out on't! *Pfuiteufel!* You naughtn't to look, missus, so you naughtn't when a lady's ashowing of her elemental. (*U* 9: 61–73)

Stephen pointedly segregates the sexes, listing male theosophists – Daniel Dunlop, editor of *The Irish Theosophist*, William Quan Judge, the Irish-American co-founder of the Theosophical Society, A. E., Koot Hoomi, the Tibetan 'mahatma' who supposedly precipitated spirit-messages to Blavatsky – before the women, Blavatsky and her disciple and companion, Isabel Cooper-Oakley. This gender segregation is reinforced by allusions to 'Arval', or the council of twelve prominent theosophists who led the movement, in imitation of Christ's disciples, and 'Brotherhood of the great white lodge', the association of benign Masters who watched over the faithful from a higher spiritual plane.[26] Stephen's internal monologue thus maps out a modulating and ideologically loaded reinterpretation of the 'family of man' metaphor. He draws upon the movement's well-known motto – 'A Universal Brotherhood of Humanity without distinction of race, creed, sex, class or colour' – to emphasise how theosophy reassessed the family of man not as a reproductive unit, but as the terminal stage of biological and social development; a sterile siblinghood. By displacing 'Allfather, the heavenly man' with 'brothers of the great white lodge', Stephen draws attention to the way theosophy's particular brand of celibate egalitarianism censored the dangerous dynamics of sexual reproduction from a familiar metaphor. The process of this displacement is emphasised with 'Christ with the bridesister', where Stephen linguistically demarcates the point of transformation, as 'bride' mutates into chaste 'sister'. As Stephen suggests, the sibling relationship offered theosophists a safely celibate paradigm for the containment of potentially transgressive desire. As Gerty MacDowell puts it in a rather different context, 'They would be just good friends like a big brother and sister without all that other' (*U* 13: 665–6).

Such containment, however, is immediately queried by an imagined scenario which provocatively forces open the fissures implicit in theosophy's vision of a chaste 'universal brotherhood of man'. Stephen recalls Madame Blavatsky's insistence that her 'elemental' or ghost would appear to her followers after her death, and Isabel Cooper-Oakley's much-publicised claim to have been so visited. Whilst Blavatsky is in Stephen's pastiche of

---

[26] See Jenkins, 'Theosophy in "Scylla and Charybdis"', 35–48, and Don Gifford, *Annotations to James Joyce's 'Ulysses'* (Berkeley: University of California Press, 1989), 196–8 for full glossing of Joyce's allusions.

theosophical discourse 'our very illustrious sister', she is also a perverse sexual exhibitionist, flaunting her 'elemental' to her friend, and Stephen's pun on 'elemental'/ 'genital' here transforms sisterhood into a predictable dirty joke, disclosing a repressed lesbian longing lurking beneath the celibate facade. Stephen suggests that theosophy's conspicuous disdain for heterosexuality or 'straight sex' in favour of an asexual sibling bond in fact masks a sexuality which contemporary standards would have judged perverted or corrupt.[27] It is thus significant that Stephen's internal meditation on theosophical brotherhood is prompted by George Russell's theory that 'Art has to reveal to us ideas, formless spiritual essences' (*U* 9: 48–9). Stephen notes how Russell's aesthetics stems from his theosophy, and retaliates by placing that connection under scrutiny. In Stephen's reading of Shakespeare's life, he repeats this wry suggestion that the sibling bond so venerated by theosophy displaces and disguises an insidious and secretive form of sex. Russell's impatient objection, 'But this prying into the family life of a great man' (*U* 9: 181) is revealingly defensive, since Stephen's focus upon 'that brother motive' (*U* 9: 956) forcefully satirises theosophy's view of brotherhood as egalitarian and asexual. If theosophy presented 'universal brotherhood' as a benignly spiritualised alternative to the disruptive dynamism of sexuality, then Stephen reappraises the relationship, building upon his insinuations about Blavatsky and Cooper-Oakley to present the sibling bond not as an evasion of sex, but as a bizarre perversion of it.

Stephen argues that Ann Hathaway's 'misconduct with...the brothers' (*U* 9: 963) ensured that 'the theme of the false or the usurping or the adulterous brother or all three in one is to Shakespeare, what the poor are not, always with him' (*U* 9: 996–9). He detects the brothers' names in *Richard III* and *King Lear* and reads *Hamlet* as an autobiographical account of sexual rivalry to lock the Shakespeare siblings into a stifling sexual bond.[28] Arguing that 'The images of other males of his blood will repel him. He will see in them grotesque attempts of nature to foretell or to repeat himself' (*U* 9: 433–5), Stephen reinterprets brotherhood as a relationship of sexual jealousy, fear and revulsion. His account of Shakespeare

---

[27] Interestingly, the 'companionate marriage' of the sexologist Havelock Ellis to Edith Lees, a lesbian who featured in one of Ellis' case studies of 'inversion', was much admired in theosophical circles. See Burfield, 'Theosophy and Feminism', 45.

[28] These hints of a shocking sexual taboo are confirmed and compounded, as Susan Sutliff Brown has brilliantly shown, by Joyce's perplexing concealment of the names of his own three brothers, George, Stanislaus and Charles within *Ulysses*. As Brown notes, all appear 'in sexually explicit or suggestive connection with either Stephen or Bloom or both', a curious coincidence Brown interprets as a covert attack upon contemporary psychoanalysis. ('The Joyce Brothers in Drag: Fraternal Incest in *Ulysses*', *Gender in Joyce*, ed. Jolanta W. Wawrzycka and Marlena G. Corcoran (Gainesville: University of Florida Press, 1997), 8–28.

in psychological thrall to these 'brothers-in-love' (*U*9: 1046) thus boldly challenges theosophy's ideological investment in brotherhood as a model for safely celibate human interaction. The challenge is extrapolated when Stephen introduces the spectre of homosexual incest; 'a bodily shame so steadfast that the criminal annals of the world, stained with all other incests and bestialities, hardly record its breach' (*U* 9: 850–2). The impact of these insinuations is indicated when Stephen responds to Eglinton's 'severe' rebuke, 'The doctor can tell us what those words mean' (*U* 9: 738) by declining his interpretation of incest as requiring the psychoanalysis of 'the new Viennese school' (*U* 9: 780). Instead, Stephen displaces Freud with Aquinas to elaborate upon his vision of Shakespeare as enthusiastic and exploitative capitalist, a 'moneylender, with ten tods of corn hoarded in the famine riots' (*U* 9: 743–4). He asserts that incest is 'an avarice of the emotions', since 'the love so given to one near in blood is covetously withheld from some stranger who, it may be, hungers for it' (*U* 9: 781–3). Incest is here presented as a perversely obsessive form of self-absorption, where sex, like gold, is hoarded from the outside world. Through Shakespeare, Stephen provocatively insists that 'brotherhood' is a turning away from life, an unhealthy repression of or internalisation of or hoarding of sexual energy, rather that the utopian state theosophists suggested. This sustained hypothesis of a correspondence between brotherhood and sexual claustrophobia insinuates that sterile frustrations lie behind an emphasis upon platonic restraint. Elsewhere in 'Scylla', Stephen builds upon these hints that theosophy conceals an insular and obsessive sexual solipsism.

III

Stephen's revision of 'brotherhood' into a form of sexual claustrophobia exemplifies a sustained rhetorical strategy. Elsewhere too he interrogates theosophy's enthusiasm for celibacy by eroticising its ideology and language. If theosophy's interpretation of 'brotherhood' as a sanitised alternative to sexuality is wilfully undercut, then so is another central aspect of its belief and practice. Whilst theosophy was committed to 'brotherhood', it was most notoriously concerned not with relationships between the living, but with those between the living and the dead. It developed from the late-Victorian popular occult practices which indicated to spiritualist believers a secret spectral sphere.[29] Blavatsky was an acclaimed spiritualist

---

[29] For an account of the connections between spiritualism and theosophy, see Alex Owen, *The Darkened Room: Women, Power and Spiritualism in Late-Victorian England* (London: Virago, 1989), 94, 136.

medium during the late 1870s, and she began to promote spiritualism's faith in the paranormal within the context of wider occult lore.[30] With *Isis Unveiled* (1877) and *The Secret Doctrine* (1889), she drew heavily on esoteric Buddhism to interpret paranormal events as evidence for a new religious faith, insisting that 'divine wisdom' was telepathically disclosed to her through automatic writing by the Mahatmas, Tibetan spirit guides.[31] As we shall see, theosophy's appropriation of Buddhism and other Eastern doctrines thus crucially relied upon the paraphernalia of late-Victorian spiritualism; automatic writing, séances and spirit manifestations.

Joyce's impatience with such paranormal visitations was stylishly demonstrated in 1904, when, together with Buck Mulligan's prototype, Oliver StJohn Gogarty, he broke into the Dublin Theosophical Lodge shortly before a meeting. There, the two discovered what Stephen remembers as a 'Yogibogeybox in Dawson Chambers' (*U* 9: 279), a spirit cabinet usually taking the form of a curtained box or large cupboard accessible only from the front. Next to this 'Yogibogeybox' stood a packing case belonging to Joyce's future would-be publisher George Roberts, at the time combining his theosophical investigations with a day-job as a travelling underwear salesman. Joyce purloined a particularly elaborate pair of drawers, stringing them aloft in the centre of the room suggestively balanced on a broom handle, whilst Gogarty attached a note reading 'I never did it' and signed 'John Eglinton' as a final flourish.[32] These high jinks take on a particularly arch resonance, since billowing Edwardian knickers produced from a packing case reproduce the culturally expected image of ghosthood, a nebulous apparition clothed in white draperies. Joyce and Gogarty's biting visual pun thus placed on show that sexuality which theosophy tried to repress. Their student prank burlesqued theosophy's ostentatious chastity by questioning the nature of the repressed spectres which haunted its members' imaginations.

When Stephen begins his discussion of Shakespeare with the loaded question 'What is a ghost?' (*U* 9: 147), he provocatively names the privileged object of theosophical quest. His answer may be more intellectually complex than Joyce's 1904 practical joke, but it relies upon similar methods

---

[30] For an account of Blavatsky's 1870s séance activities in Cairo and the USA, see Richard Hutch, 'Helena Blavatsky Unveiled', *The Journal of Religious History* 11: 2 (1980), 322.

[31] *Ibid.*, 326, 330–2. Blavatsky's occult practices gained theosophy a widespread notoriety seven years later, when the movement was sufficiently established to be investigated by Richard Hodgson of the Society for Psychical Research. Hodgson's damning and widely circulated report presented Blavatsky as a charlatan and fraud, who faked the paranormal materialisations and automatic writings on which she based her authority.

[32] Ellmann, *James Joyce*, 174.

of provoking unease. For Stephen also manipulates his audiences' expectations and preconceptions about ghosts to draw a parallel between the erotic and the occult. John Eglinton, the most obvious butt of Joyce and Gogarty's wit, introduces this substitution:

– He will have it that *Hamlet* is a ghoststory, John Eglinton said for Mr Best's behoof. Like the fat boy in Pickwick he wants to make our flesh creep. (*U* 9: 141–3)

Eglinton's commonplace misreading of Dickens is significant, since the fat boy refers not to a paranormal occurrence, but to his vision of the middle-aged lovers Miss Wardle and Mr Tupman 'a-huggin and a-kissin' in a summerhouse.[33] Eglinton's mistake operates as something of a Freudian slip, as he substitutes a ghost story for a sexual secret. Stephen takes up this confusion, as his initial attempt to define 'What is a ghost' as 'One who has faded into impalpability through death, through absence, through change of manners' (*U* 9: 147–9) is soon displaced by an erotically charged account of ghosthood. Stephen's argument that Shakespeare should be identified with the ghost of King Hamlet relies upon the two men's shared identity as cuckolds sexually betrayed by their own brothers. King Hamlet's ghost is 'endowed with knowledge' of 'The poisoning and the beast with two backs that urged it' by his 'creator', Shakespeare 'weary of the creation he has piled up to hide himself from himself, an old dog licking an old sore' (*U* 9: 469–75). Stephen entangles ghosthood with sexual obsession: his ghosts remain haunted by the body, its desires, its humiliations. These touches are consolidated when Stephen responds to Eglinton's objection to his lascivious portrait of Ann Hathaway. 'Carping', Eglinton complains 'Her ghost at least has been laid for ever' (*U* 9: 215). For Stephen, however, Hathaway's ghost is laid in another sense:

That memory, *Venus and Adonis*, lay in the bedchamber of every light-of-love in London . . . If others have their will Ann hath a way. By cock, she was to blame. She puts the comether on him, sweet and twentysix. The greyeyed goddess who bends over the boy Adonis, stooping to conquer, as prologue to the swelling act, is a boldfaced Stratford wench who tumbles in a cornfield a lover younger than herself. (*U* 9: 249–60)

The excess of innuendo in this passage snidely reinterprets Eglinton's suggestion that Ann Hathaway's ghost has been 'laid for ever'. Instead, she is resuscitated with such lecherous fervour that Russell, disgusted, rises to leave for *The Homestead*, his departure prompting a flurry of invitations to an evening party from which Stephen is pointedly excluded.

---

[33] Charles Dickens, *The Posthumous Papers of the Pickwick Club*, London: Odham's Press, n.d., 108.

When Stephen resumes, he significantly offers a metaphor which imagines ghosthood as an indelible physical trace:

And as the mole on my right breast is where it was when I was born, though all my body has been woven of new stuff time after time, so through the ghost of the unquiet father the image of the unliving son looks forth. (*U* 9: 378–81)

Stephen's simile provocatively confuses the spirit and the flesh, likening the 'mark' of the father's spirit on the son to the birthmark leaving an indelible physical trace. This confusion is taken further elsewhere in *Ulysses*, where ghosts are inevitably rendered disconcertingly physical as they are entangled with sexual encounters or imagery. In 'Proteus', Stephen's recollection of his dying mother, 'The ghostcandle to light her agony. Ghostly light on the tortured face' is curiously spliced to his fantasy of the primal scene of his conception: 'The man with my voice and my eyes and a ghostwoman with ashes on her breath. They clasped and sundered, did the coupler's will' (*U* 3: 46–7). In 'Hades', this association between ghosts and the erotic is taken up by Bloom, who rephrases the occult as a form of aphrodisiac: 'Tell her a ghost story in bed to make her sleep. Have you ever seen a ghost? . . . Still they'd kiss all right if properly keyed up. Whores in Turkish graveyards' (*U* 6: 754–7). Later Bloom expands on the quasi-necrophiliac implications of this scenario:

And even scraping up the earth at night with a lantern like that case I read of to get at fresh buried females or even putrefied with running gravesores. Give you the creeps after a bit. I will appear to you after death. You will see my ghost after death. My ghost will haunt you after death. (*U* 6: 997–1001)

This connection between ghosts and sex is reprised in 'Circe', where Bella Cohen commands Bloom 'Tell me something to amuse me, smut or a bloody good ghoststory' (*U* 15: 3052–3), and where the Croppy Boy 'gives up the ghost' as 'A violent erection of the hanged sends gouts of sperm spouting through his deathclothes onto the cobblestones' (*U* 15: 4548–9). These macabre associations between ghosts and sexuality chime in with Stephen's Shakespeare theory to disturb theosophy's insistent privileging of the spectral over the somatic.

The connection between body and spirit are pointedly addressed in 'Cyclops', where Alf Bergan claims to have seen Paddy Dignam in Capel Street that morning. His companions are superstitiously appalled: '– You saw his ghost then, says Joe, God between us and harm' (*U* 12: 326). Alf's spectral sighting introduces an interlude which pastiches the séance reports frequently written up in theosophical journals. 'In the darkness spirit hands were felt to flutter' as Dignam's 'etheric double' is disclosed through 'a faint but increasing luminosity of ruby light... orangefiery and scarlet rays emanating from the sacral region and solar plexus' (*U* 12: 338–44). The 'etheric double' was a specific type of ghost defined in Charles Webster Leadbeater's *The Astral Plane* as the spectral state closest to the flesh and comparable to purgatory, since the virtuous swiftly moved along into 'the devanchic condition where alone his spiritual aspirations can find full fruition'.[34] Joyce's 'etheric double' of Paddy Dignam, as Leadbeater predicts, is indeed preoccupied with the body. He requests buttermilk, worries about funeral costs and instructs 'his dear son Patsy that the other boot which he had been looking for was at present under the commode in the return room' (*U* 12: 367–8), whilst maintaining that the spirit world is equipped with such incongruous modern conveniences as 'tālāfānā, ālāvātār, hātākāldā, wātāklāsāt' (*U* 12: 354). Dignam's spirit particularly resembles the 'etheric double' of the 'victim of sudden death', abruptly severed from an 'earth-life low and brutal, selfish and sensual':

Crowds of these unfortunate creatures hang around public houses or other even more disreputable places – wherever the gross influences in which they delight are to be found and where they encounter men and women still in the flesh who are like-minded with themselves.[35]

Dignam's haunts include Capel Street, a slumland backstreet where disreputable amusements like mutoscope parlours are to be found (*U* 13: 794), Barney Kiernan's pub, and later Nighttown outside Bella Cohen's brothel, where he addresses Bloom 'I am Paddy Dignam's spirit. List, list, O list!' (*U* 15: 1218). More strikingly still, Leadbeater insisted that the 'auric egg' or spirit mist could be classified through colour, and that 'a lurid, flaming red' indicated 'animal passions'. Significantly, not only is Dignam's 'auric egg' of the appropriate debased shade, but also the 'orangefiery and scarlet rays' shine forth from a suggestive zone of the body, the 'sacral region', a coy euphemism for the groin.[36]

[34] Charles Webster Leadbeater, *The Astral Plane* (London: Theosophical Publishing Society, 1895), 35. I cite Leadbeater as Joyce's source here since, although Leadbeater did not invent these concepts, he was the first to interpret and theorise them extensively and publish tracts explaining them to believers. See Gregory Tillett, *The Elder Brother: A Biography of Charles Webster Leadbeater* (London: Routledge and Kegan Paul, 1982) for a full account of Leadbeater's influence. As Stanislaus Joyce tells us, the young Joyce was an avid reader of Leadbeater's guides to theosophy (*My Brother's Keeper*, 140).
[35] Leadbeater, *The Astral Plane*, 40.
[36] Charles Webster Leadbeater, *The Aura: An Inquiry into the Nature and Function of the Luminous Mists Seen Around Human and Other Bodies* (London: Theosophical Publishing Society, 1897), 25.

Joyce's parodic vision of ghosthood as a disconcertingly somatic condition thus demonstrates the specificity of his knowledge of theosophy's doctrinal nuances. Dignam's etheric double behaves exactly as Charles Leadbeater predicted the ghost of an 'impure' man who met a sudden death would act: he is preoccupied with the banal and the worldly, he manifests in the disreputable places he favoured in life, he even emits the fiery red aura of 'animal passions' from his groin. These close coincidences argue for Joyce's willingness to subvert the minutiae of theosophical doctrine for his own purposes. To read 'Cyclops' and 'Scylla' together is to note how closely Joyce engaged with a fiercely contested issue within theosophy: the problem of unruly spirit manifestations and the affiliated question of supernatural desire. Many converts found comfort in the idea of an asexual paradise awaiting the faithful beyond the grave. For Charlotte Despard, 'In the spiritual world there is no sex. "There", said a Master, "shall be neither marrying nor giving in marriage; but they shall be as the angels of God in heaven." '[37] For W. T. Stead 'love beyond the borderland' was reassuringly distinct from this life's 'temporary passion which is not love, but self-indulgence of the worst shape'.[38] For G. R. S. Mead, editor of the occult journal *The Quest*, the masters dwelt on 'lofty planes of pure morality', whilst as we have seen, Gretta Cousins longed for a future world where sex would be transcended.[39] However, Charles Leadbeater provided a controversial and opposing view of an afterlife saturated with taboo sexual desires. *The Astral Plane* addressed a disconcerting faultline in contemporary occultism: if the afterlife transcended the body's material concerns, how to account for the startling atmosphere of sexual excess which came to dominate séances?

IV

By the turn of the century, the kinds of materialisation séances Joyce spoofs in 'Cyclops' had acquired a certain notoriety. Young, pretty female mediums entered the spirit cabinet as exemplary figures of Victorian decorum, then emerged as spirits whose appearance and behaviour was in tantalising contrast to their conventionally modest demeanour.[40] The acclaimed medium Elizabeth D'Esperance produced 'Yolande, a beautiful Arab girl,

---

[37] Despard, *Theosophy and the Women's Movement*, 7.

[38] W. T. Stead, *Letters from Julia, or Light from the Borderland* (London: Grant Richards, 1897), 19.

[39] G. R. S. Mead and Herbert Burrows, *The Leadbeater Case: The Suppressed Speeches of Herbert Burrows and G. R. S. Mead* (Manchester: E. E. Marsden Press, 1908), 18.

[40] Owen, *The Darkened Room*, 219–56.

olive-skinned and dark haired' who appeared in the flimsiest interpretation
of Egyptian costume, whilst her rival Florence Cook's 'Katie King' dressed
in diaphanous robes, accepted bouquets and gifts, kissed and sat on the
laps of male admirers, and invited enthusiasts to 'pass their hands over her
dress in order that they might satisfy themselves she wore only a robe'.[41]
Other spectacular evidences of supernatural presences, such as the ectoplasmic extrusions from later mediums' mouths, nipples and, on occasion,
genitals, compounded existing suspicions that it was sex, not ghosts, that
occult practitioners were really liberating.[42] These suspicions were encouraged by a hostile medical establishment, which repeatedly linked occultism
to hysteria, a condition with unsavoury sexual connotations.[43] For Henry
Maudsley, one of the leading Victorian medical psychopathologists, the
ecstatic state of mediumship was mere 'emotional incontinence' resulting
from 'irregularities of menstruation and suspected self-abuse' and an excess
of 'heavily disguised venereal passions'.[44]

These responses indicate how closely supernatural belief was linked to
diseased sexuality, placing Joyce's own lively responses to seances in sudden relief. In this context, flaunting ladies' bloomers in Ely Place in 1904
seems a loaded allusion to the suspicions which sullied the reputation of
contemporary occultism, as Joyce's practical joke unmistakeably suggests
what commonly issued from the spirit cabinet; scantily clad 'ghosts', who
disconcertingly resembled the smutty postcards, indecent stereoscopes and
tableaux vivants of popular erotica. The allusion is expanded in 'Scylla',
where Stephen's seemingly gratuitous references to Elizabeth Tudor's hoard
of underlinen, oppressive stream of innuendo and discussion of ghosthood
as a condition of sexual obsession similarly hints at an occultism easily
constituted as a displaced form of 'venereal passions'. These suggestions
are rendered particularly specific in the chapter's closing pages, where Buck
Mulligan effervescently 'reads' Stephen's theory to disclose its hidden slur.

---

[41] *Ibid.*, 223–30. Florence Marryat went further still when invited 'to place my hands inside the loose
single garment she was wearing and feel her nude body. I did so thoroughly. I felt her heart beating
rapidly beneath my hands and passed my fingers through her long hair. I can testify that if she be
"of psychic force", psychic force is very like a woman', 227.

[42] For an account, with illustrations, of 'the extraordinary erotic charge' surrounding materialisation
séances, see Tom Gunning, 'Phantom Images and Modern Manifestations: Spirit Photography,
Magic Theater, Trick Films and Photography's Uncanny', in *Fugitive Images: From Photography to
Video*, ed. Patrice Petro (Bloomington: Indiana University Press, 1992), 42–71.

[43] Owen, *The Darkened* Room, 139.

[44] Henry Maudsley, *The Physiology and Pathology of Mind* (London: Macmillan and Co., 1873), 79. See
also *The British Medical Journal*'s suggestion that 'hysteria is doubtless the disease which more than
any other furnishes the most abundant crop of fruit to the Spiritualists', *British Medical Journal* 2
(1871), 99.

Mulligan repeatedly constitutes masturbation as the concealed vice of 'that hermetic crowd', alluding, as we shall see, to sustained and well-publicised contemporary cultural anxieties.

In 1906, a Chicago theosophist discovered a letter to her thirteen-year-old son from Charles Leadbeater, then deputy leader of the London Theosophy Society and acclaimed by many theosophists as 'the world's greatest occultist and seer'.[45] Written in a simple code, it instructed her son to masturbate twice weekly, and included the damning line 'Glad sensation is so pleasant.'[46] Called before a disciplinary committee of London theosophists, Leadbeater argued that he was 'clairvoyantly aware' of the 'sex problems' tormenting his young pupils, and so advocated masturbation as a 'a preventative against unchastity'.[47] His 'safety-valve' defence radically departed from the social purity orthodoxy outlined above in chapter 3; the belief that masturbation was a debilitating evil in itself, leading to physical decay, mental instability, emasculation and further immoralities. It failed to convince a London committee dominated by shocked social purists, and Leadbeater was expelled.[48] The Theosophy Society's investigation and expulsion of Leadbeater confirmed rumours prevalent since 1897, when he began to urge parents to entrust the spiritual development of their sons to him.[49] His flamboyant chastity further exacerbated suspicions: he pointedly refused to shake hands with women at meetings, and, when a guest of married couples, insisted they occupy separate bedrooms for the duration of his stay, eccentricities which prompted one host to comment 'his tastes ran mainly to boys and tapioca pudding'.[50] However, his influence as 'one of the world's foremost scientists in spiritual research' meant that the scandal could not be so easily contained.[51]

Those who hoped in 1907 for an 'end to this wretched controversy' which had for the past decade 'threatened to plunge theosophy into the foul masturbation abyss' were to be disappointed.[52] Supporters of Leadbeater were

---

[45] For a brief summary of Leadbeater's influence as the most prolific publisher of theosophical texts, see Tillett, *The Elder Brother*, 5.
[46] A full account of the scandal, where the letter is quoted in full, is given in 'Serious charges preferred: the fallen prophet', chapter 9 of Tillett, *The Elder Brother*, 77–90.
[47] Mead and Burrows, *The Leadbeater Case*, 5.
[48] The committee, chaired by G. R. S. Mead, included Edith Ward, author of *The Vital Question: An Address on Social Purity* mentioned above, and Isabel Stead, wife of purity crusader W. T. Stead. See Mead and Burrows, *The Leadbeater Case*, 1.
[49] During 1897, Leadbeater published a series of articles in *Lucifer*, the journal of the London Theosophical Society on the theme 'Our Relation to Our Children'. They promoted the theosophical youth group he was founding. See Tillett, *The Elder Brother*, 65.
[50] Tillett, *The Elder Brother*, 199; Washington, *Madame Blavatsky's Baboon*, 118.
[51] Tillett, *The Elder Brother*, 5.   [52] Mead and Burrows, *The Leadbeater Case*, 18.

numerous enough to force the London committee to reaffirm their decision at an appeal in 1909.[53] Throughout 1909 the London paper *John Bull* insisted that 'the Theosophical society is gathering into it's ranks an army of morbid moral degenerates whose teachings are calculated to undermine the character and sap the manhood of our race', and *The Times*, *The Daily Telegraph* and *The New Statesman* concurred.[54] The controversy rumbled on for many years, following Leadbeater to India in 1912, where his adoption of two Hindu boys prompted their father to initiate a bizarre lawsuit combining charges of deification and sodomy, and to Australia in 1922, where a series of articles in the *Sydney Daily Telegraph* led to a full-scale police investigation.[55] Such publicity threatened to render 'the public propagation of theosophy impossible', despite the London Theosophical Society's vigorous efforts to rid the movement 'of this foul blot upon its name and fame'.[56]

Given the highly public nature of 'the Leadbeater affair', one might speculate that Joyce, an avowed sceptic who borrowed from key Leadbeater texts in 'Cyclops', relished this global scandal. Certainly, speculation that Joyce knew of theosophy's seamier side are encouraged in the closing pages of 'Scylla'. For masturbation is central to Buck Mulligan's parody of the Dublin theosophists assembled in the National Library, and its centrality must have been bitingly resonant by 1919–20, when Joyce was composing the chapter and theosophy had already endured more than two decades of persistent scandal over the solitary vice. Mulligan builds upon a theme slyly introduced by Stephen, who draws an implicit parallel between Hamlet, 'glorified man, an androgynous angel, being a wife unto himself' (*U* 9: 1052) and his listeners: 'Unwed, unfancied, ware of wiles, they fingerponder nightly each his variorum edition of *The Taming of the Shrew*' (*U* 9: 1061–2). The bawdy ramifications of Hamlet's sexual self-reliance ('a wife unto himself') are drawn out with the word 'fingerponder', an intrusion of the manual freighted with double entendre. Stephen associates his listeners with the kind of forestalled sexuality which Mulligan will later castigate as particularly Irish in 'Oxen of the Sun', and these insinuations

[53] Supporters argued firstly that Leadbeater 'had the clairvoyant vision to see what thought-forms were hovering about the boys', secondly that his teachings were 'dictated to him verbatim by one of the Masters', and thirdly that expulsion violated the principle of 'universal brotherhood', Mead and Burrows, *The Leadbeater Case*, 18.
[54] Mead and Burrows, *The Leadbeater Case*, 20; 'A Teacher of Filth', *John Bull*, 9 February 1909; Editorial, *John Bull*, 13 February 1909; 'Deified and Defiled: Two Boys and A Beast', *John Bull*, 16 November 1912. For further details of newspaper coverage, see Tillett, *The Elder Brother*, 180.
[55] Washington, *Madame Blavatsky's Baboon*, 118; Tillett, *The Elder Brother*, 200.
[56] Tillett, *The Elder Brother*, 5.

are voluble in the context of theosophy's contemporary reputation. Stephen presents both Hamlet and his audience as ghosthunters terrified of procreative, interactive sexuality and instead confined to the sexual cul-de-sac of autoeroticism.

These hints that theosophical sexuality is strangulated, sterile and furtively self-indulgent are taken up by Mulligan, who offers Eglinton the parting-shot 'Monsieur Moore...lecturer on French letters to the youth of Ireland' (*U* 9: 1101–2). Mulligan's allusion to contraception is loaded since, in 1904, Annie Besant, the one-time feminist campaigner for birth control, had recently taken over the leadership of the London Theosophical Society with Leadbeater as her deputy after the death of Helena Blavatsky. Despite Besant's high-profile recantation, her role must have added to the aura of sexual impropriety which threatened to 'render the public propagation of theosophy impossible'. Mulligan makes the associative leap between contraception, or 'conjugal onanism' as it was widely known, and masturbation with his parody of Yeats' 1903 poem 'Baile and Aillinn'. Yeats' poem would no doubt have delighted the Dublin Hermetists, since it celebrated lovers who transcended sexual union in favour of the higher spiritual affinities to be found in the afterlife, thus evading the decay and disappointments of sexuality:

> Their love was never drowned in care
> Of this or that thing, nor grew cold
> Because their bodies had grown old.
> Being forbid to marry on earth
> They blossomed to immortal mirth.[57]

Yeats' quasi-theosophical vision of love purified on a higher plane is drastically burlesqued by Mulligan, who transforms a virtue into a necessity. Yeats' 'curlew cry' becomes a 'purlieu cry' (*U* 9: 1043), the lure of Dublin's red-light area Joyce later presented as Nighttown. Yeats' chaste lovers are displaced by a more incongruous pairing, Eglinton and the minor Revivalist Frederick M'Curdy Atkinson, bound together through a chastity produced not through restraint so much as incapacity. Atkinson's 'wooden leg' and Eglinton/Magee's 'chinless mouth', 'That never dared to slake his drouth' (*U* 9: 1147, 49, 50) are cruelly visceral metonyms of impotence, in ironic contrast to Yeats' lovers, whose chaste progress to the afterlife spares them somatic decay. Mulligan ascribes their purity not to spiritual strength, but to mental and corporeal weakness: 'Being afraid to marry on earth / They

[57] W. B. Yeats, *A Critical Edition of the Major Works*, ed. Edward Larrissy (Oxford: Oxford University Press, 1997), 359.

masturbated for all they were worth' (*U* 9: 1150–1). With his spoof play for 'the mummers',

> – *Everyman His Own Wife*
> *or*
> *A Honeymoon in the Hand*
> (*a national immorality in three orgasms*) (*U* 9: 1171–6),

and its hero 'Toby Tostoff, a ruined Pole' (*U* 9: 1181), he extends his view of Eglinton's and Atkinson's sexuality to the whole of the Dublin theosophical-literary establishment. Mulligan's puns on 'French letters', his parody of Yeats and his spoof play for the Abbey together read theosophy's various cultural enterprises as substitutions for and evasions of sexual creativity.

'Scylla and Charybdis' is thus structured to reveal pervasive cultural associations between a revivalism intimately connected to theosophy, and a secretive sexual deviancy. Stephen's Shakespeare theory allegorically interrogates theosophy to unfold provocative connections with a cautious, concealed and claustrophobic sexuality; Mulligan's verbal play names this sexuality as masturbation, thus alluding to a highly contentious contemporary scandal which theosophy was trying to conceal. If the Leadbeater affair is a submerged intertext in 'Scylla', then the chapter parallels the repressive hypothesis which dogged contemporary occultism. The Leadbeater controversy was so eloquent to theosophy's critics because it articulated in a particularly obvious manner the sexuality suspected to lurk beneath theosophy's high-minded façade, exposing faultlines in that facade already evident in speculations over spiritualism's salacious séance manifestations, Annie Besant's former enthusiasm for contraception and Blavatsky's unfortunately crooked cucumber. This repressive dynamic is similarly encoded within 'Scylla', where Mulligan's remarks explicate Stephen's Shakespeare monologue. His naming of masturbation as the dark side of theosophical chastity offers to retrieve what the movement's sexual politics buried. Masturbation in 'Scylla' is thus deeply politically resonant, as Joyce uses Mulligan to signpost the implications of Stephen's monologue in that 'history of cultural conflict' which Len Platt defines as central to 'Scylla'.[58] If 'Scylla' is an episode dominated, as Platt suggests, by snide attacks and bitter asides, by submerged hostilities and battles for cultural possession and prestige, then Stephen's assault upon theosophy's sexual pretensions is a particularly effective instance of this maliciously playful sniping.

[58] Platt, 'The Voice of Esau', 740.

V

Writing to Harriet Shaw Weaver at *The Egoist* in October 1918, Joyce hinted at a further dimension to his assault upon theosophical sexuality. Regretting 'My book *Ulysses* appears to be giving you a great deal of trouble', Joyce consoled her with the prospect of a new instalment: 'I am writing now the Hamlet episode ("Scylla and Charybdis")' (*L* 1: 120). Joyce's movement here from Weaver's difficulties in finding a printer willing to risk the obscenity laws to his ongoing creative enterprise implies a connection between composition and censorship which became increasingly evident as the months progressed. Joyce was composing the first draft of 'Scylla' from late 1918 through to February 1919, months when he was simultaneously preoccupied with *Ulysses'* disjointed serial progress through *The Egoist* in London, and Margaret Anderson's and Jane Heap's New York journal *The Little Review*.[59] *The Little Review* was first suppressed in January 1919, when the New York Society for the Suppression of Vice confiscated the 'Lestrygonians' number for violation of the Comstock law prohibiting material deemed obscene from being distributed through the postal system.[60] Further confrontation with these moral vigilantes was to come: 'Scylla' itself was confiscated in May 1919, 'Nausicaa' in August, and in February 1921 social purity triumphed over *Ulysses* when *The Little Review* was convicted of obscenity.[61] Meanwhile, Weaver's difficulties in London increased. The November–December 1918 issue announced

As our efforts to find a British printer willing to print the complete text of Mr James Joyce's new novel *Ulysses* have been unsuccessful, we regretfully abandon the proposal to bring that work out as a separately printed supplement.[62]

The next issue carried an extract from 'Nestor', footnoted by Weaver: 'As printing difficulties have made it impossible to publish *Ulysses* in full in serial form, a series of extracts will be printed in *The Egoist* during the next few months.'[63] This unhappy resolution, however, was shortlived. Extracts appeared sporadically in an increasingly sporadic journal, and within a year *The Egoist* had closed in order to prioritise the publication of *Ulysses* 'in book form'.[64] Joyce's sustained ridicule of theosophical sexuality in 'Scylla'

[59] Ellmann, *James Joyce*, 441–3.
[60] The Post Office acted on information given by the New York Society for the Suppression of Vice, who objected to Bloom's thoughts on Dr Hy Franks' remedies for 'the clap', the Revd Mr MacTrigger, and his memories of lovemaking with Molly on Howth Head. See Paul Vanderham, *James Joyce and Censorship: The Trials of Ulysses* (London: Macmillan, 1998), 171.
[61] *Ibid.*, 3.   [62] 'Notice', *The Egoist*, November–December 1918, 139.
[63] 'Episode Two: Nestor', *The Egoist*, January–February 1919, 11.
[64] 'Notice to Readers', *The Egoist*, December 1919, 70.

during these months takes on another layer of political resonance in the light of these struggles against censorship. In particular, the various revisions made to the chapter invite an obvious interpretation: was Joyce's insistence upon the connections between theosophy and a perversely hypocritical sexuality a form of coded commentary upon his censors?

Anderson and Heap had struggled with the New York Society for the Suppression of Vice for some years, and they attempted to appease the vigilantes with ill grace in the May 1919 issue of *The Little Review*. There, 'Scylla' was prefaced with a complaint over the confiscation of the 'Lestrygonians' issue earlier that year:

To avoid a similar interference this month, I have ruined Mr Joyce's story by cutting certain passages in which he mentions natural facts known to everyone.[65]

Anderson deleted 'Sons with mothers, sires with daughters, nephews with grandmothers, queens with prize bulls', Stephen's reference to 'the holy office an ostler does for the stallion' and Mulligan's skit 'A Honeymoon in the Hand'. Nonetheless, what she left in was enough to move the Society for the Suppression of Vice to act, and the May number was also prohibited from passing through the US mails.[66] However, whilst in the USA such 'natural facts' were being excised, in Europe Joyce was adding them. Successive drafts of 'Scylla' disclose a process of revision with a distinct flavour of bloody-mindedness. The revision process began in late 1918, when Joyce added specific theosophical details to *The Little Review* proofs; 'Allfather, the heavenly man. Hiesos Kristos, magician of the beautiful', 'The life esoteric is not for ordinary person. O.P. must work off bad karma first' and 'the name ineffable' (*JJA* 12: 351). However, after 'Scylla's' suppression in May 1919, Joyce's revising pencil was directed not so much towards theosophy, but more to the chapter's disputed sexual content.

In November 1920, Joyce's alterations for Sylvia Beach's planned Shakespeare and Company Paris edition exacerbated the allusions queried by the New York Society for the Suppression of Vice further. 'Argive Helen' became 'the wooden mare of Troy in whom a score of heroes slept' (*JJA* 18: 182), the passage describing various 'incests and bestialities' which Anderson and Heap reluctantly removed was elaborated with 'lesbic sisters, loves that dare not speak their name' (*JJA* 18: 198).[67] Joyce added also 'between conjugial love and its chaste delights and scortatory love and its foul pleasures' (*JJA* 18: 190), and, more provokingly still, transformed Ann Hathaway into

---

[65] *The Little Review* 6: 1 (May 1918), 21.   [66] Vanderham, *James Joyce and Censorship*, 31.
[67] The 'lesbic sisters' presumably recapitulated Stephen's earlier speculation about the sisterly friendship between Blavatsky and Cooper-Oakley.

a faded, jaded tract-reading Puritan, a dangerous equivalent to contemporary purity censors:

> She read or had read to her his chapbooks, preferring them to *The Merry Wives* and thought over *Hooks and Eyes For Believer's Breeches and The Most Spiritual Snuffbox to Make the Most Devout Souls Sneeze.* (*JJA* 18: 197)

In late 1921, making final revisions to the Beach galley proofs in the aftermath of *The Little Review*'s suppression that February, 'Scylla' becomes more confrontational still. 'Prologue to the swelling act' is added to Stephen's initial portrait of Ann Hathaway, 'jailbirds with keyholes' to the catalogue of 'incest and bestialities' (*JJA* 23: 248, 332). Most tellingly, the final couplet of Mulligan's Yeats parody, 'Being afraid to marry upon earth / They masturbated for all they were worth' (*JJA* 23: 340) only appears on this final revision. Until then, Joyce avoided naming so explicitly the solitary vice which made theosophy infamous. His modifications emphasise, rather than tone down, the connections between theosophy and sexual disorder, changes surely designed to provoke the social purists pursuing *Ulysses* through the courts.

Two early poems, 'The Holy Office' (1904) and 'Gas From a Burner' (1912) further suggest theosophy's role in Joyce's strategy of defiance. Both respond to early experiences of censorship. 'The Holy Office' was distributed after *The Irish Homestead* refused to take any more *Dubliners* stories since 'readers had complained' (*L* 1: 98), and after Joyce's essay 'The Day of the Rabblement' attacking the Irish Literary Theatre for producing moral but mediocre Irish plays had been rejected by *St Stephen's Magazine*.[68] 'Gas from a Burner' commented on the collapse of negotiations with George Roberts to publish *Dubliners* and the subsequent refusal of printer John Falconer to sell the sheets on to Joyce, a setback acknowledged in the poem's initial title, 'Mr Falconer Addresses the Vigilance Committee' (*JJA* 1: 287).[69] These poems foreshadow Joyce's critical method in 'Scylla' because both associate censorship with theosophy. 'The Holy Office' singled out Yeats, Roberts, Russell and Eglinton for particular censure; 'But all these men of whom I speak / Make me the sewer of their clique. / That they may dream their dreamy dreams / I carry off their filthy streams' (*Poems* 98). Joyce's insistence that 'my office of Katharsis' (*Poems* 98) ventilated the kinds of somatic desires theosophists feared to acknowledge was repeated in 'Gas from a Burner'. Ventriloquising Roberts, Joyce complained 'I printed mystical books in dozens: / I printed the table book of Cousins / Though (asking

---

[68] Ellmann, *James Joyce*, 166, 200.   [69] *Ibid.*, 328.

your pardon) as for the verse / T'would give you a heartburn on your arse'
(*Poems* 104). Assuming a corollary between Roberts' timid refusal to print
Dubliners and his role as a staunch supporter of theosophical effusions,
Joyce again insists that mysticism and bad verse masked a furtive, secretive
and dishonest sexuality: 'In the porch of my printing institute / The poor
and deserving prostitute / Plays every night at catch-as-catch-can / With
her tight-breeched British artilleryman' (*Poems* 105). Joyce's striking image
metonymically discloses the underbelly of Maunsel and Co.'s daytime reputation for moral probity. Sexual transgression hovers figuratively on the
porch, under cloak of darkness. So Joyce suggests it lurks in the shadows
of Irish theosophy, a disavowed yet nonetheless present force.

These broadsides offer an intriguing perspective on 'Scylla' because they
emphasise how closely the young Joyce's earliest experiences of censorship
were bound up with and attributed to Irish theosophical prudery. In 'Scylla',
written fifteen years after his flight from Dublin, Joyce addresses the contemporary censorship threat at one remove, returning to the Dublin of his
youth, where theosophy was the strand of social purity ideology most influential in Irish literary circles. There, theosophy stands in for social purity: its
sexual timidity exemplifies a wider climate of artistic censorship with which
Joyce was permanently in conflict. His assault upon theosophy is thus a
pre-emptive and metonymic assault upon a movement which would force
The Little Review's suppression, an assault made clear through the chapter's
revisions, where, during the months of *Ulysses'* suppression and eventual
trial, Joyce elaborated and amplified his provocative insinuations of a fundamental connection between theosophy and the obscene. His revisions
make bold one of 'Scylla's' themes; how sexual tensions disrupt the moralising façade. Sexuality seethes through 'Scylla', most obviously in Stephen's
innuendo-laden Shakespeare theory which playfully subverts theosophy's
doctrinal enthusiasms for brotherhood and ghosthood as states of inviolable
purity. Stephen reappraises 'universal brotherhood' as a stiflingly incestuous
bond, fissured by sexual jealousies, and suggests a belief in ghosts is a deflection of sexual obsession. The episode slyly substantiates the resonances
of his argument through submerged allusions to the contemporary suspicions and scandals which theosophy was unable to contain. By anchoring
theosophy to the kinds of scandals it unsuccessfully attempted to ignore,
from spiritualism's associations with sexual hysteria to, more specifically,
the long-running Leadbeater controversy over masturbation, Joyce places
moralising discourses of sexual proscription upon an eloquent continuum.
The prostitute on the porch of Maunsel and Co. in 'Gas from a Burner' is
marginal, extraneous to the institution, in its shadow. In 'Scylla', Joyce goes

one step further, representing sexuality not as a force prudishly excluded from theosophy and clamouring at the door to be let in, but rather as intrinsic to it, submerged within a discourse of chastity which, as the Leadbeater case so devastatingly suggested, incites whilst it prohibits. Joyce's depiction of theosophy in 'Scylla and Charybdis' argues that rather than repressing and controlling sexuality, moralising propagandists covertly participate in and amplify the desires they deny. 'Scylla' thus contributes to a sustained Joycean theme: the underground correlation between vice and vigilance.

CHAPTER 5

Making a spectacle of herself: Gerty MacDowell through the mutoscope

If the suppression of 'Scylla and Charybdis' in May 1919 provided an inti-
mation of an oncoming crisis, then that crisis was eventually precipitated
when *The Little Review* published the third instalment of 'Nausicaa' in its
July–August 1920 issue. The chapter had been drafted whilst Joyce received
bulletins of *Ulysses*' unsteady progress through the New York journal, as he
noted in February that year when sending his manuscript to Frank Budgen:
'Hope you got *Nausikaa*. Do you like it? . . . USA govt. burned whole May
issue and threaten to suppress review on account of me' (*L* II: 458). Eventually, the catastrophe Joyce predicted came about when John Sumner, the
secretary of the New York Society for the Suppression of Vice, initiated
the court proceedings against the July–August 1920 number of *The Little
Review* which would proscribe *Ulysses* from publication in the United States.
As Sumner explained in the Society's Annual Report,

A citizen wrote a letter to the District Attorney stating that it had been sent to his
young daughter without solicitation and from a source unknown. A careful perusal
of one of the stories by a foreign writer disclosed an apparently clear violation of
the law against 'the publication and circulation of lewd and filthy material'. The
magazine boasts that it 'makes no compromise with the public taste'. Its publishers
contend that 'art' is above the law. They were arraigned in the Magistrates Court
and have been held on bail for trial. We shall see whether our laws are sufficiently
comprehensive to prevent the indiscriminate circulation here of the degenerate
ideas of an alien exploited by misguided Americans whose only claim to recognition
is derived from self-advertisement and the misuse of good printers' ink.[1]

The prosecution of the 'Nausicaa' episode was thus a test case, designed to
crush the avant-garde pretension that ' "art" is above the law', and thereby
upping the stakes in Joyce's ongoing struggle with social purity. As the
Society for the Suppression of Vice made clear, prosecution was necessary
for two distinct reasons. Firstly, 'Nausicaa' was sexually explicit, describing a

[1] The New York Society for the Suppression of Vice, *Annual Report*, 47 (1920), 13–14.

middle-aged man masturbating whilst stimulated by a young girl's deliberate exhibitionist display. Secondly, the offending extract had been mailed to an unnamed adolescent, the daughter of a lawyer who complained to the District Attorney.[2] This accident unfortunately collided with one of the New York Society for the Suppression of Vice's fervently held beliefs, that those circulating 'lewd and filthy material' deliberately attempted to pollute 'young minds':

School roll-books are the directories for the vendors of obscene matter, etc., which furnish them with the names of our boys and girls. *Children have thrust upon them, unsolicited, these death traps.* Their curiosity is piqued, and unconscious of danger, they often send for the matter advertised, simply to gratify inquisitiveness.[3]

The Little Review fitted into this paradigm, since Anderson's attempts to win new subscribers could be interpreted as part of a nationwide conspiracy to imperil the young. The journal unambiguously jeopardised the 'young person'; a juvenile, innocent, often female reader in danger of corruption by sexually suggestive writing.[4] This Victorian incarnation dominated debate on the censorship of literature, and with 'Nausicaa' Joyce violated two of her breed, the offended 'citizen's daughter', and Gerty MacDowell herself. Writing in *The Little Review*, Jane Heap appreciated the irony. Noting that the New York Society for the Suppression of Vice was ostensibly 'founded to protect the public from corruption', she added

When asked *what public?* its defenders spring to the rock on which America was founded, the cream puff of sentimentality, and answer chivalrously 'Our young girls'. The present case is rather ironical. We are being prosecuted for printing the thoughts in a young girl's mind.[5]

'Nausicaa' supplies a particularly arch and resonant subversion of social purity premises and rhetorical strategies. There, Joyce's intricate assault upon the 'young person' of the social purity imagination takes the form of a competition of intertexts. The first is the respectable nineteenth-century sentimental best-seller *The Lamplighter.* The second, however, is the technologically novel and distinctly shady mutoscope; a *fin de siècle* optical toy which destabilised the ideas of youth, femininity and violated innocence upon which social purity rhetoric depended.

[2] Paul Vanderham, *James Joyce and Censorship: The Trials of Ulysses* (London: Macmillan, 1998), 2.
[3] Anthony Comstock, *Traps for the Young*, ed. Robert Bremner (Cambridge, Mass.: Harvard University Press, 1967), 135, italics in the original. Comstock was the founder of the New York Society for the Suppression of Vice.
[4] See 'Adventures of the Young Person', Walter Kendrick, *The Secret Museum: Pornography in Modern Culture* (New York: Viking, 1987), 67–94.
[5] Jane Heap, *The Little Review* 8: 2 (October 1921), 7.

I

The 'young person' was inevitably figured as vulnerable, suggestible, and in danger from a popular culture social purists perceived to be increasingly sexualised. One response was the production of a distinct genre of didactic fiction considered morally suitable for juvenile consumption, a task embraced by a range of social purists, from the Pure Literature Society to W. T. Stead through his 'Masterpiece Library'. It is perhaps no coincidence that the decade that saw the 'young person' identity enshrined in law with the Obscene Publications Act (1857) also saw the publication of a classic of the genre, the transatlantic best-seller *The Lamplighter* (1854) by Maria Susannah Cummins. Suzette Henke, S. L. Goldberg and Kimberley Devlin have each identified 'that book *The Lamplighter* by Miss Cummins, author of *Mabel Vaughan* and other tales' (*U* 13: 632–4) as the inspiration for 'Nausicaa's' coloured narrative.[6] All offer convincing studies of the relationship between *The Lamplighter* and 'Nausicaa', and the respective heroines, Gertrude Flint and Gerty MacDowell, and all note that MacDowell falls short of the ideal of proper female conduct presented by Flint. For Flint is the paragon of the 'young person', poor but honest, decorous and self-sacrificing, and, most importantly, sexually modest and completely lacking in physical self-awareness.[7] After many trials from unsuitable admirers and vindictive female rivals, her virtues are rewarded by marriage to her childhood sweetheart, who through a final plot twist is suddenly endowed with riches from an unexpected bequest.[8] Crucially, for Cummins' heroine, the economically fortunate marriage and the physical modesty are intimately associated. Although other characters in *The Lamplighter* repeatedly compliment Flint's unaffected and uncultivated beauty and simple taste in dress, and although she is bombarded with suitors, the narrator reassures us such loveliness is 'undoubtedly greatly enhanced by an utter unconsciousness, on her part, of possessing any attractions at all'.[9] Cummins' exemplary heroine is thus sexually innocent to an unusual degree. She is blind to the value of her sexuality as a commodity. As Joyce well understood, Gertrude

[6] Suzette Henke, 'Gerty MacDowell: Joyce's Sentimental Heroine', in *Women in Joyce*, ed. Suzette Henke and Elaine Unkeless (Urbana: University of Illinois Press, 1982), 133; S. L. Goldberg, *The Classical Temper: A Study of James Joyce's Ulysses* (London: Chatto and Windus, 1961), 141; Kimberley Devlin, 'The Romance Heroine Exposed: "Nausicaa" and *The Lamplighter*', *James Joyce Quarterly* 22: 4 (1985), 383.

[7] As Devlin points out, Flint thus conforms to the conventions of romantic fiction theorised by Tania Modleski, where the heroine must be artless, lacking in self-consciousness and innocent of consciously cultivating her beauty, lest she be confused with her 'scheming' rival, 'The Romance Heroine Exposed', 386–7.

[8] See Henke, 'Gerty MacDowell', 133 for a plot-summary.

[9] Maria Susannah Cummins, *The Lamplighter* (London: Blackie, 1916), 165.

Flint is the ideal 'young person' of the social purity imagination. She was the kind of unsullied young girl the vigilantes at the New York Society for the Suppression of Vice were purporting to protect even into the second decade of the twentieth century.

As Devlin notes, 'Nausicaa' stands in 'ironic contrast' to this classic of 'young person' fiction. Whilst Gertrude Flint is pointedly oblivious to the striking personal beauty that wins her compliments from all, Gerty MacDowell's charms are 'artful, as most charms by definition are'.[10] Devlin's astute study underlines how central the interwoven issues of feminine display, spectacle and spectatorship are to the 'young person' identity in both Cummins' novel and Joyce's subversion of it. To demonstrate this point, Devlin compares two significant and obviously paralleled incidents in *The Lamplighter* and 'Nausicaa', the first where Gertrude Flint takes off her bonnet to swing it by its string, and the narrator comments that 'this was a habit she had always had since childhood, so we will acquit her of any coquettish desires to show an unusually fine head of hair.'[11] Joyce 'lifts' this scene and rewrites it as Gerty's self-conscious play with her hat:

Gerty just took off her hat for a moment to settle her hair and a prettier, a daintier head of nutbrown tresses was never seen on a girl's shoulders – a radiant little vision, in sooth, almost maddening in its sweetness... She could almost see the swift answering flash of admiration in his eyes that set her tingling in every nerve. She put on her hat so that she could see from underneath the brim and swung her buckled shoe faster for her breath caught as she caught the expression in his eyes. He was eyeing her as a snake eyes its prey. (*U* 13: 509–17)

In sharp contrast to Gertrude Flint's innocence of 'coquettish desires', Gerty MacDowell is acutely conscious of herself as an enticing sight, not only removing and replacing her hat to display her 'unusually fine head of hair', but also tilting it so she can monitor the effect of her display on Bloom. As Devlin notes, Joyce thus places the issue of spectacle and spectatorship at the heart of his subversion of the 'young person', filtering the affiliated questions of innocence and agency through the visual.

However compelling and convincing Devlin's study of *The Lamplighter* intertext may be, she, along with Henke and Goldberg, disregards certain puzzling aspects of *The Lamplighter*'s publication and reception history which query the implicit assumption that 'Nausicaa' is simply a male Modernist parody of the 'silly lady novelists' of a century before. The novel was widely derided as sentimental didactic pap for the 'young person' many decades before Joyce's belated critique. In 1855, Nathaniel Hawthorne's well-known protest against 'a damned mob of scribbling women' singled out

[10] Devlin, 'The Romance Heroine Exposed', 383.   [11] Cummins, *The Lamplighter*, 97.

The Lamplighter for particular opprobrium, whilst eight years later, Charles Kingsley was able to refer to it in *The Waterbabies* as 'The Pumplighter', a 'little book' written by 'little people'.[12] Whilst the novel became an overnight best-seller on both sides of the Atlantic, selling 100,000 copies in the first year, by the turn of the century it was frequently abridged and marketed as a morally improving children's story, and as such was included in Stead's Masterpiece Library.[13] Joyce's pastiche thus seems to break a butterfly on a wheel, since by 1904, and still more by 1920, it would have seemed strangely redundant. *The Lamplighter* is more fully understood as a palimpsest intertext, its obsolescence written over and its message ironically disrupted by a directly contemporary icon of disorderly modernity. This chapter will take up Devlin's observations to propose a more immediately contemporary and, crucially, *visual* intertext to 'Nausicaa' which competes with *The Lamplighter* to ironise further Gerty MacDowell's proximity to the 'young person'. Mutoscopes foregrounded the series of questions about spectacle, femininity and its commodification *The Lamplighter* attempted to erase, for this forgotten precursor of cinema soon acquired an unsavoury reputation as the purveyor of cheap and accessible soft pornography. Accordingly, like 'Nausicaa' itself, the mutoscope was a culturally contested artefact, censored and suppressed by social purists. The relationship between 'Nausicaa' and the popular cultural sources on which Joyce so clearly draws is more subtle and complex than has hitherto been figured. By displacing *The Lamplighter* with the mutoscope, 'Nausicaa' argues for the belatedness and obsolescence of social purity's imagined 'young person'.

II

After Bloom has enjoyed Gerty MacDowell's high kicks on Sandymount Strand, he places the spectacle in a technologically novel context:

A dream of well filled hose. Where was that? Ah, yes. Mutoscope pictures in Capel street: for men only. Peeping Tom. Willy's hat and what the girls did with it. Do they snapshot those girls or is it all a fake? *Lingerie* does it. Felt for the curves inside her *deshabille*. (*U* 13: 793–6)

---

[12] Nathaniel Hawthorne, *Letters 1853–1856*, ed. Thomas Woodson, James A. Rubino, Neal Smith and N. H. Pearson (Ohio: Ohio State University Press, 1984), 174; Charles Kingsley, *The Waterbabies* (London: Macmillan, 1898), 27.

[13] Frank Luther Mott, *Golden Multitudes* (London: Macmillan, 1947), 124–5; John Garret Leigh, 'What Do the Masses Read?', *Economic Review* 14 (1904), 166–77. Leigh's 1904 survey of an unnamed Lancashire community revealed that *The Lamplighter* was almost as widely read as the Bible or *Pilgrim's Progress*, although it lacked the prestige of either.

Bloom's erotic reverie is inspired by a contemporary motion picture device containing a sequential series of photographs mounted on a cylinder. When the viewer looked through a peephole, inserted a coin and turned a hand-crank, these cards could be rotated to produce the effect of movement.[14] Invented after Thomas Edison's more technologically advanced kinetoscope, the mutoscope has often been dismissed as a 'blind alley' in the history of the development of cinema.[15] Nonetheless, within eighteen months of their introduction in the British Isles in January 1897, the British mutoscope and Biograph Company managed to float nearly one million pounds of nominal capital on the London stock market.[16] As the company explained, 'the coin-operated mutoscope excels all other automatic devices as a money-earner', since it was easy to operate and powered manually not electrically 'requires neither nurse nor attendant to keep it in order'. An ubiquitous article of urban furniture, 'It follows people in their hours of leisure, and will serve them at the seaside, meet them at the football game; it awaits them at railway stations, or stands by whilst one takes a glass of Scotch'.[17] Above all, however, one contemporary advertisement alluded to the secret of the mutoscope's success (see figure 5). Captioned 'The mutoscope and How it Makes Money', it showed Anna Held, a Ziegfeld actress who appeared in several films, turning the handle of the machine and peering into it.[18] 'Money' is printed in large type down, rather than along the page, so that reading from left to right, the images 'Mutoscope', 'attractive woman' and 'Money' gesture towards an unsavoury reputation. Mutoscopes showed a wide range of films, ranging from images of royalty, military parades, news-reels and slapstick comedies. However, they were also known as 'What the Butler Saw Machines', since the best-selling films showed suggestive images of young women in flesh tights, skimpy lingerie and, occasionally, entirely nude.

Mutoscope parlours were therefore usually disreputable, and imaginative names such as 'cinnimatograph' and 'tabascoscope' invited the passer-by to speculate about how 'spicy' the films were.[19] In Dublin, customers could visit the smart 'Mutoscope Palace' on fashionable Grafton Street,

[14] Barry Anthony, 'Shadows of Early Films', *Sight and Sound*, 59: 3 (1990), 194–7.

[15] *Ibid.*, 197.

[16] Richard Brown and Barry Anthony, *A Victorian Film Enterprise: The History of the British Mutoscope and Biograph Company 1897–1915* (Trowbridge: Flicks Books, 1999), 1.

[17] International Mutoscope Syndicate, *The Age of Movement* (London: International Mutoscope Syndicate, 1901), 30–2.

[18] Advertisement issued 1899.

[19] Charles Musser, *The Emergence of Cinema: The American Screen to 1907* (Berkeley: University of California Press, 1994), 184.

Figure 5 Promotional poster for the mutoscope featuring the Ziegfeld actress Anna Held looking into the machine (American Mutoscope and Biograph Company, 1902).

but showmen often surreptitiously opened less wholesome establishments down side streets and in vacant shops. One such parlour, on Parliament Street, just south of the river from Capel street, is probably the 'men only' establishment which Bloom recalls.[20] As Austin Briggs notes, the films Bloom remembers were the American mutoscope and Biograph Company's

---

[20] Information kindly supplied by Bob Monks in his lecture 'Irish Film Making – the Hidden Years', *The BKSTS Bernard Happé Lecture*, 8 October 1998, at the National Film Theatre, London.

What the Girls Did with Willie's Hat (1897) and any one of several 'Peeping Tom' films, including *Peeping Tom* (1901) by George W. Smith, the maker of other popular sex films including the 1899 *A Kiss in the Tunnel* and the 1900 *Things Seen Through my Telescope*.[21] Both *Willie's Hat* and *Peeping Tom* were cited in *Hansard* by social purity MPs as examples of moral torpor. *Peeping Tom* was 'an undressing film with every possible obscene suggestion', whilst *Willie's Hat* showed 'girls in short frocks engaged in kicking at a hat, there being at each attempt a liberal display of underclothing'.[22]

Mutoscopes, then, were a vital part of that sexualised popular culture that the purity leagues were determined to stamp out. The device attested to the precariousness of contemporary boundaries between the prostitute and her representation, a precariousness explored by Christine Stansell, who argues that for late-Victorian and Edwardian moral reformers, the prostitute was a theatricalised figure, defined not by her actions but by her appearance.[23] The invisibility of the act of sex in the prostitution exchange meant that reform anxieties and surveillance frequently devolved upon the demoralising spectre of the 'fallen woman' in public space, 'flaunting', 'soliciting', 'thronging the thoroughfare'; identifiable upon the basis of such nebulous characteristics as 'dress, conversation and general bearing'.[24] This dissolution of the boundary between the prostitute and her image was particularly articulated by the mutoscope. The British mutoscope and Biograph Company may have lauded its product for the way it 'finds its way on excursion steamers, lurks in hotel and theatre lobbies, frequents the popular shops', but its 'silent but eloquent plea for coins by its patient presence' in such venues only emphasised its similarities with soliciting prostitutes.[25] These similarities were compounded by the mutoscope's disreputable appearance. Each machine had to fight hard for attention and the practice arose of pasting sensational illustrations, usually 'stills' and plot summaries above the machines.[26] Furthermore, mutoscope parlours were gaudy places, loudly proclaiming their risqué delights, an assault to the respectable eye, and accordingly the device was often included in purity-sponsored

---

[21] Austin Briggs, ' "Roll Away the Reel World, the Reel World": "Circe" and Cinema', in *Coping With Joyce: Essays from the Copenhagen Symposium*, ed. Morris Beja and Shari Benstock (Columbus: Ohio State University Press, 1989), 146–7.

[22] For 'Willie's Hat', see Samuel Smith, *Hansard*, vol. 85 (13 July 1900), col. 1549; for 'Peeping Tom', see William Caine, *Hansard*, vol. 99 (5 August 1901), col. 1308.

[23] Christine Stansell, *City of Women: Sex and Class in New York 1789–1860* (New York: Alfred A Knopf, 1986), 173.

[24] *Ibid.*, 175–7.   [25] International Mutoscope Syndicate, *The Age Of Movement*, 32.

[26] Details of the demoralising effects of frames pasted above machines, and of the sale of mutoscope stills as 'dirty postcards' provided by William Caine in *Hansard*, vol. 93 (6 May 1901), col. 756, and vol. 99 (5 August 1901), col. 1305.

parliamentary debates on the regulation of prostitution. In one such debate in 1899, a group of MPs affiliated to the National Vigilance Association informed the House that 'exhibitions of obscene pictures took place in a mutoscope in a gentleman's lavatory in Rhyl, but owing to public denunciation in the streets of that town, they have been stopped', and demanded measures to monitor 'prostitution and the related evil of the mutoscope'.[27] In Rhyl, the similarities between mutoscopes and prostitutes as affiliated public nuisances were particularly drawn out, since the local paper claimed that citizens wishing to use the lavatory for its proper purpose were prevented from doing so due to the unseemly swarms of 'men and youths who are attracted there by these questionable pictures. We are told that the place is at times overcrowded and people have to be turned out.'[28] The mutoscope's unseemly fusion of sex and profit, together with its promotion of new and morally suspect technologies of the visible, meant it shared the prostitute's shameless visibility, as it solicited passers by and profited from the corruption of morals.

This sense in which the mutoscope collapsed the distinction between prostitute and pornography is pertinent to 'Nausicaa', where the disreputable equation between profit and sexual display that the device made explicit is a scarcely elided subtext. Gerty MacDowell's desire to attract is blatantly motivated by her bleak financial prospects. Living in a household beset by indigence, domestic violence and alcoholism, she labours for her father in 'Wandering Rocks', and has often witnessed 'her own father, a prey to the fumes of intoxication, forget himself completely' (*U* 13: 299–300). Marriage is her most plausible preservative from want, yet, as Maria Luddy has shown, from 1901 to 1911, female celibacy levels in Ireland doubled, indicating a steadily increasing prospect of a poor, crippled Catholic woman who would 'never see sweet seventeen again' being left on the shelf.[29] Accordingly, Gerty's pretence that her 'dreamhusband' (*U* 13: 431) is the tall, dark, handsome figure of romantic fiction is swiftly displaced by a submerged emphasis upon his financial position. Like Miss Devlin in 'A Mother', who sensibly perceives how the dull but solvent Mr Kearney 'would wear better than a romantic person' (*D* 134), Gerty prudently contemplates an older man, 'perhaps his hair slightly flecked with grey' (*U* 13: 211). A 'sterling good daughter...with a little heart worth its

[27] *Hansard*, vol. 75 (24 June 1899) col. 71, and vol 75 (13 July 1900) col. 1544.
[28] 'The Council Making Money Out of Obscene Pictures', *The Rhyl Recorder and Advertiser*, 8 July 1899, 5.
[29] Maria Luddy, *Women and Philanthropy in Nineteenth-Century Ireland* (Cambridge: Cambridge University Press, 1995), 13.

weight in gold' (*U* 13: 325–6), Gerty perceives her 'heart' as a commodity
with its measured price, and seeks a 'sterling man' (*U* 13: 694) willing to
pay it, to whom she can be 'Dearer than the whole world...and gild his
days with happiness' (*U* 13: 654–5). This punning collision of money with
sex cumulates with her 'fireworks' (*U* 13: 718), where she is covered with 'a
stream of rain gold hair threads and they shed and ah! they were all greeny
dewy stars falling with golden' (*U* 13: 739–40). Like Danae rather than
Nausicaa, through sexual interchange with the dark stranger, Gerty is covered with gold from the heavens. The slang term 'to spend', so ubiquitous in
Victorian pornographic literature, contains in linguistic microcosm Gerty's
commodification of her image. It is unsurprising, then, that Gerty's cameo
appearance in 'Circe', soliciting Bloom with the bloodied clout signalling
loss of virginity, has provoked speculation that her commodification of her
sexuality extends to prostitution.[30] It is a hint Joyce compounds through
her 'coquettish little love of a hat of wideleaved nigger straw' (*U* 13: 156),
in other words, the black straw hat which signals the prostitute in *Stephen
Hero* and 'Eumaeus'.[31] Out alone after dark, wearing a black straw hat,
showing her knickers to a stranger, Gerty accrues the familiar props and
gestures of prostitution, and Bloom, in recalling the prostitute 'in Meath
street that night' (*U* 13: 868–9) and the mutoscope as parallel contexts for
his encounter with Gerty, attests to the instability of the contemporary
boundary between the commodification of sex and of sexual spectacle.

The mutoscope's associations with prostitution blurred a distinction between looking and touching also compromised in 'Nausicaa', where, as
Suzette Henke notes, Bloom 'can penetrate Gerty with nothing more dangerous than a burning gaze'.[32] Such a distinction was further problematised
by the mutoscope's encouragement of an oddly physical form of voyeurism
through its handcrank mode of operation. As Abigail Solomon-Godeau
has argued, what photographic pornography supplied which lithographic
or pictorial pornography withheld was a more immediate sense of physical
presence, since it brought the viewer into a newly intimate relation to the
depicted female body 'which once was really there before the camera'.[33]

---

[30] Mark Shechner, *Joyce in Nighttown: A Psychoanalytical Study* (Berkeley: University of California
Press, 1974), 165.
[31] 'The woman in the black straw hat gave something before she sold herself to the state. Emma will
sell herself but give nothing', *SH* 180; 'The face of a streetwalker glazed and haggard under a black
straw hat peered askew round the door of the shelter' (*U* 16: 714–15). Molly too has a black straw
hat resting on the commode (*U* 17: 2104).
[32] Henke, 'Gerty MacDowell', 67.
[33] Abigail Solomon-Godeau, *Photography at the Dock: Essays on Photographic History, Institutions and
Practices* (Minneapolis: University of Minnesota Press, 1991), 233.

Linda Williams extends Solomon-Godeau's observations, as she theorises that optical toys displaying pornographic images provided more than the 'entirely metaphorical notion of ocular possession' often understood to define the relation between male consumer and objectified female in pornography.

Rather, such devices supplied a sensation of possession beyond metaphor:

This touch should be conceived not as the impossible, metaphorical touch of the absent object by the spectator, but literally as the real touch of spectator-observer's bodies with both the machinery of vision and themselves.[34]

Few machineries of vision are more suggestive of this doubled 'real touch' than the mutoscope, since, standing at five feet high, the handcrank was positioned suggestively at groin level.[35] The device drew the spectator into intimate relation to the machine, as he watched alone through a peephole, cranking the handle to unfold the film at the pace and rhythm he found most satisfying. A 1920s stag film, *A Country Stud Horse*, elucidates what Williams calls 'the manual nature of these repeatable pleasures', as it shows a man watching a striptease through a mutoscope, cuts to what he sees, and then cuts again to a long shot of the spectator, clutching the handcrank with one hand, his exposed penis with the other.[36] *A Country Stud Horse* provides an unexpected parallel with what happens in 'Nausicaa', where Bloom operates his own somatic handcrank as he watches Gerty's high-kicks. Later in 'Circe', the mutoscope is revisited when Bloom ushers Boylan through to Molly's bedroom, and is invited to 'apply your eye to the keyhole and play with yourself while I just go through her a few times' (*U* 13: 3788–9), and Bloom asks for permission to take a 'snapshot', (*U* 13: 3792), or, in other words, to see what the butler saw. As Joyce surely understood, the mutoscope's handcrank provided a startlingly indiscreet metaphor for the kinds of solitary practices its pictures encouraged. Its way of seeing provides a remarkably acute and culturally loaded model for the onanistic, voyeuristic exchange 'Nausicaa' describes.

[34] Linda Williams, 'Corporealised Observers: Visual Pornographies and the "Carnal Density of Vision"', in *Fugitive Images: From Photography to Video*, ed. Patrice Petro (Bloomington: Indiana University Press, 1995), 14.

[35] Austin Briggs has queried my positioning of the mutoscope crank, pointing out that many models had cranks a few inches below the eyepiece ('The Mutoscope Crank', *James Joyce Broadsheet*, 51 (October 1998), 3). Although some mutoscopes were so constructed, the most decorative version, the Model D. Clamshell, widely exported throughout England and Ireland, had the distinctive groin-level crank, as figure 5 shows, and I like to speculate that these were the models which attracted Joyce's attention.

[36] Stills from *A Country Stud Horse*, featuring the mutoscope, reproduced in Williams, 'Corporealised Observers', 18.

The intimate intertextual relationship between mutoscope erotica and 'Nausicaa' becomes still more apparent in the choreography of Gerty's display. Although the handcrank incited the disreputable manual pleasures noted above, its ostensible purpose was to democratise the protocinematic motion studies carried out by Eadweard Muybridge, who broke down the movement of animals and humans into single photographs, then, by means of his own handcrank device, the zoopraxiscope, sped these photographs up to create the illusion of continuous motion.[37] Mutoscopes alluded to this trajectory between photograph and motion picture by marketing some stills as postcards, pasting some above the machines and, most persuasively, allowing the first photograph in a series of flickercards to be visible through the viewfinder.[38] What erotic mutoscope films thus encouraged was the surveillance of a woman in tableau, a spectacle Bloom particularly relishes. Glimpsing a woman's ankle as she mounts her carriage outside the Grosvenor Hotel in 'Lotos Eaters', he craves a handcrank to capture the film still of maximum revelation:

Watch! Watch! Silk flash rich stockings white. Watch!
A heavy tramcar honking its gong slewed between.
Lost it. Curse your noisy pugnose. Feels locked out of it. Paradise and the peri. Always happening like that. The very moment. Girl in Eustace street hallway Monday was it settling her garter. Her friend covering the display of. *Esprit de corps*. Well, what are you gaping at? ...
Flicker, flicker: the laceflare of her hat in the sun: flicker, flick. (*U* 5: 130–40)

Bloom's pique suggests a cameraman where the tram has spoilt his shot, 'flicker, flicker [...] flicker, flick' suggesting both the shutter of a camera and the wavering of a film reel. Similarly, he experiences the clichéd parameters of female sexuality, whore and virgin, as film stills, possessing both 'that dirty bitch in that Spanish photo' (*U* 18: 564) and his 'splendid masterpiece

---

[37] Linda Williams, *Hard Core: Power, Pleasure and the 'Frenzy Of The Visible'* (London: Pandora, 1990), 38–41. Williams offers a compelling analysis of Muybridge's dissections of motion as proto-pornography, since contemporary responses to his lectures detected an inappropriate fascination with sexual difference. Similarly, when one lecture showed 'a series of pictures of female dancers pirouetting', an uneasy reviewer queried 'the propriety of exhibiting semi-nude figures to a promiscuous audience', Musser, *The Emergence of Cinema*, 56.

[38] William Caine managed to buy such stills and produce them in the House of Commons: *Hansard*, vol. 93 (6 May 1901), col. 756, and vol. 99 (5 August 1901), col. 1305. Working mutoscopes may be viewed in the National Museum of Film and Television, Bradford, the Museum of the Moving Image, London, the Brighton Museum and Art Gallery, Sussex, the Hove Museum and Art Gallery, in Victorian amusement arcades on the piers of Hastings, Brighton and Blackpool, and at the Mechanical Museum, Cliff House, San Francisco, and in all these the first frame of the picture is visible before you insert your penny.

in art colours' (*U* 4: 370), the *Photo-Bits* nymph.[39] Most pointedly, when the nymph steps down from her oakframe in 'Circe', she resembles the first frame of the mutoscope sequence springing into life at the turn of the handcrank.[40] Accordingly, Gerty is introduced in 'Nausicaa' in just such a tableau, holding an 'artistic' pose, 'as fair a specimen of winsome Irish girlhood as one could wish to see' (*U* 13: 80–1). Captured in freeze-frame before miraculous motion begins, the undertone of stasis is implied through her pallid marble loveliness. Like the National Museum statues which fascinate Bloom, Gerty has 'hands . . . of finely veined alabaster' (*U* 13: 89) to match 'The waxen pallor of her face . . . almost spiritual in its ivorylike purity' (*U* 13: 87–8) and 'her throat, so slim, so flawless, so beautifully moulded it seemed one an artist might have dreamed of' (*U* 13: 582–3). Playing Galatea to Bloom's Pygmalion, Joyce makes his heroine simulate the first frame of a mutoscope reel, perfectly still yet waiting for the penny to drop and the handcrank to turn.

Once Gerty is sure of the handcranking attentions of her audience, 'a telltale flush, delicate as the faintest rosebloom, crept into her cheeks' (*U* 13: 120–1). Making good use of the very prop in *What the Girls Did with Willie's Hat,* she removes and replaces her hat in a theatricalised gesture suggestive of the formulaic flirtatious preliminaries to striptease, and lifts her skirt 'a little but just enough' (*U* 13: 362) to show her 'wellturned ankle' (*U* 13: 168) in 'transparent stockings' (*U* 13: 426) and 'the bright steel buckles of her shoes' (*U* 13: 425). Gerty perfectly pitches her performance towards her audience, staging the kind of display Bloom, particularly susceptible to the mutoscope, might relish. For mutoscope advertisements boasted that not only did photographs come to life before one's eyes, one could slow down, speed up or stop the picture through varying the speed of the handcrank.[41] As one commentator enthusiastically noted,

---

[39] Joyce's perception that *Photo-Bits* and the mutoscope were affiliated erotic commodities is confirmed in an early draft of 'Nausicaa', where Bloom wonders 'a dream of well filled hose? Where was that? Picture I saw *Photo-Bits*?', and Joyce superscribes 'Mutoscope pictures: for men only' (*JJA* 13: 223).

[40] The mutoscopic promise of a picture coming to life was made explicit in the American Mutoscope and Biograph Company's 'Living Pictures' series, where in films like *The Birth of the Pearl* (American Mutoscope and Biograph Company, 1901), a naked model posed as Botticelli's Venus. A film still from 'Birth of the Pearl' is printed in Kemp R. Niver and Bebe Bergsten, *Biograph Bulletins 1896–1908* (Los Angeles: Locare Research Group, 1971), 57.

[41] See Musser, *Emergence of Cinema*, 176; International Mutoscope Syndicate, *The Art of Movement*, 31. Many ingenious and educational uses were suggested for the new invention: a surgeon wondered if 'the various phases of an operation from the first cut of the knife' could be shown to medical students on the mutoscope, a scheme to give 'copies of all interesting subjects to the British Museum so that people of a hundred, nay, a thousand years hence may see them by merely turning a handle' was proposed, and *Punch* ran a cartoon showing 'A Mutoscope of the Pictures in the Royal Academy for the use of Visitors in a Hurry'. See 'The Cinematograph in Surgery', *Chambers Journal*, 26 August 1899; 'The Mutoscope', *Pearson's Magazine*, February 1899; *Punch*, 10 May 1899. Gerty might have

The spectator is absolute master of the revolution, and if a detail interests him particularly, he can arrest it and examine the latter at leisure. In a subject that represents a fencing bout, for example, he can, at any given moment, analyse the thrust if he is desirous of seeing how it was executed.[42]

Not all spectators were so innocent, and it might safely be assumed that Bloom is the sort of mutoscope customer guilty of hunting for those frames in a sequence which most revealed the actress' body. Gerty imitates the mutoscope's unique mechanics of viewing, striking poses which dissect her gradual gestures of disclosure to provide opportunities for uninterrupted scrutiny, from her initial pose 'gazing far away into the distance' (*U* 13: 80) to other moments where she 'gazed out towards the distant sea' (*U* 13: 406) or, lame, sits perfectly still showing off her 'graceful beautifully shaped legs' (*U* 13: 698) whilst her companions 'run like rossies' (*U* 13: 688). Even her interior monologue is suggestively punctuated by 'stills'; she recalls how when Reggie Wylie embraced her, she adopted the pose of the lovely statue or freeze frame, turning 'white to the very lips' (*U* 13: 202–3); she imagines herself in studied stage-lit picturesque, 'mus[ing] by the dying embers in a brown study without the lamp because she hated two lights' (*U* 13: 294); or, incongruously, in the outside privy admiring her 'arms that were white and soft' (*U* 13: 341) in imitation of the grocer's almanac tableau of 'oldtime chivalry' (*U* 13: 335). These struck poses, inviting the admiration of an onlooker, bring to life the mutoscope's promise to 'arrest and examine at leisure' its enticing images.

Gerty's command of the oscillation between motion and stasis which the mutoscope so profitably permitted is, however, most obvious at the climax of her performance. As she watches Bloom's handcranking ('his hands and face were working and a tremour went over her', *U* 13: 694–5), she leans back to display her legs 'supply soft and delicately rounded' (*U* 13: 699) as 'she seemed to hear the panting of his heart, his hoarse breathing' (*U* 13: 699–700). As John Hagan has noted, citing films like *It's A Shame to Take the Money* (American Mutoscope and Biograph Company, 1901), in which a bootblack finds a glimpse of his customer's ankle payment enough, women's legs and feet functioned as ubiquitous fetish objects.[43] In *Three Jolly Girls and the Fun they had with the Old Swing* (American Mutoscope and Biograph Company, 1897), where two girls take turns to

---

read in the February 1899 issue of *Pearson's Magazine* that, after consultation with the Vatican, Pope Leo XIII was also filmed blessing the faithful through the peephole in 1898, before the mutoscope's profane reputation was firmly established.

[42] *The New York Herald*, 1897, quoted in Musser, *Emergence of* Cinema, 151.

[43] John Hagan, 'Erotic Tendencies in Film 1900–1906', in *Cinema 1900/1906: An Analytical Study*, ed. Roger Holman (Brussels: International Federation of Film Archives, 1982), 234–5.

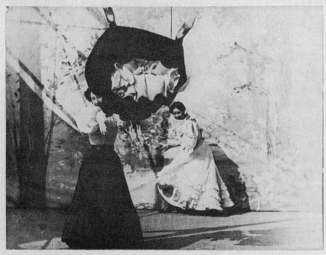

Figure 6 An image from Kemp R. Niver and Bebe Bergsten, *Biograph Bulletins 1896–1908* (Los Angeles: Locare Research Group, 1971), 24.

push a third towards the camera, the predictable display of stocking tops and frilly drawers offers a particularly close approximation to what Gerty puts on show. The film was particularly condemned for the suggestive motion towards the camera.

However, it is not only what Bloom sees on Sandymount Strand, but, crucially, how Joyce writes what he sees that so closely coincides with mutoscope erotica:

And she saw a long Roman candle going up over the trees, up, up, and, in the tense hush, they were all breathless with excitement as it went higher and higher and she had to lean back more and more to look up after it, high, high, almost out of sight, and her face was suffused with a divine, an entrancing blush from straining back and he could see her other things too, nainsook knickers, the fabric that caresses the skin . . . and she let him and she saw that he saw and then it went so high it went out of sight a moment and she was trembling in every limb from being bent so far back that he had a full view high above her knee where no-one not even on the swing or wading and she wasn't ashamed and he wasn't either to look in that immodest way like that because he couldn't resist the sight of the wondrous revealment half offered like those skirtdancers behaving so immodest before gentlemen looking and he kept on looking, looking. (*U* 13: 720–33)

As Gerty builds up to this emphatically mutoscopic moment, her coloured narrative simulates the salacious slowing down of the mutoscope reel and the deconstruction of movement into a series of photographs. The staccato, dissected quality of her exhibitionism is implied through the breathless repetition of words of motion, implying the gradual, drawn out suspension of time protracted over two pages. Joyce writes the firework display not in real time but rather in 'reel time', in mutoscope slow motion and freeze frame. In the fantasy world of mutoscopes, the titillating spectacle Gerty offers was the viewer's reward, slowed down to a series of stills to allow the viewer to savour the actress 'lean[ing] back more and more'. 'Nausicaa' conforms so closely to these scenarios that it could almost be filmed: *A Saucy Fireworks Display* (American Mutoscope and Biograph Company, 1904).

III

The meticulous precision of Joyce's use of the mutoscope as a context for Gerty's performance does not, however, end with the way Bloom's masturbation and Gerty's slow, stop-start revelation of her frilly bloomers mimic the conventions of contemporary erotic films. Intriguingly, Joyce's appropriation of the specific visual dynamics of such films is filtered through

'Nausicaa' to foreground that most troubling and fascinating of the chapter's questions, the extent of Gerty's complicity. 'Nausicaa', as Fritz Senn notes, is a 'chapter of glances' and, in this most intensely visual of chapters, the issue of the improper knowledge and collusion that so differentiates Gerty from the 'young person' of social purity propaganda is explored through the politics of her looks.[44] After Gerty's coloured narrative comes to its climax, she telegraphs her 'innocence' to Bloom through a series of glances which supposedly proclaim her reluctance:

She glanced at him as she bent forward quickly, a pathetic little glance of piteous protest, of shy reproach under which he coloured like a girl. He was leaning back against the rock behind. Leopold Bloom (for it is he) stands silent, with bowed head before those young guileless eyes. What a brute he had been! At it again? A fair unsullied soul had called to him and, wretch that he was, how had he answered? An utter cad he had been! He of all men! But there was an infinite store of mercy in those eyes, for him too a word of pardon even though he had erred and sinned and wandered. Should a girl tell? No, a thousand times no. (*U* 13: 741–50)

Such glances of 'piteous protest, of shy reproach' from 'young guileless eyes' capable, nonetheless, of 'an infinite store of mercy' are the glances of the 'young person', violated and betrayed. They are, however, also part of a performance which simultaneously pastiches moralising discourses and closely accords with the kinds of titilating, collusive glances to camera which helped to provide mutoscope films with their frisson, as Bloom remembers:

Mutoscope pictures on Capel street: for men only. Peeping Tom. Willy's hat and what the girls did with it. Do they snapshot those girls, or is it all a fake? (*U* 13: 795)

Bloom is naïvely preoccupied by the enigma posed by the dramas of 'accidental' revelation on which mutoscope films commonly relied. His understanding of 'snapshot' either situates the camera as a concealed and surreptitious 'peeping tom', catching women unawares, or explains the films as deliberately staged 'fakes', where actresses feign their surprise. As Bloom suspects, mutoscope films heavily promoted the illusion that their actresses were caught by a concealed 'candid camera'. Titles such as *How the Girls Were Caught Bathing, Inside a Ladies Swimming Bath* and *Not a Man in Sight – or so the Girls Thought* suggested male infiltration of a female private space where women were (usually) free to disport themselves

[44] Fritz Senn, 'Nausicaa', in *James Joyce's 'Ulysses': Critical Essays*, ed. Clive Hart and David Hayman (Berkeley: University of California Press, 1974), 310.

undisturbed.[45] To explore the visual dynamics of such films in greater depth is to perceive how Joyce well understood this illusion, and appropriates it in 'Nausicaa' to foreground the troubling, provocative question of his 'young person's' agency in the process of her own sexual commodification.

As Tom Gunning has suggested, a distinct genre of 'through the keyhole' films emerged at the turn of the century, in response to the actual situation of mutoscope spectators, bent double at the peephole.[46] Films like *Peeping Tom*, *As Seen Through a Telescope* (George W. Smith, 1900) and *Ce que je vois de mon sixième* (Zecca, 1901) showed a male character peering at a woman through a keyhole or telescope, before cutting to what the character sees, signalled by a circular or keyhole shaped matte.[47] These 'proxy voyeur' films insisted that the erotic spectacle was accidentally given and opportunistically gathered, or, as Bloom would put it, procured by 'snapshot' rather than staged 'fake'. They played upon an illusion of spectator invulnerability by implicitly plotting the spectator into the drama as a 'peeping tom' secretly watching women supposedly unable to protest against, or return the look which surveyed them.

Bloom, however, is partly unconvinced by this fiction in 'Nausicaa', and is instead preoccupied with his own status as a 'sight':

Saw something in me. Wonder what...Ought to attend to my appearance my age. Didn't let her see me in profile. Still, you never know. Pretty girls and ugly men marrying. (*U* 13: 833–7)

His sensitivity is continued in the observation 'See ourselves as others see us. So long as women don't mock what matter?' (*U* 13: 1058–9). His anxieties seem initially curious in the context of Christian Metz's distinction between theatrical voyeurism, 'one which thrives on a reciprocity of seeing and being seen', and cinematic voyeurism, where 'the filmic spectacle, the object seen, is more radically ignorant of its spectator, since he is not there, than the theatrical spectacle can ever be'.[48] In other words, cinema imposes a distance between film space and spectator space, between screen and auditorium which is absent from the more intimate play of exhibitionism

---

[45] William Caine, *Hansard*, vol. 99 (5 August 1901), col. 1308. Caine listed several hundred such titles, and argued 'These titles were not sells: the pictures thoroughly justified the titles.'

[46] Tom Gunning, 'Symposium Session 3', in *Cinema 1900/1906*, ed. Holman, 57.

[47] See Noel Burch, *Life to those Shadows*, translated and edited by Ben Brewster (Berkeley: University of California Press, 1990), 222; Judith Mayne, *The Woman at the Keyhole: Feminism and Women's Cinema* (Bloomington: Indiana University Press, 1990), 169–70 for discussions of the 'keyhole' genre.

[48] Metz quoted in Miriam Hansen, *Babel and Babylon: Spectatorship in American Silent Cinema* (Cambridge: Harvard University Press, 1991), 35.

and voyeurism in the theatre. Such a construction of cinematic spectatorship similarly informs Laura Mulvey's influential account of voyeurism,
where 'the extreme contrast between the darkness of the auditorium and
the brilliance of the screen' facilitates the controlling and curious gaze of
male scopophilia.[49] However, both Metz and Mulvey's understanding of
a cinema spectator invisible in a darkened auditorium, anonymous in a
crowd and therefore invulnerable fails to account for the viewer glued to
the peephole of a mutoscope. In contrast, such a viewer is dangerously
overexposed:

I have just glued my ear to the door and looked through a keyhole. I am all alone.
All of a sudden, I hear footsteps in the hall. Someone is looking at me. What does
this mean?[50]

Mutoscope 'proxy voyeur' films like *Peeping Tom* dramatised this sense
of exposure by rupturing the illusion of invulnerability that their scenarios of concealment and secret infiltration of private space might be
expected to uphold. In countless knowing allusions to the mutoscope's
'naughty' reputation, the 'proxy voyeur' on screen in such films is seldom
permitted to look on undisturbed. Invariably, the 'punchline' of such films
devolves upon his discovery and punishment. *Peeping Tom* is exemplary:
there, a troupe of semi-naked girls rush over to one side of the screen to
rout the discovered voyeur peering through a window.[51] As the mutoscope
viewer is implicitly plotted into the drama, so the transformation of the
'peeping tom' on the flickercards from spectator to spectacle implies that
the threat of a similar role reversal stands over the voyeur cranking the
handle.

The mutoscope, then, provided a very different kind of spectatorship
to that on offer in the darkened space of the projected cinema. This paranoid condition of mutoscope voyeurism, where the peeping tom watching
through the keyhole occupied a precarious position of potential exposure,
provides a particularly appropriate context for the relationship between

[49] Laura Mulvey, 'Visual Pleasure and Narrative Cinema', *Screen* 16: 3 (Autumn 1975), 14.
[50] Jean-Paul Sartre, *Being and Nothingness*, quoted in Norman Denzin, *The Cinematic Society: The Voyeur's Gaze* (London: Sage Publications, 1995), 42.
[51] For analysis of the ubiquity of the punishment scenario in 'keyhole' films, see Judith Mayne, *The Woman at the Keyhole*, 178. An excellent example of such a film is also available online through the Library of Congress website – http://www.loc.gov/. In 'Mr Jack in the Dressing Room', Mr Jack ogles several scantily clad showgirls, only to be discovered in the closing frames by his wife, dressed in a Salvation Army bonnet, who belabours him about the head with her umbrella. The Library of Congress has also placed 212 other mutoscope films from its Paper Print collection on its website. To browse them, key in 'mutoscope' under a basic keyword search of the catalogue.

spectator and spectacle in 'Nausicaa'. Although Gerty MacDowell is introduced as a passive 'specimen' for Bloom's gaze, and although she holds a
pose 'lost in thought, gazing far away into the distance' (*U* 13: 79–80), pretending, like the mutoscope actresses, that there is not a man in sight, she
conceals the threat implicit in her own returned looks behind the cinematic
fantasy outlined above of the invisible voyeur and his oblivious victim. In
what appears to be a paradigmatic enactment of Laura Mulvey's well-known
argument that women in classic Hollywood cinema are treated as objects of
a male controlling and curious gaze, Gerty insists that 'he was eyeing her as a
snake eyes its prey' (*U* 13: 517). However, Gerty's apparent conformity to
the gendered role of the passively surveyed female is disingenuous, for she
uses the identity of 'specimen' to disguise her own reciprocal voyeurism.
She monitors her audience through a constant battery of glances concealed
behind a pretence of 'unconscious loveliness', for example appearing to
cast a picturesque glance out to sea whilst confirming 'Yes, it was her he
was looking at, and there was meaning in his look' (*U* 13: 411–12). This
technique of masking her glances towards Bloom behind her good looks
culminates when she removes her hat to display 'a prettier, a daintier head
of nutbrown tresses' and replaces it 'so that she could see from underneath
the brim' (*U* 13: 509–15). Fritz Senn may well characterise 'Nausicaa' as
a 'chapter of glances', but Gerty, claiming she 'could see without looking
that he never took his eyes off of her' (*U* 13: 495–6), asserts that there are
(at least) two kinds of 'glance' in play, Bloom's open and desirous 'looking'
and her own subversive, secretive 'seeing'.[52]

The demarcation of the gendered roles of spectacle and spectator is
perhaps most disconcertingly assaulted in one of the passages explicitly
objected to by the New York Society for the Suppression of Vice:

Bertha Supple told her once in dead secret and made her swear she'd never about
the gentleman lodger that was staying with them out of the Congested Districts
Board that had pictures cut out of papers of those skirtdancers and highkickers
and she said that he used to do something not very nice that you could imagine
sometimes in the bed (*U* 13: 701–5).[53]

With the introduction of Bertha Supple's lodger, any remaining distinction
between watcher and watched collapses. The gentleman lodger, masturbating over pictures of highkickers, indulges in the kind of manual pleasures which the mutoscope's handcrank mechanics metaphorically staged.

---

[52] Senn, 'Nausicaa', 310.
[53] For this and the other passages in 'Nausicaa' objected to by the New York Society for the Suppression
of Vice, see 'Appendix: The Censor's *Ulysses*', Vanderham, *James Joyce and Censorship*, 178–83.

Meanwhile, his absorption in his own spectatorship makes him vulnerable to that 'step in the hallway' that Sartre described as the scourge of the
voyeur bent double at the keyhole. The lodger in turn becomes the victim
of a female, retaliatory spectatorship when Bertha peers through the keyhole of his bedroom, and later tells Gerty what she saw. Like 'Nausicaa'
itself, the Supple scenario could also be filmed as a short mutoscope film,
How Bertha Caught the Lodger Unawares (James Joyce, 1904), showing a
young woman creeping stealthily to a door, peeping through it, and then,
via a keyhole shaped matte, cutting to what she sees. However, Joyce's film
would throw into confusion those gendered boundaries of public and private space which films like *Peeping Tom*, showing a man peering into a
woman's boudoir, enforced. Joyce stages an alternative form of mutoscope
spectatorship, where his voyeur performs a doubled transgression, firstly by
inverting the model of female spectacle and male spectator, and secondly
by occupying that space at the keyhole more commonly assigned to a man.

The mutoscope facilitated this kind of female infiltration of designated
'men only' space.[54] As Charles Musser notes, most parlours were equally
open to both men and women, and mutoscope films showing bodybuilder
Eugene Sandow clad only in a fig leaf and flexing his muscles, whilst presumably aimed at a heterosexual male audience interested in physical culture, were potentially also of considerable erotic interest to some female
spectators.[55] Whilst such films did occasionally offer proscribed sights of
semi-naked male bodies, more importantly mutoscopes made previously
'men only' pleasures accessible to curious women who could take Bertha
Supple's place at the keyhole. For, as Joyce carefully makes clear, Bertha's
pleasure is supplied not only by the sight of her lodger, but by the sight
of what arouses him, the 'pictures cut out of papers of those skirtdancers
and highkickers' (*U* 13: 704). Like Bloom in 'Wandering Rocks', who reads
Sweets of Sin imagining Molly reading, Bertha too savours pornography over
the shoulder of its designated consumer. Similarly, Gerty yearns to infiltrate
a proscribed male world via the transgressive look over the shoulder of a
male consumer of erotic spectacle. Her familiarity with 'those skirtdancers
behaving so immodest before gentlemen looking' (*U* 13: 732–3) and 'the
fallen women off the accommodation walk beside the Dodder that went
with the soldiers' (*U* 13: 661–3) undercuts her insistence that 'From everything in the least indelicate her finebred nature instinctively recoiled'

---

[54] Musser, *Emergence of Cinema*, 78.
[55] *Ibid.*, 184. One might similarly speculate that images of Sandow were also popular with homosexual
men.

(*U* 13: 660–1). In a twist on the Supple scenario, what Gerty sees over Bloom's shoulder is herself, in the mask of the 'skirtdancer' of popular pornography: 'Gerty could see without looking that he never took his eyes off of her' (*U* 13: 495–6). She occupies two seemingly irreconcilable positions simultaneously: the actress is also a peeping tom.

The complications manifest in Gerty's subtension of these two roles were particularly encouraged by what Tom Gunning has designated 'the cinema of attraction', a particular aesthetic which dominated the first decade of film development:

Contrasted to the voyeuristic aspect of narrative cinema analysed by Christian Metz, this is an exhibitionist cinema. From comedians smirking at the camera, to the constant bowings and gesturings of conjurers in magic films, this is a cinema that displays its visibility, willing to rupture a self-enclosed fictional world for the chance to solicit the attention of the spectator.[56]

Gunning argues that this aesthetic of confrontation partly derived from the practice of exhibiting early films as one item in a vaudeville entertainment, sandwiched in amid 'star turns', comic songs and magic tricks.[57] As music-hall stars directly addressed the audience, often encouraging sing-alongs and heckling, so actors in early films similarly gestured towards their viewers. Early cinema's connection to vaudeville was particularly pronounced in Ireland, where, until Joyce opened the Cinematograph Volta in 1909, Dublin was the only capital in Europe to lack a permanent purpose-built picture house.[58] The direct look towards the camera did not become taboo until the late 1900s, when in 1909, the Selig Polyscope Company officially prohibited it.[59] This development contextualises the glances Gerty gives at the climax of her performance, when, rather than concealing her looks behind the conventions of feminine scopic modesty, she finally meets Bloom's gaze: 'She looked at him a moment, meeting his glance, and a light broke in upon her. Whitehot passion was in that face, passion silent as the grave, and it had made her his' (*U* 13: 690–2). The breathless, aroused or, as Joyce

---

[56] Tom Gunning, 'The Cinema of Attraction: Early Film, its Spectator and the Avant-Garde', *Wide Angle* 8: 3–4 (Fall 1986), 68.

[57] Gunning, 'The Cinema of Attraction', 5.

[58] Projected films in Dublin were shown at Dan Lowrey's Star of Erin Theatre of Varieties, later the Empire Palace Theatre, and the first run of pictures in January 1897 'eclipsed' the accompanying music-hall acts. See Kevin Rockett, Luke Gibbons and John Hill, *Cinema and Ireland* (London: Routledge, 1988), 3–5. A playbill for a performance at the Empire Palace in 1903 promised Marie Kendall, a comic turn and a film showing the Gordon Bennett Cup motor race (featured in 'After the Race'). Playbill shown by Bob Monks, 'Irish Film Making – the Hidden Years'.

[59] Burch, 'Life to those Shadows', 214.

put it, 'tumescent' prose appears to signal that Gerty has lost control of her masquerade, that she is at last 'wild, untrammelled, free' (*U* 13: 673).[60]

This spectacle of Gerty's supposed loss of inhibitions, however, simultaneously communicates the reciprocal glance from performer to audience which formed the central 'attraction' of many early films exhibiting a woman's body. For instance, the comic film *Photographing a Female Crook* (American Mutoscope and Biograph Company, 1904) moves towards the pursuit and capture of the subject's look to camera. A woman is restrained by two policemen as the camera dollies in towards her, and resists by squinting, pulling faces and twisting her head away. The film ends as she looks directly into the lens and acknowledges her defeat by bursting into tears. Here, as Judith Mayne observes, what is being exhibited is the woman's femininity, in contrast to the policemen and the presumed male agency of the camera: her final capitulation to the lens' scrutiny is the climax of the film.[61] This emphasis upon the desirability of the woman's look into the lens unsurprisingly crosses over into early erotic films. In *Le Coucher de la mariée* (Pathé, 1904), the bride addresses her wedding-night striptease not towards her new husband, a proxy voyeur peering out from behind a dressing-screen, but to the camera, winking, nodding and smiling into the lens.[62] This overt look is present in many other erotic films where the performer participates in staging herself as spectacle. For instance, in *Annabelle Butterfly Dance* and *Annabelle Serpentine Dance* (American Mutograph and Biograph Company, 1900), a woman swirls the voluminous swathes of her costume in a fashion which both conceals and reveals her body, whilst glancing coquettishly towards the camera. In *Trapeze Disrobing Act* (Thomas Edison, 1901), two men seated in a theatre box watch a woman on a trapeze strip, whilst her looks oscillate between the proxy voyeurs and the camera.[63] The prevalence of such come-hither glances to camera in these early erotic films suggests that Gerty's sudden capitulation to Bloom's 'burning gaze' is not, as it may first appear, an impulsive shrugging aside of inhibition, but rather, the climax of her skilled masquerade.

Intriguingly, Gerty's 'looks to camera' fall between the two polarities of coercion and complicity exemplified in 'Photographing a Female Crook' and '*Le Coucher de la mariée*'. For Gerty masks her desire to solicit Bloom's

---

[60] According to Joyce's Gorman-Gilbert schema for *Ulysses*, 'Nausicaa's' 'Technic' was 'Tumescence, detumescence'. See Richard Ellmann, *Ulysses on the Liffey* (London: Faber and Faber, 1974), 189.
[61] See Judith Mayne, *Woman At The Keyhole*, 163–5, for discussion and stills of *Photographing a Female Crook*.
[62] See Burch, 'Life to those Shadows', 214–15, for discussion and stills of *The Bride Retires*.
[63] Judith Mayne, *Woman at the Keyhole*, 169–70.

attention behind the suggestion that her looks, at first covert, later overt, are drawn from her against her will. Thus, after she has met Bloom's glance, she endeavours to disguise her exhibitionist pleasure behind a masquerade of reluctance, giving Bloom 'a pathetic little glance of piteous protest, of shy reproach' which telegraphs the accusation 'What a brute he had been!' (*U* 13: 742, 746). Gerty constitutes herself as a 'fair unsullied soul' (*U* 13: 746) who, like the female crook, has capitulated to the force of a masculine scopic drive she finds herself powerless to withstand. Whilst Gerty's 'reluctance' is obviously compromised, she also falls short of the unashamed blatancy of the bride's arch nods, winks and grins to camera. Constance Balides' study of 'the cinema of attraction' focuses on a body of early erotic films which mediate between these two extremes, and thus provide the closest parallel for Gerty's performance. Importantly, these films sexualised women's bodies in the context of everyday public space. Unlike films such as *Trapeze Disrobing Act* and *Annabelle Serpentine Dance*, they did not rely upon the pretext of a theatrical situation to supply a reason for exposure. Rather, the public visibility of women in the everyday provided sufficient narrative justification for the 'accidental' disclosure of their bodies.

Films Balides places in this category include *A Windy Day on the Roof* (American Mutoscope and Biograph Company, 1904), where a gust of wind blowing up the skirt of a woman hanging laundry on the roof of her tenement building permits a house painter a good look up her skirt, *Pull Down the Curtains, Susie* (American Mutoscope and Biograph Company, 1904), where a young woman undresses in front of a window, apparently unaware she can be seen by men passing on the street outside, and *What Happened on 23rd Street, New York City* (1902), where a woman finds her skirts blown up when she passes a subway grate. These women are engaged in mundane activities – hanging out washing, getting changed, walking down the street – when they are transformed into erotic spectacles in the public sphere.[64] In 'Nausicaa' too, the public space of Sandymount Strand, the 'women's work' of minding children, and the more-or-less everyday activity of watching a fireworks display provides the stage and pretext for the display of Gerty's body. Furthermore, to sustain the naturalist effect, women in this 'everyday' cinema of attractions reserve their looks to camera

---

[64] See Constance Balides, 'Scenarios of exposure: Women in the cinema of attractions', *Screen* 34: 1 (Spring 1993), 19–37 for stills and discussions of *A Windy Day on the Roof* and *What Happened on 23rd Street, New York City*, and Judith Mayne, 'Uncovering the Female Body', in *Before Hollywood: Turn of the Century American Film*, ed. John Fell (New York: Hudson Hills Press, 1987), 234 for stills and discussion of *Pull Down the Curtains, Susie*.

or proxy voyeur until the final frames of the film. When the woman hanging out laundry discovers the painter looking up her skirt, she throws a bucket of water over him; when Susie starts to strip further than her underwear, she realises her exposure and hurriedly pulls down the curtain; when the woman on 23rd Street finds her skirts blown round her thighs, she screams, tries (inefficiently) to hold them down, and casts an accusatory look to camera. Each woman directs what approximates to Gerty's 'glance of piteous protest, of shy reproach' towards her voyeur, a glance which subtends both the look expressing her coercion given by the heroine of *Photographing a Female Crook*, and that glance of collusion bestowed by more 'theatrical' stripteasers.

These films of everyday exposure thus masked the choreographed conditions of their production behind a drama of fortuitous display. Here, the look towards the voyeur, which according to Tom Gunning solicits the audience's gaze, foregrounds the question of the spectacle's complicity in the spectator's desire. An advertisement for *What Happened on 23rd Street* addresses the centrality of this issue:

As our picture was being made, a young man escorting a young lady comes into view and walks slowly along until they stand directly over the air shaft. The young lady's skirts are raised to, you might say, an almost unreasonable height, *greatly to her horror.*[65]

The actress is supposedly exonerated from responsibility, yet her pantomimic expressions of 'horror', directed towards the camera and drawing attention to the spectacle, suggests otherwise. The look into the camera has a specialised resonance in erotic films, for it responds to Bloom's query 'Do they snapshot those girls or is it all a fake?' by announcing the actress' collusion in presenting herself as an alluring sight. Gerty's returned look to Bloom in the closing frames of her performance thus imitates the collusive glance to camera of the mutoscope heroine in these scenarios of everyday life, who reveals her mutual longing along with her body. This doubled act of disclosure places the unmasking of desire previously concealed beneath the proprieties of feminine modesty alongside the conventional striptease, making Gerty's revelation of her body a physical metaphor for a psychological process.

What Gerty's suddenly overt glance to camera thus appears to stage is a revelation of the real Gerty behind the mask, an 'exposure' of the sexual longing she has, until this point, attempted to conceal. Such a revelation

[65] Advertising synopsis quoted in Balides, 'Scenarios of exposure', 24. Italics added.

clearly appeals to Bloom, and unleashes a series of predictable fantasies: 'Virgins go mad in the end I suppose' (*U* 13: 781), 'Yours for the asking. Because they want it themselves. Their natural craving' (*U* 13: 790–1), 'Don't want it they throw it at you' (*U* 13: 792). The way a reading of Gerty's glance as evidence of her 'natural craving' concurs with these kinds of fantasies is suspicious, since little in Gerty's performance can be described as 'natural'. Indeed, Gerty's sudden capitulation to a desire she can no longer withstand seems theatricalised, not so much unwittingly exposed as self-consciously *exhibited*. If there is a real Gerty somewhere behind the artful pose, it would seem that this 'real self' is not so much the heroine of pornographic fantasy, who finally casts off her inhibitions to respond to the desire of a male consumer, as a shrewd young woman, painfully conscious of her precarious economic situation and therefore determined to affiliate herself to a particularly lucrative form of sexual commodification. Like the eyebrowleine, Queen of Ointments and other products Gerty assimilates in order to promote herself as a contemporary icon of alluring femininity, the mutoscope and the strategies of display it introduced is one of Gerty's props. Her impersonation of the mutoscope heroine in the 'cinema of attraction' through her self-conscious glances to camera hints at her mastery of her role, indicating that her masquerade is the pragmatic response of a skilled performer and her final glance of desirous collusion her masterstroke. By placing her image rather than her body on the market, by imitating successful strategies of mutoscope display, Gerty reproduces modernity's commodification of the visible and shrewdly allies herself with the perfect product. Above all, her artful deployment of her glances, so closely coinciding with contemporary erotica, attests not just to her complicity but to her control of her performance, emphasising an agency which pointedly differentiates her from the innocent, bashful 'young person' in need of social purity protection.

IV

The mutoscope, therefore, is a far more apposite and accurate model for Gerty MacDowell's strategies of sexual display than *The Lamplighter*, from which Joyce clearly derives Gerty's saccharine coloured narrative. 'Nausicaa's' piquancy stems from the collision of these two intertexts. Joyce's heroine attempts to mask her improper knowledge and indecorous motivations behind the 'young person' identity championed in Maria Cummins' conduct novel, yet her efforts are disrupted by her dangerous, and to Bloom immediately recognisable proximity to popular erotica. Through this ironic and ingenious competition of intertexts, Joyce argues for the obsolescence of the 'young person' archetype social purists so stridently sought to protect. For 'Nausicaa' oscillates between the outdated, the redundant, the clichéd *Lamplighter*, a byword for mid-Victorian sentimentality for decades, and the new, technologically innovative mutoscope, a cultural artefact standing at the threshold of a new century and signalling the arrival of a new representational phenomenon, cinema. Gerty's masquerade as 'a fair unsullied soul' with 'young guileless eyes' (*U* 13: 745–6), a belated 'young person' innocent of the strategies of calculated, profitable sexual display, is radically undercut by her unmistakeably accurate appropriation of the methods, conventions and techniques of sexual exhibition perfected in mutoscope films. Drafting 'Nausicaa' as *Ulysses* lurched towards that catastrophic conflict with social purists which would outlaw not only *The Little Review* but the novel itself from the English-speaking world, Joyce daringly ridiculed the vice crusaders' pretensions to protect a figment of a bygone cultural imagination by, as Jane Heap astutely observed, 'printing the thoughts in a young girl's mind'.

Joyce's anticipatory ridicule of reformers like the New York Society for the Suppression of Vice is typically provocative in the light of the centrality of the mutoscope to social purity's campaign against a popular culture it perceived as increasingly sexualised. As Edward Bristow notes, 'the diversions of the poor were obvious objects of scrutiny as potential sources of incivility and dissidence', and the bawdy, easily accessible mutoscope arcades, ubiquitous in seaside resorts, the larger cities and fairgrounds, were sitting targets for purity suppression.[66] In July 1897, within six months of the device's invention, Revd Frederick Bruce Russell of the New York Society for the Suppression of Vice personally raided a number of Coney Island mutoscope parlours in order to halt the showing of the very film Bloom remembers, *What the Girls Did With Willie's Hat*.[67] Meanwhile in Britain, *The Vigilance Record* regularly reported on its crusade against the mutoscope. Samuel Smith MP addressed the Sixteenth Annual Conference of the National Vigilance Association in June 1901 to insist that 'unless we can put down vile mutoscope and other pictures, the prospects before our country are dark indeed'.[68] The journal carried one typical account of Dublin White Cross Vigilance Association proceedings against mutoscope films in Fanning's Irish–American Marionett Company on Great Britain Street, Dublin:

---

[66] Bristow, *Vice and Vigilance: Purity Movements in Britain since 1700* (Dublin: Gill and Macmillan, 1977), 201.
[67] Musser, *Emergence of Cinema*, 189.   [68] *The Vigilance Record*, June 1901, 1.

Several of the pictures were obscene. They were calculated to debauch and demoralise the youth of the city. They were intended to be most pernicious in their sequence. They offended against purity and chastity, and the man who said they were not did not know the meaning of the English language, and the man who brought them to Dublin did not understand the temperament of the Dublin people. This might be an illustration for London or any other part of England, but not for Ireland. It was a most loathsome exhibition. It did not suit the temperament of this country at all.[69]

Notwithstanding the insistence that the mutoscope was particularly abhorrent in Dublin, this kind of unease was articulated by social purity prosecutors in magistrates' courts from Southend-on-Sea to Blackpool throughout the 1900s, and soon these individual prosecutions flourished into a full-blown purity campaign. Together with two fellow purity MPs Robert Corfe and William Caine, Smith coordinated a letter-writing campaign to *The Times* and repeatedly interrogated the Home Secretary about mutoscopes, prompting 'A Patron of the mutoscope' in *The British Journal of Photography* to protest 'We cannot help wondering how these people acquire their altogether abnormal scent for the improper.'[70] Such sustained social purity anxiety over mutoscopes could, however, be traced to one primary source of disquiet: the loaded questions mutoscopes raised about the 'young person' as the implied consumer of the sexually provocative.

Mutoscopes, as we have seen, were relatively cheap and easily accessible, supplying entertainment for a penny a time. Their cheapness, ubiquity, associations with pleasure resorts and home in gaudy arcades made them 'calculated', as *The Vigilance Record*'s report from Dublin declared, 'to debauch and demoralise the youth of the city'. Accordingly, purity testimony repeatedly protested that mutoscope spectators were predominantly juvenile. One police raid on a parlour in the Brompton Road, Kensington in May 1902 uncovered '80 girls and young men', despite the clear labels 'For Gentlemen Only' on the walls.[71] Mutoscope parlours profited from 'holiday pennies from Sunday School treats', despite protests that 'far better for children is a day in God's green fields than at some seaside place or holiday centre that is planted thick with penny illustrated guides to

---

[69] 'Mutoscopic Pictures – Police Prosecution', *The Vigilance Record*, January 1903, 8.
[70] For examples, see 'Demoralising Moving Pictures', *The Times*, 1 August 1899; 'Incentives to Vice', *The Times*, 1 June 1901. House of Commons Debates, *Hansard* vol. 75 (13 July 1900), col. 1539–1546; vol. 99 (5 August 1901), col. 1327–34. 'A Patron of the Mutoscope', *The British Journal of Photography*, 15 August 1901.
[71] 'Indecent Pictures in Mutoscopes', *The Vigilance Record*, May 1902, 39. Similarly, reported examples of the age of mutoscope viewers during 1899–1900 gave fifteen to twenty at Folkestone in Kent, twelve to fifteen at Rhyl in North Wales and ten to fifteen in 'a Midland town'. See Brown and Anthony, *A Victorian Film Enterprise*, 96.

vice'.[72] Campaigning MPs continued the theme: for Samuel Smith, it was 'hardly possible to exaggerate the corruption of the young that comes from exhibiting, under strong light, nude female figures represented as living and moving', for Robert Corfe, 'mutoscopic outrages' awaited 'the young children of the nation directly school is over', for William Caine 'every day tens of thousands of young people were being polluted and degraded', since parlours were overrun by 'hundreds of young lads and lasses looking at these machines and roaring with laughter'.[73]

The mutoscope thus unleashed a complex network of anxieties about the policing and protection of children and adolescents. One National Vigilance Association purity pamphlet, *The Dangers of False Prudery*, devoted a whole chapter to 'The Cinematograph, the mutoscope and Kindred Perils', explicating the several interconnected arguments for why the mutoscope was a 'trap for the young and the innocent'.[74] Firstly, the parlours themselves attracted undesirables, men who would 'make acquaintance' with a young girl by 'recommending to her a particular picture, at the same time dropping in the money himself'.[75] Pointing out that it 'depended on the girl's own moral code what results', the author predicted 'case after case where girls have gone away with Chinamen of their own accord' as a direct result of mutoscope watching.[76] Mutoscopic seductions were not always so blatant, however. Films like *What Happened when she was Asleep*, showing a man stealing into the bedroom of a sleeping woman, lifting up her skirt and removing her garter could have a devastating effect on 'a boy and his girl companion. Isn't it almost sufficient to encourage him to go and do likewise to her?'[77] More pernicious still were suggestive mutoscope titles and films which cut off shortly before the final revelation, providing the young with 'unwholesome stimuli', since 'an unchecked imagination is a dangerous plaything'.[78] Behind these arguments one can sense a fundamental unease permeating social purity. If the 'young person' needed so much protection, perhaps she was not as pure as she seemed? The girls in these scenarios were all, as purists admitted, in mutoscope parlours of their own accord, watching racy films, flirting with boys, indulging in innuendo and sexual fantasy, even allowing themselves to be picked up by disreputable men. It is the 'unchecked imagination', the 'moral code' of these young people which

[72] 'Incentives to Vice', *The Times*, 1 June 1901.
[73] Samuel Smith MP, 'Demoralising Moving Pictures', *The Times*, 3 August 1899; Robert Corfe MP, 'Incentives to Vice', *The Times*, 1 June 1901; William Caine MP, *Hansard*, vol. 99 (3 August 1901), col. 1304–6.
[74] Anon., *The Dangers of False Prudery* (London: National Vigilance Association, 1912), 44.
[75] *Ibid.*, 45.   [76] *Ibid.*, 46.   [77] *Ibid.*, 48.   [78] *Ibid.*, 53.

above all prompts the anxiety of these reformers. Underneath the rhetoric of innocence and pollution lies the fear that the modern 'young person' was no longer a vulnerable and virtuous Gertrude Flint, but instead a Gerty MacDowell, a collusive and sophisticated consumer of popular culture.

The mutoscope's notoriety as the premier Edwardian attraction for crowds of rowdy, sexually precocious young people thus discloses its significance to 'Nausicaa', demonstrating the provocativeness and the precision of Joyce's attempts to court a confrontation with the vice crusaders. Joyce places the deconstruction of the 'young person' at the heart of this most controversial of chapters, since his 'fair specimen of winsome Irish girlhood' is simultaneously actively collusive in a blatantly erotic popular culture. This technologically modern intertext exposes Gerty's relationship to the 'young person' as one fatally compromised, since her highkicking performance is identified with precisely the kind of cultural pollution organisations like the New York Society for the Suppression of Vice tried to protect girls like her from. Whilst Gerty MacDowell closely approximates to the stereotype of the 'young person', being young, lower class, female, virginal and ostensibly in danger from the advances of a predatory older man, the troubling question of her titillating and staged exhibitionism means she undercuts that ideal. The New York Society for the Suppression of Vice recognised this well, since it objected explicitly to passages which disclosed Gerty's improper knowledge, particularly the lines revealing her interest in the masturbatory activities of Bertha Supple's lodger and where Bloom speculates that Gerty recognises he was masturbating.[79] As they surely recognised, 'Nausicaa' blows open the social purity ideal of the pristine 'young person' by foregrounding the troubling question of Gerty's complicity in the vice that supposedly imperils her.

Joyce's bleakly compassionate vision thereby highlights what many social purists preferred to overlook; the economic factors compelling women and girls, if not towards actual prostitution, towards some form of barter of their sexuality for a subsistence. Accordingly, Gerty masters the strategies, conventions and choreography of sexual display in the mutoscope's 'cinema of attraction', prudently allying herself, in her desperate bid to gain some little economic security, with a particularly successful machine for the commodification of sexuality. For Gerty, the 'young person' identity is a façade, as a masquerade of virtuous innocence designed to disguise her expedient co-option of mutoscope erotica. 'Nausicaa' thus radically destabilises the vice societies' view of the 'young person' as *bovariste*, passively corrupted

[79] Vanderham, *James Joyce and Censorship*, 3.

by what she consumes. If the raucous, laughing girl-patrons of mutoscope parlours briefly glimpsed through the prism of solemn *Vigilance Record* reports seem worlds away from this stereotype, then so too does Gerty MacDowell. Her returned glance, which approximates so very closely to those seductive, challenging and deeply ambiguous glances towards the camera in films like *What Happened on 23rd Street*, plot the issue of Gerty's problematic agency at the heart of the chapter. As Joyce implies, Gerty does not need the kind of questionable 'protection' social purity groups attempted to impose, a protection easily interpreted as a covert form of control. Rather, it is Gerty who is in full control of her performance, allowing Bloom to look but not to touch, promoting yet containing desire, keeping him guessing. As the chapter closes, Bloom remains uneasy about what he has seen, disconcerted by that mutoscope enigma, the mystery of her returned glances and the collusive desire they may or may not suggest. No wonder he is puzzled: 'Do they snapshot those girls, or is it all a fake?'

CHAPTER 6

Vice crusading in Nighttown: 'Circe', brothel policing and the pornographies of reform

On 4 October, 1920, the New York Society for the Suppression of Vice initiated the proceedings against the 'Nausicaa' issue of *The Little Review* which would lead to *Ulysses'* proscription from the English-speaking world for the next twelve years. The journal's conviction for obscenity four months later was swiftly followed by the withdrawal of Joyce's American publisher Ben Huebsch:

A New York court having held that the publication of a part of the novel in *The Little Review* was a violation of the law, I am unwilling to publish the book unless some changes are made in the manuscript as submitted to me by Miss Weaver who represents Joyce in London. In view of your statement that Joyce declines absolutely to make any alterations, I must decline to publish it.[1]

Meanwhile in Paris, Joyce was nervously in the dark, increasingly suspicious of an ominous silence from New York and attempting to complete 'Circe' whilst 'reduced [...] to a state of helplessness in the face of many material difficulties' (*L* I: 146). His letters reveal two unremitting preoccupations; anxious speculations on events in New York ('Huebsch is crying off *Ulysses*' – *L* I: 144), and struggles to finish the fifteenth episode. 'Circe', 'half written' (*L* I: 144) in July 1920, was redrafted over and over again during the months leading to the February 1921 trial as Joyce waited for some word from New York. He wrote hopefully to defence lawyer John Quinn on 3 September with a chapter outline drawing attention to the two episodes preoccupying him, 'The cross represents the episode ['Nausicaa'] which *The Little Review* is publishing at present and the asterisk represents the chapter or episode ['Circe'] which I am engaged on' (*L* I: 145). Yet Joyce was still in ignorance of the precise direction of events across the Atlantic. As late as 29 September, he wondered 'Has no number of the *Little Review* appeared since May–June?' (*L* III: 23), apparently unaware that the confiscation of the July–August edition had halted serialisation. Instead, he seemed more concerned about

[1] Paul Vanderham, *James Joyce and Censorship: The Trials of Ulysses* (London: Macmillan, 1998), 44–8, 56.

the recent prosecution of one of his sources for 'Circe', the British soft porn magazine *Photo-Bits*, a longstanding target of purity hostility.[2]

These uncertainties haunted the process of 'Circe's' composition. It is not until 3 November that Joyce's letters at last reveal his grasp of the seriousness of the situation in New York:

the American police, roused by the daughter of the attorney-general of the state of New York, confiscated the review. The first hearing took place on the 22nd ult. There will be a stink as soon as the damned book is published. (*L* III: 27)

Enlightenment had come from 'two very long letters from Mr Quinn of New York concerning *Ulysses* and *The Little Review*' (*L* I: 149), yet, as he was keen to assure Harriet Shaw Weaver, the composition of *Ulysses* continued: 'I shall try to finish the *Circe* episode before Christmas. The next one ['Eumaeus'] is already drafted but this has cost me an incredible amount of labour' (*L* I: 150). 'Circe' was finally sent to be typed in early January, but the six months from July 1920 until then provide a startlingly vivid illustration of the hypothesis that the threat of vice-crusading censorship was, for Joyce, intimately bound up with his creative life. 'Circe' and to a lesser extent 'Eumaeus', both composed during these tortuously anxious months, provide a paradigmatic illustration of the impact of social purity repression upon the shape and character of Joyce's fiction. It is unsurprising, then, that 'Circe', played out against the suggestive backdrop of red-light district and brothel, is Joyce's most savage, exuberant and ingenious assault upon the 'purity snoopers' (*FW* 254: 21). The episode covertly ridicules and subverts social purity's most prominent campaign; its sustained assault upon brothels, streetwalkers and tolerated prostitution. Through his portrait of that compromised, voyeuristic would-be reformer Leopold Bloom, Joyce devastatingly satirises contemporary moral crusades to erase spectacles of vice from the urban scene.

I

In early 1885, Josephine Butler and Catherine Booth of the Salvation Army approached W. T. Stead, the pioneering 'new journalist' and editor of *The Pall Mall Gazette*. They sought help to 'rouse the nation' into support of social purity's inaugural law, the Criminal Law Amendment bill, intended to raise the age of consent from thirteen, and challenge the double standard by

---

[2] The editor of *Photo-Bits*, recently renamed *Bits of Fun* had been prosecuted and fined after a particularly racy number. Joyce warned Budgen 'whatever else in that way you send had better be enclosed in a copy of the *Christian Hero* or some such paper' (*L* I: 148).

displacing state surveillance from prostitute to client. Stead's crucial intervention in the nascent purity campaign to pass this bill is now well known. He set up a 'special commission' to explore the nether world of London prostitution, and, disguised as an elderly rake with a false beard resting on top of his own, spent several months early in 1885 roaming mean streets and brothels, drinking champagne, smoking cigars and interviewing young prostitutes. He published his findings in a four-part series, 'The Maiden Tribute of Modern Babylon', which ran in the *Pall Mall Gazette* during the first week of July, and sensationally cumulated with the story of 'Lily', thirteen-year old Eliza Armstrong. Stead had commissioned an accomplice, reformed prostitute Rebecca Jarrett, to prove a child could be bought in London for £5. Jarrett persuaded Eliza's mother that her daughter was going into service, paid her £5, and took Eliza to a brothel. There, Eliza's virginity was certified by a midwife; she was chloroformed, undressed, put to bed, and awoke to find Stead, disguised as an old roué, hovering over her:

And then there arose a wild and piteous cry- not a loud shriek, but a helpless, startled scream like the bleat of a frightened lamb . . . 'There's a man in the room. Take me home, oh, take me home!' And then all once more was still.***[3]

Eliza was removed inviolate from the brothel the next day and placed with nuns in France, where her virginity was once more certified for Stead's protection. The impact of these revelations was unprecedented. Issues of *The Pall Mall Gazette* sold out so fast that rioting crowds gathered outside the *Gazette* offices demanding more copies. Josephine Butler and the Salvation Army organised a mass demonstration in Hyde Park to exploit public feeling, and a float of white-clad girls bearing placards reading 'The Innocents – Shall They Be Slaughtered?' accompanied a petition to Parliament. The Criminal Law Amendment bill became law within weeks, and Stead donated the profits from the 'Maiden Tribute' issues of the *Pall Mall Gazette* to found the National Vigilance Association.[4] The year 1885 was truly an *annus mirabilis* in the history of Victorian sexual politics.

   With the birth of social purity, then, came the birth of the chief suspicion that would dog the movement; the proximity of vigilance to vice. Stead's breathless, excited prose, his sensational headlines such as 'I order Five Virgins', and 'Why the Cries of the Victims are not heard', and his curious

[3] W. T. Stead, 'The Maiden Tribute of Modern Babylon', *The Pall Mall Gazette*, 6 July 1885, 4.
[4] The 'Maiden Tribute' controversy has been excellently and thoroughly analysed elsewhere. See Judith R. Walkowitz, *City of Dreadful Delight: Narratives of Sexual Danger in Late-Victorian London* (London: Virago, 1998), 81–134, and Lucy Bland, *Banishing the Beast: English Feminism and Sexual Morality 1885–1914* (London: Penguin, 1995), xii–xx.

slippage between first and third person narrative underscored the shadowy borderland between social purity activities and what they attempted to police.[5] The implication that he was in some way complicit in the murky sexual practices he had tried to expose soon became pointed. Eliza Armstrong's mother complained to the police that her daughter had been taken from her under false pretences, and late in 1885 Stead was tried and convicted on charges of child abduction. Stead's imprisonment made him social purity's first martyr, but it also fuelled widespread media speculation that his account of London brotheldom might be little more than the product of his 'feverish sin-stained dreams'.[6] The 'Maiden Tribute' affair condensed cultural anxieties not only about the state of the late-Victorian sex industry, but, more significantly, about the methods and motives of investigators of the sexual underworld. It is intriguing, then, that both Stead and Joyce chose the same overarching metaphor for their explorations of prostitution:

> After a time, the eye grows familiar with the foul and poisonous air, but at best you wander in a Circe's Isle, where the victims of the foul enchantress' wand meet you at every turn. But with a difference, for whereas the enchanted in olden time had the heads and voices and bristles of swine, while the heart of a man was in them still, these have not put on in outward form 'the inglorious likeness of a beast', but are in semblance as other men.[7]

Stead's image of London red-light zones as a 'Circe's Isle' is resonant for any reader of *Ulysses*, since his vision of men transformed by lust into swine anticipates Joyce's meditation on the theme of 'swine and yet with men's memories'.[8] As Stead's explorations figured for a mass Victorian public the dangers and pleasures of rambling urban space intent upon reform, so Leopold Bloom's adventures in Nighttown mimic the strategies and conventions of such reform to emphasise its disreputable underbelly. Both 'The Maiden Tribute' and 'Circe' pose a vital question: just how vulnerable were social purists to the enticing spectacles of vice they tried to police?

As we shall see, Bloom stands in a similar ironic proximity to purity reformers like Stead as Gerty MacDowell does to the 'young person' such

---

[5] Walkowitz, *City of Dreadful Delight*, 101.

[6] *The National Reformer*, 30 August 1885.

[7] Stead, 'The Maiden Tribute Of Modern Babylon', *Pall Mall Gazette*, 6 July 1885: 3.

[8] Richard Ellmann, *James Joyce* (Oxford: Oxford University Press, 1983), 495. Possible connections between Stead and Joyce have been thoroughly explored in two studies by Grace Eckley, *The Steadfast Finnegans Wake* (Lanham: University Press of America, 1994) and, more recently, *The Steadfast James Joyce: A Social Context for the Early Work* (San Bernardino, California: Borgo Press, 1997). Whilst I concur with Eckley that Joyce knew about Stead, most plausibly through his friend, the Stead disciple Francis Sheehy-Skeffington, and was most likely familiar with the 'Maiden Tribute' scandal, this chapter will not follow her biographical speculations about Joyce's admiration for and dense network of coded allusions to an individual reformer.

reformers sought to protect. Bloom's thwarted attempts to masquerade as a vice crusader isolate and amplify the doubts about complicity and motive social purity practice foregrounded, since he uses the vice-crusading identity as an unconvincing pretext for rambling through a notorious part of town. Ostensibly, he has ventured into Nighttown in pursuit of Stephen Dedalus, who he wishes to 'rescue' from his dissolute companions, a rescue, of course, eventually accomplished when Bloom intervenes to save Stephen from police trouble, and escorts him to the cabman's shelter at the chapter's close. 'Rescue' appears strikingly when Bloom deflects Josie Breen's accusatory archness ('Mr Bloom! You down here in the haunts of sin! I caught you nicely! Scamp!' – *U* 15: 395) by declaring a philanthropic motive: 'Interesting quarter. Rescue of fallen women. Magdalen Asylum. I am the secretary' (*U* 15: 401–2). It is further confirmed when, apprehended by the First Watch ('Caught in the act. Commit no nuisance' – *U* 15: 680) whilst feeding a stray dog, he resorts to the reformer's defence 'I am doing good to others' (*U* 15: 682). These transparent defence mechanisms are later elaborated into fantasy, as 'the famous Bloom' is acclaimed 'the world's greatest reformer' (*U* 15: 1459) and declares 'I stand for the reform of municipal morals and the plain ten commandments', (*U* 15: 1685–6). Reform supplies a dubious alibi for the suspect spectatorship Bloom is engaged in, 'down in the haunts of sin'. Through Bloom, Joyce interrogates contemporary social purity initiatives to police the unruly city, exposing the voyeuristic complicities which fissured reform's supposedly detached, altruistic gaze. He dramatises the perilously self-reflexive quality of the social purity project through a 'reformer' both susceptible to the pleasures he purports to discipline, and thereby vulnerable to the policing strategies he claims to operate.

Speculation about the reformer's questionable contact with the vice he or she sought to regulate and contain has left an unexpected semantic legacy. The 1909 *Oxford English Dictionary* supplied two definitions of 'pornography', the second still familiar – 'A description of the life, manners, etc. of prostitutes and their patrons; hence, the expression or suggestion of obscene or unchaste subjects in literature or art' – but the first declaring a fascinating ambivalence: 'a description of prostitutes or of prostitution, as a matter of public hygiene'.[9] This Edwardian understanding of the pornographic drew upon the nineteenth-century practice of surveying, regulating, theorising and writing about what was coyly known as 'the social problem', and such investigations into commercial sex particularly flourished towards the

---

[9] *A New English Dictionary on Historical Principles*, ed. J. A. H. Murray (Oxford: Clarendon Press, 1909), 1131. Intriguingly, the *Dictionary* listed W. T. Stead's *If Christ Came To Chicago* (London: Review of Reviews, 1894) as one of three sources for the word 'pornographic'.

century's close. Between 1875 and 1885, an annual average of only eighty six brothels were prosecuted in the United Kingdom, whereas from 1885 until 1914, the figure leapt to over 1,200 a year, a dramatic shift directly attributable to the rise of social purity activity in the aftermath of the first Criminal Law Amendment Act.[10] This new drive to regulate the sex industry continued the established tradition of urban exploration narratives, where the haunts of sin of the modern city provided a curious middle class with a sensation scene, a nether region of illicit sex and crime. Voyeurism was inseparable from these narratives: their authors were drawn both to read and represent red-light districts as spectacles, with their 'dark mean streets', 'warrens of the poor', and flaunting prostitutes.[11] Accordingly, cultural commentators betrayed an understandable nervousness about the potentially titillating, compromising activity of 'rescuing fallen women'. The pioneering social hygienist, Alexandre Parent-Duchâtelet, summarised an ubiquitous anxiety, declaring 'Because I devote myself to research on prostitutes, must I necessarily be stained by contact with these unfortunate women?'[12] His question resonated throughout later studies. One reviewer of William Acton's *Prostitution* (1857) condemned it as a 'mere guidebook to vice', adding

It is to be regretted that the author should have allowed himself to introduce sensational matter into his history of a most repulsive subject . . . Still more objectionable are highly-coloured autobiographies of women of loose character, or picturesque descriptions of evenings spent at Cremorne and elsewhere.[13]

Similarly, as Leonora Davidoff has explored, the nocturnal perambulations of William Gladstone in search of prostitute women to 'rescue' troubled Gladstone himself, his friends and political allies.[14] Even Ellice Hopkins, to an extent preserved from such suspicions by her gender, was rueful about the social consequences of her rescue work, telling one colleague 'Nature has made me a singing bird but Grace has made me a sewer-rat.'[15] These concerns suggest the tone of a sustained cultural unease about prostitution investigation. As W. T. Stead discovered, the grave literature of prostitution

[10] Edward Bristow, *Vice And Vigilance: Purity Movements in Britain since 1700* (Dublin: Gill and Macmillan, 1977), 154.

[11] Walkowitz, *City of Dreadful Delight*, 15–39, 192–6.

[12] Alexandre Jean-Baptiste Parent-Duchâtelet, *De la prostitution dans la ville de Paris, considérée sous le rapport de l'hygiène publique, de la morale et de l'administration*, I (Paris: J.-B. Ballière et Fils, 1857), 37.

[13] Anonymous review of William Acton's *Prostitution*, *Sanitary Review and Journal of Public Health*, III (1857–8), 327.

[14] Leonora Davidoff, 'Gender and Class in Victorian England: The Diaries of Arthur J. Munby and Hannah Cullwick', *Feminist Studies* 5 (Spring 1979), 93.

[15] Bristow, *Vice and Vigilance*, 94.

reform could all too easily be confused with the obscene representation of what prostitutes do.

Such a confusion is eloquently inscribed upon the geography of 'Circe', where Bella Cohen's brothel at 81 Mecklenburgh Street stood next door to the headquarters of the city's most active prostitution reform organisation, the White Cross Vigilance Association at number 82.[16] Joyce's decision to set 'Circe' in the brothel adjacent to the vice society headquarters is pointedly symbolic, since at the turn of the century no city in the British Isles presented a more striking object for reform than Dublin, and no area of Dublin more obviously demanded such reform than its infamous red-light district, Monto. For, as Judith Walkowitz suggests, the prostitute was 'the quintessential female figure of the urban scene', a 'central spectacle in a series of urban encounters and fantasies' who condensed the more general anxieties about poverty, infection, dirt and disease which characterised concern about the city.[17] Reform discourse assimilated the prostitute to the waste-clogged social body of the expanding nineteenth-century metropolis, and consequently subjected her to similar regimes of inspection.[18] This connection between prostitute and slum as twin urban spectacles for a fascinated yet repulsed bourgeois gaze offers an inviting context for 'Circe', located in a landscape where the two strikingly converge.

In 1899, an international sense of crisis over housing, disease and poverty in cities was shown to have a particularly Irish provenance when in Dublin the death rate reached 33.6 in the thousand, dramatically exceeding both British and European averages, and far surpassing London's 19.7.[19] By 1900, one third of Dublin's population, 21,475 families, lived in single-room tenements, a proportion of poor again far exceeding that discovered in London.[20] Ten years later, the situation had barely improved: the census showed that 22.9 per cent of the city's population occupied single-room tenements, once more considerably higher than elsewhere in the United Kingdom, and commentators repeatedly insisted that poverty and filth were more conspicuous in Dublin than elsewhere in the British Isles.[21] Meanwhile, slum converged with brothel in Monto, an area spanning barely

---

[16] John Finegan, *The Story of Monto* (Dublin: Mercier Press, 1979), 14.   [17] *Ibid.*, 21.

[18] Charles Bernheimer, 'Parent-Duchâtelet: Engineer of Abjection', chapter one of *Figures of Ill-Repute: Representing Prostitution in Nineteenth-Century France* (London: Duke University Press), 1997, 8–33.

[19] Statistics from Jacintha Prunty, *Dublin Slums 1800–1935: A Study in Urban Geography* (Dublin: Irish Academic Press, 1998), 153.

[20] Kevin Kearns, *Dublin Tenement Life: An Oral History* (Dublin: Gill and Macmillan, 1994), 10.

[21] Prunty, *Dublin Slums*, 172. Contemporaries were quick to note the spectacular nature of Dublin's degeneration. For D. P. Moran, slums were 'hideous eyesores', supplying intensely visual images of 'sordid misery, dilapidation and dirt', *The Leader*, 25 January 1913. In 1898 *The Daily Nation* ran a series of articles on 'Our North Slums', where headlines such as 'More Deplorable Filth', 'A

a quarter of a mile, yet crammed with tenements, ramshackle back courts, unadopted lanes, streetwalkers and brothels. It featured in an article on prostitution in the 1902 edition of *The Encyclopaedia Britannica*:

> Dublin furnishes an exception to the usual practice in the United Kingdom, in that the city police permit 'open houses' confined to one street, but carried on more publicly than even in the south of Europe or Algiers.[22]

The Dublin police had the example of an earlier crackdown on prostitution before them, when in the aftermath of a 1870s brothel clearance in French and Clarendon Streets in the south of the city, the prostitutes 'went to the banks of the canal. But now they are scattered in different outlying parts, Mecklenburgh Street... You move them from one site to another, you do not put them down.'[23] Faced with the dilemma which still haunts policing strategies today, the Dublin Metropolitan Police chose to follow what was disparagingly referred to as 'the continental system' by trying to contain sexual commerce within a designated area in the north-east of the city. In 1894, a decade after the Criminal Law Amendment Act had bestowed upon police stringent powers to close brothels and prosecute prostitutes and their keepers, Dublin Metropolitan Police statistics recorded seventy-four known brothels within Monto, yet had closed only four of them down.[24]

Dublin's best-known nicknames 'Dear Dirty Dublin' and 'Strumpet City' thus neatly condensed the twinned notorieties for slumland dereliction and sexual commerce which so compelled contemporary reformers. Segregation may have been intended to tuck prostitution out of sight, but in fact, by concentrating sexual commerce within one area rather than dispersing it across the city, Dublin vice became all the more spectacular. Its shameful visibility outraged the anti-Catholic polemicist Michael

Terrible Picture' and 'Further Horrible Scenes' drew attention to the shocking *visibility* of festering slaughterhouses, derelict tenements and overflowing privies, 'Our North Slums', *The Daily Nation*, 5, 10 and 12 September 1898. Occasionally, words failed: 'your readers can more readily imagine for themselves the condition of these horrible places [unflushable dirt closets] than I can describe them', *The Daily Nation*, 10 September 1898. *The Lancet's* report on 'the submerged population and social wrecks who throng the back courts and alleys of Dublin' focused with particular horror upon the proximity of slums to vice: since a typical tenement back court 'saw little or no traffic, people go there to defecate in quietude and at night it is frequented by the worst class of prostitute', *The Lancet*, 25 November, 30 December 1899.

[22] 'Prostitution', *The Encyclopedia Britannica*, tenth edn, IX (Edinburgh: Adam and Charles Black, 1902).

[23] Osbourne Morgan, Senior Surgeon of the Westmoreland Lock Hospital, testimony to *House of Commons Select Committee on the Administration, Operation and Effects of the Contagious Diseases Acts of 1865–1869*, HC 1881 (351) viii, Qs. 6461, 6473.

[24] 'Statistical Returns of the Dublin Metropolitan Police', table xxxv, *Parliamentary Papers*, 55 (1895), c. 7734.

McCarthy, who designated it 'the greatest blot upon the social life of Dublin and Ireland' where 'the trade in immorality is carried out as openly as any branch of legitimate business' and 'the principal houses are as attractively painted and fitted up on the outside as private hotels which are legitimately licensed for the sale of drink in the principal streets of the city'.[25] McCarthy's objection that prostitution in Dublin was unacceptably conspicuous, whilst 'there was no such area in London or any other town in Great Britain' was frequently reiterated; 'the principal cities of London, Brussels, Germany and France have by no means the air, whatever be the reality, which enter our thoroughfares at the fall of night', 'Vice is not so open in Paris as it is in Dublin', 'Must we endure the shocking sights of depravity nightly enacted in our thoroughfares and public spaces?'[26] Dublin's unique containment strategies made the city's prostitutes, like its slums, frighteningly flamboyant. Monto intensified the social anxieties articulated by late-Victorian moral reformers, compressing panic over the city and sexual danger into a tightly enclosed urban space.

'Nighttown' accordingly incited a variety of surveillance philanthropies, such as the St Vincent de Paul Society and its Protestant rival, the Dublin Visiting branch of the Irish Church Mission.[27] However, the majority of the reform campaigns directed at Monto responded to its reputation as infamous red-light area, and interspersed between shabby tenements and 'flash houses' were several institutions for prostitute rescue. Homes for 'penitent Magdalens' included the Protestant Dublin Midnight Mission and Female Refuge on Marlborough Street, the Rescue Mission Home on Gardiner Street Lower, and Catholic asylums on Gloucester Street, Marlborough Street and 76 Mecklenburgh Street Lower, a few doors down from Bella Cohen's.[28] Yet, most significantly, Monto also provided the ideal site for the more aggressive experiments in urban reform initiated by social purity crusaders in the wake of Stead's notorious investigations. From 1885, Monto was patrolled by the Dublin White Cross Vigilance Association, that 'band of earnest, thoughtful men who love Ireland and Irish chastity' whose attempts at 'moral moonlighting' involved the attempted intimidation of brothel customers by men's patrols.[29] Operating from the small office next

[25] Michael McCarthy, *Priests and People in Ireland* (London: Hodder and Stoughton, 1908), 282–3.
[26] *Ibid.*, 282; *The Irish Times*, 14 October 1910, 7; *The Irish Times*, 21 October 1910, 8. The debate continued in *The Irish Times*, letters pages from 18 to 30 October 1910.
[27] Prunty, *Dublin Slums*, 237–9.
[28] *Ibid.*, 267.
[29] *The Vigilance Record*, September 1902. Rosa M. Barrett, *Ellice Hopkins: A Memoir* (London: Wells Gardner, 1907), 175–83 gives an account of the foundation of the Dublin White Cross Vigilance Association by Ellice Hopkins in 1885.

door to Bella Cohen's brothel, by 1891 the organisation had founded fourteen branches in Dublin, with 530 members scattered throughout the city,
recruits enough to field patrols of two dozen men through Monto every
night from 9.30 until 2 a.m., 'as circumstances may depend, so that wet
or dry their attendance may be relied upon'.[30] Such patrols kept 'a system-
atic watch on evil houses with a view to clearing them out and rescuing
the inmates from their shameful life'.[31] The unique spatial organisation of
Nighttown meant that the Dublin branch were effectively pioneers of this
kind of purity work. Their efforts attracted special praise from William
Coote, chairman of the National Vigilance Association, who noted that
'moral moonlighting' was only suited to 'towns of moderate size, where men
are known. The same technique was adopted in one of the London suburbs
and had to be given up.'[32] These tactics indicate how Joyce's Nighttown
was a compressed theatre of vice and crime, inciting the reforming gaze.
The area displayed upon its streets that proximity of vice to vigilance exemplified in the contemporary double meaning of 'pornography'. Monto's
notoriety as an isolated, sensational landscape of vice, which solicits and
then absorbs the reformer's gaze, enfolding him into complicity with the
social problems he would police, resonates through 'Circe' and defines
Bloom's perambulations through it.

II

Joyce's construction of Monto as a striking object for reform is evident in
the opening scene of 'Circe': 'red and green will-o-the-wisps' and 'danger
signals' mark out 'the Mabbot street entrance of nighttown', populated by
a spectacular underclass who display their abjection upon their bodies; a
'deafmute idiot with goggle eyes', a 'pigmy woman swing[ing] on a rope', a
tramp sleeping against a dustbin, a 'crone', a 'gnome' scavenging for rags and
bottles on a rubbish tip and a 'slut' combing 'the tatts from the hair of a scro-
fulous child' (*U* 15: 1–41). As Alan Mayne has argued, nineteenth-century
representations of slums form a genre dependent upon 'highly stylised sets
rather than locations, one-dimensional types rather than people, and prepared scripts rather than spontaneous social exchanges'.[33] Mayne's thesis is
amply illustrated in 'Circe', where 'one-dimensional types' and a 'highly
stylised set' filters Monto through a lens of hyperbole, transforming a scene
of urban danger into a theatre of deformity which parades its own status

[30] *The Vigilance Record*, April 1891.   [31] *Ibid.*, 15 April 1887.
[32] William Coote, *A Romance of Philanthropy* (London: National Vigilance Association, 1916), 37.
[33] Alan Mayne, 'Representing the Slum', *Urban History Yearbook* 17 (1990), 69.

as a sight. 'Circe' unveils a melodramatic sensation scene, vying with reform classics such as 'The Maiden Tribute', where vice and crime could
not be contained within the conventions of realist narrative and impar-
tial reportage. Stead's Nighttown was a 'strange and inverted world, the
world of the streets and the brothel', a 'London inferno' part-veiled by
'foul and poisonous air', the backdrop for a Gothic fairytale with a sim-
plistic cast of villains, victims and Sir Galahads.[34] Joyce's Nighttown too is
characterised by this theatricality, with a cast of 'stunted men and women'
looming from a 1900s version of dry ice: 'From drains, clefts, cesspools,
middens arise on all sides stagnant fumes' (*U* 15: 138–9). 'Circe' presents
Monto's streets and their inhabitants as things to be looked at as they solicit the gaze of the reformer through the histrionic projections of their
degeneration, and 'Circe's' spectator is, of course, Bloom, whose enthusiasm for reform as he traverses Dublin is matched by his preoccupation
with seeing. His fantasy of being declared 'the world's greatest reformer'
(*U* 15: 1685) is anticipated elsewhere in *Ulysses*; for instance in 'Hades', he
proposes a corporation tramline to transport cattle and hearses to quays
and cemetery, and suggests burying corpses vertically would save scarce
graveland (*U* 6: 400–8, 764), whilst in 'Lestrygonians' he advocates the
use of anaesthetics in childbirth and the bestowal of government grants to
newborns (*U* 8: 377–88). Bloom's sensitivity to municipal and social problems, his compassionate yet prurient vision, finds its natural focus in Monto,
which staged the spectacular social problems which attracted the reforming
gaze.

Tellingly, then, the prostitute Zoe solicits Bloom by humouring his defensive masquerade as a socially concerned, detached reformer intent upon
street rescue: 'Are you looking for someone? He's inside with his friend'
(*U* 15: 1283). Once inside, Bloom calls Zoe 'a necessary evil' (*U* 15: 1980),
a key cliché of rescue rhetoric, and asks twice about her origins 'Are you a
Dublin girl?' (*U* 15: 1344), 'Where are you from? London? (*U* 15: 1980–1).
He reproduces a standard strategy of eliciting individual prostitutes' stories, since reform texts incorporated numerous 'case-histories' of prostitute
women, giving details of their former lives and their 'first fall'.[35] Stead,
William Acton and Josephine Butler all relied upon the kind of prostitutes'
confessions which occurred again and again in the annual reports of social
purity leagues, magdalen asylums and reform journalism:

---

[34] Stead, 'The Maiden Tribute of Modern Babylon', *Pall Mall Gazette*, 6 July 1885, 3.
[35] See Judith R. Walkowitz, *Prostitution and Victorian Society: Women, Class and the State* (Cambridge:
Cambridge University Press, 1980), 13–21 for a summary of such case-histories.

The story begins with no father or mother, an aunt who kept a whiskey store in Cork, an artilleryman who came to the whiskey store and saw and seduced the girl. By and by his regiment was ordered to the Curragh. The girl followed him, being then with child. 'He blamed me for following him' said she. 'He'd have nothing to do with me. He told me to come here and do like other women did. And what could I do? My child was born here in this very place, and glad I was when the child died – thank the Blessed Mary! What could I do with such a child? His father was sent away from here and good riddance. He used me very bad!'[36]

These ubiquitous confession narratives are burlesqued when Bloom's enquiries about Zoe's background mutate into a fantasy-encounter between the three whores and the revivalist preacher Elijah. Kitty and Florry's conventional stories of seduction and betrayal – 'I forgot myself. In a weak moment I erred and did what I did on Constitution Hill... It was a working plumber was my ruination when I was pure' (*U* 15: 2226–9), 'It was in consequence of a portwine beverage on top of Hennessy's three star. I was guilty with Whelan when he slipped into the bed' (*U* 15: 2233–4) – are brusquely undercut by Zoe's defiant 'I let him larrup it into me for the fun of it' (*U* 15: 2231). The connection between Bloom's prying questions and these playfully disingenuous responses is highlighted through Elijah's sly wink to his audience as he pleads 'help me save our sisters dear' (*U* 15: 2222).

Bloom's barely contained voyeurism is emphasised through the juxtaposition of the two distinct forms of gaze he casts upon Nighttown. Whilst Bloom traverses Dublin musing upon a wide variety of reform strategies, he is also intent upon an ostensibly different kind of spectatorship; the covert, libidinous desire to look which makes him constantly alert for a glimpse of ankle. 'Circe' emphatically revisits moments elsewhere in *Ulysses* where Bloom is particularly open to visual pleasure. His near-accident with the sandstrewer as he enters Nighttown prompts him to connect the driver with 'the fellow balked me this morning with that horsey woman' (*U* 15: 205–6), recalling the moment when his view of a woman mounting her carriage outside the Grosvenor Hotel was frustrated by 'A heavy tramcar honking it's gong slewed between' (*U* 5: 131). Similarly, the girls from 'Nausicaa' escape into 'Circe': Edy Boardman and Bertha Supple gossip together, Cissy Caffrey strolls with the soldiers, Gerty herself appears 'leering' and 'ogling', displaying a sign of her lost virginity, 'her bloodied clout' (*U* 15: 371, 372).

---

[36] See Walkowitz, *City of Dreadful Delight*, 20–1, 88–9, 100–1 for Henry Mayhew, Butler and Stead; Walter Kendrick, *The Secret Museum: Pornography in Modern Culture* (New York: Viking, 1987), 30–1 for Acton. Prostitute's confession from James Greenwood, 'The Plain Facts and Figures of Prostitution: The Wrens of the Curragh', chapter 17 of *The Seven Curses of London* (London: S. Rivers and Co, 1869), 234.

Such reminders of past scopic pleasures disquietingly qualify Bloom's detached reforming gaze. This disquiet becomes pointed during Bloom's first
encounter with Zoe when he gropes her breast 'with the unparalleled em-
barrassment of a harassed pedlar gauging the symmetry of her peeled pears'
(*U* 15: 1993–4), yet leers 'The mouth can be better engaged than with
a cylinder of rank weed' (*U* 15: 1350–1). Bloom oscillates uncomfortably
between the roles of brothel client and investigative journalist blushingly
feigning interest in the purchase of sex before making his excuses and
leaving. Through Bloom, Joyce dramatises the understandable suspicion
that men who busied themselves patrolling red-light districts after dark,
conversing with prostitutes or hunting down obscenity, might themselves
be unwholesomely preoccupied with what they attempted to suppress.
Such scepticism was encouraged by phenomena such as the aftermath of
the Jack the Ripper killings, when hundreds of disturbed men roamed
Whitechapel as vigilantes, some bizarrely cross-dressed as decoy prostitute
women, prompting media speculation that perhaps the murderer was 'a
purity man gone mad on religion', or the 1887 Shropshire scandal where
the local chairman of the National Vigilance Association, a Revd H. G.
Wakefield, was found to have sent many 'most revoltingly obscene letters'
to local servant girls.[37] Vice societies were alert to the dangers of this ubiquitous allegation. The Dublin White Cross Vigilance Association published
a list of rules clarifying their activities, where they forbade male members to
'kneel down with women at midnight [prayer] meetings, especially behind
a pew', to confront prostitutes alone, and to 'voluntarily enter into conversation with women of bad or doubtful character'.[38] However, Joyce's
critique is not limited simply to demonstrating his would-be reformer's
predictable vulnerability to absorption in the spectacles of sex he desires to
discipline. More disturbingly, 'Circe' revenges itself upon the social purity
movement by staging Bloom's oscillation between the unstable identities
of 'rescuer of fallen women', and 'reformed rake' (*U* 15: 1781) who prompts
the City Recorder to declare 'I will put an end to this white slave traffic
and rid Dublin of this odious pest' (*U* 15: 1167–8).

Such a slippage is anticipated in the opening pages of 'Circe', where
Bloom enters 'the Mabbot street entrance of nighttown' (*U* 15: 1) both eager

[37] Walkowitz, *City of Dreadful Delight*, 212; *The Vigilance Record*, February 1888, 9. It is worth noting
that these suspicions still haunt modern reactions to Victorian purity campaigners: Edward Bristow
suggests that Frederick Charrington, a purity zealot whose zeal in closing East End brothels in the
late 1880s forced the Ripper's victims onto the streets, might be considered as a suspect for the
Whitechapel murders (Bristow, *Vice and Vigilance*, 167).
[38] *The Vigilance Record*, April 1891.

to see its disreputable sights, yet also terrified of being observed. 'A concave mirror' (*U* 15: 145) presents Bloom with a distorted image of himself, whilst 'gallant Nelson's image' (*U* 15: 145) looks on, 'Grave Gladstone sees him level' (*U* 15: 146), and he is 'struck by the stare of truculent Wellington' (*U* 15: 147–8). Caught in the crossfire of these competing imperial stares, Bloom pauses, 'sweated under the bright arclamp' (*U* 15: 150–1), ducks into Olhausen's butcher, and walks on to where 'The glow leaps again' (*U* 15: 165). Joyce scripts the alternating states of shadow and light as Bloom walks from streetlamp to streetlamp as a malign drama of exposure. Seeing a fire burning south of the city, he panics 'What is that? A flasher? Searchlight' (*U* 15: 167), and is immediately lit up by 'Two cyclists, with lighted paper lanterns aswing' (*U* 15: 178) and the sandstrewer's 'huge red headlight winking' (*U* 15: 186). These sudden flashes of light present him in a state of visibility antipathetic to the Victorian urban explorer's desire to remain disguised. Henry Mayhew, for instance, attended a midnight mission rescue meeting, where prostitutes 'recounted their woes and the struggles and published their shame amid the convulsive sobs of the others' whilst he stood discreetly taking notes 'barely visible' at the back of a 'dimly lit' church hall.[39] In sharp contrast, Bloom is conspicuous, accosted by a 'Gaelic League spy' (*U* 15: 220) who 'From under a wideleaved sombrero . . . regards him with evil eye' (*U* 15: 212–4), his father, Rudolph, who peers at him through 'horned spectacles' and asks 'What you making down this place? Have you no soul?' (*U* 15: 259) and 'an elderly bawd' who warns 'Don't be all night before the polis in plain clothes sees us' (*U* 15: 370–1). The subversive implications of Bloom's precarious conspicuousness are particularly clear in the context of the precise forms of moral regulation practised on the streets of Monto in 1904.

From 1885 until 1910, Monto was policed each night by the Dublin White Cross Vigilance Association:

As a rule, about six young men are appointed to watch each house. One of the patrol was provided with a notebook and pencil, while others possessed lanterns. As soon as a man came up to the house he was stopped by the patrol, the light from the lantern flashed onto his face, and the note-book brought into full play. The members of the patrol were then asked if they recognised this person. In every instance his name and address were demanded, and in many cases were correctly given. Where the person was known, it needed very few words to persuade him to forego his evil intention and return home.[40]

By 1892, the association claimed to have put thirty-five houses out of business using this method, forcing one proprietor to offer a £1,000 bribe, and another three to syndicate to share their losses.[41] These methods of surveillance, particularly the vigilantes' claim that they asked amongst the patrol to see if any recognised the miscreant, 'since often the person was known' curiously contradicts more usual nineteenth-century representations of metropolitan mean streets as places of anonymity where the accomplished urban flâneur could wander without fear of detection. However, as Clair Wills notes, Dublin was disqualified 'as a Baudelairean city of the chance encounter... Dublin was surely the most intractable of cities for the budding flâneur.'[42] These 'moral moonlighting' activities supply a striking context for what happens in 'Circe'. No sooner has Bloom declared himself secretary of the Magdalen Asylum and rescuer of fallen women than he is accosted by 'two raincaped watch... silent, vigilant' (U 15: 674–5). These moral vigilantes declare 'Caught in the act' (U 15: 680) and charge him with 'Unlawfully watching and besetting' (U 15: 733), oblivious to his protests that his mission too is philanthropic; 'I am doing good to others' (U 15: 682). Their techniques strongly suggest contemporary Dublin White Cross Vigilance Association tactics, especially since the confusion which ensues when Bloom claims to be 'Dr Bloom, Leopold, dental surgeon' (U 15: 721) as the card proclaiming him 'Henry Flower. No fixed abode' (U 15: 733) tumbles out of his hat dramatises the scenes one might expect frequently took place at nightfall in White Cross territory. As Joyce's ability to ascertain the names of individual prostitutes and their madams also confirms, visitors to and residents of Dublin's red-light district were particularly vulnerable to recognition.[43]

III

Bloom's manoeuvres in Nighttown between the identities of detached, invisible observer of vice and potential target for exposure and reform is intimately connected to his responses to prostitution elsewhere in *Ulysses*. His lengthiest exposition of his views on 'the social evil' comes in 'Eumaeus' when 'The face of a streetwalker glazed and haggard under a black straw hat peered askew round the door of the shelter palpably reconnoitring on her own with the object of bring more grist to her mill' (U 16: 704–6). Bloom defensively averts his eyes and insists to Stephen on the necessity for the policing, examination and registration of prostitutes:

---

[41] *The Vigilance Record*, April 1888; April 1892; see also Bristow, *Vice and Vigilance*, 163.
[42] Wills, 'Joyce, Prostitution', 88.
[43] See Richard Ellmann, *James Joyce* (Oxford: Oxford University Press, 1983), 367–8 for Joyce's use of the names of individual prostitutes.

– It beats me, Mr Bloom confided to Stephen, medically I am speaking, how a wretched creature like that from the Lock hospital reeking with disease can be barefaced enough to solicit or how any man in his sober senses, if he values his health in the least. Unfortunate creature! Of course I suppose some man is ultimately responsible for her condition... The elder man, though not by any manner of means an old maid or a prude, said it was nothing short of a crying scandal that ought to be put a stop to *instanter* to say that women of that stamp (quite apart from any oldmaidish squeamishness on the subject), a necessary evil, were not licensed and medically inspected by the proper authorities, a thing, he could truthfully state, he, as a *paterfamilias*, was a stalwart advocate of from the very first start. (*U* 16: 728–45)

Oddly, Bloom presents his scheme as novel and bold whilst anachronistically recapitulating arguments which were implemented and vigorously contested during the first two decades of his life. Supported by a disparate coalition of reforming bodies, including the British Medical Association, most of the Anglican clergy and even prominent Malthusians such as Charles and George Drysdale, the Contagious Diseases Acts of the 1860s and 1870s provided for the fortnightly gynaecological inspection of women deemed 'common prostitutes' in a series of 'prescribed districts', ports and garrison towns.[44] Diseased women were forcibly confined in 'lock hospitals' until cured, or, in the case of syphilis, until their symptoms had subsided.[45] The architects of these Acts perceived them as the cornerstone of a grand plan of urban regeneration, 'the first stage in the creation of a moral and sanitary utopia'.[46] Bloom's perception of prostitution as a 'necessary evil', his eagerness to ally himself with medical authority ('medically I am speaking'), his self-presentation as a 'paterfamilias' concerned for the common good and, above all, his suggestion that prostitute women should once more be 'licensed and medically inspected by the proper authoritites' closely shadows the arguments and rhetoric of this specific strand of prostitution regulation.

Bloom's enthusiasm for a bygone measure is, however, curiously appropriate to the exhausted and redundant aura of 'Eumaeus', since, as we have seen, this mid-Victorian interpretation of prostitution reform as regulation had been displaced by the early 1880s through Josephine Butler's feminist libertarian campaign to repeal the measures Bloom would impose. Agitators against the Contagious Diseases Acts successfully argued that the Acts were not only medically inefficient, but more importantly violated the civil liberties of 'inscribed' women and gave legal consent to the double standard.[47] Above all, they insisted the Acts, with their implicit suggestion

---

[44] Walkowitz, *Prostitution*, 80–1.   [45] *Ibid.*, 1–2.   [46] *Ibid.*, 70.   [47] *Ibid.*, 2.

that prostitution was 'a necessary evil', were complicit with vice, since their primary concern was not to decrease prostitution nor 'rescue' prostitute women, but was rather to secure a pool of 'clean' women for general sexual use.[48] Repeal rhetoric repeatedly emphasised this complicity. The speculum examination at the heart of the Acts was 'instrumental rape', an unnatural, voyeuristic intrusion giving state doctors similar gratification to that gained by the inscribed women's customers; prostitutes were arrested and tried by the policemen and magistrates who were often their covert clients; the MPs and doctors who supported the legislation were themselves far from pure.[49] These arguments emphasised the confusion implicit in the contemporary ambiguity over the meaning of 'pornography' by suggesting a compromising continuity between the punitive policing of deviant sexuality, and deviant sexuality itself.

The Contagious Diseases Acts were suspended in 1883, to be repealed three years later, and those involved in the campaign for repeal, including Josephine Butler's lieutenants Ellice Hopkins, Alfred Dyer, William Coote and W. T. Stead, went on to channel their energies towards attaining a national standard of social purity. Since the repeal of the Contagious Diseases Acts was integral to the foundation of the social purity movement, it is curious, then, that Bloom should voice his support for the very measures early social purists campaigned to displace. However, Joyce's critique does not inhere solely in Bloom's belated enthusiasm for a discredited reform. Rather, the acuity of Joyce's pastiche relies upon the tension between the Butlerite strand of prostitution reform and the coercive brand of social purity which had come to flourish in the first decade of the twentieth century. For, as became rapidly apparent, the social purity movement that emerged in 1885 from the repeal crusade markedly diverged from its libertarian origins, as purity energies swiftly shifted from safeguarding the civil liberties of prostitute women, to a reactionary return to the disciplining of prostitution.[50] Through Bloom's repressive suggestions, Joyce draws attention to the disconcerting similarities between the loathed Contagious Diseases Acts of the 1860s and 70s, and the Edwardian attempts to regulate

---

[48] *Ibid.*, 111.

[49] *Ibid.*, 108–10. Repealer J. J. Garth Wilkinson's pamphlet *The Forcible Introspection of the Women for the Army and Navy by the Oligarchy Considered Physically* (London: 1870) suggested the Acts were motivated by a combination of 'the medical lust of handling and dominating women' and 'the police lust of hunting and persecuting women' (p. 15). Butler's reports for her repeal journal *The Shield* similarly addressed official hypocrisy: one of her favourite anecdotes concerned one 'unfortunate' who, when committed to gaol, commented 'It did seem hard, ma'am, that the magistrate on the Bench who gave the casting vote for my imprisonment had paid me several shillings a day or two before, in the street, to go with him', *The Shield*, 2 May 1870.

[50] Walkowitz, *Prostitution*, 246.

prostitution orchestrated by the National Vigilance Association. In so doing, Joyce contributes to a prevailing radical critique of the vice societies,
articulated by the dissident feminists, civil libertarians and sex radicals with
whom he was naturally in ideological accord.

Josephine Butler's campaign against the measures Bloom recommends
left an uneasy legacy in a succession of laws and responses to them which
demonstrate social purity's increasing tendency towards coercion. Whilst
the first Criminal Law Amendment Act of 1885 was ostensibly passed to raise
the age of consent and thus protect juvenile prostitutes, the Act also contained clauses facilitating the closure and prosecution of brothels and their
inmates which tended to preoccupy the National Vigilance Association. As
we have seen in Dublin, purity vigilantes subsequently orchestrated local
campaigns to erase the tacit red-light districts which, before 1885, had been
allowed to flourish. Such campaigns could very easily spill over into the
surveillance, harassment and intimidation of individual prostitutes who,
with the lack of real alternatives, were forced from the comparative safety
of the brothels to the hazards of streetwalking. Between 1885 and 1914, an
average of 1,200 brothels were prosecuted in England and Wales each year,
fourteen times the annual average of prosecutions in the ten years preceding
1885, and, whilst reports in *The Vigilance Record* insisted upon a marked
decline in the visibility of prostitution, it is probable that such tactics re-
sulted in the sex trade becoming more dispersed, covert and dangerous.[51]
Meanwhile, as purists were busy clearing the cities of brothels, the National
Vigilance Association was agitating for a yet more repressive law; the second Criminal Law Amendment Act eventually passed in 1912 in the wake
of Stead's martyr's death on the Titanic. Providing police and vigilantes
with increased powers against procurers and brothel-keepers and requiring landlords to evict prostitute tenants, the Act's coercive impulses were
symbolised by a provision allowing the whipping of male procurers and
brothel-keepers. As with the 1885 Act, the practical result was the increased
persecution of prostitutes and their associates.[52] These developments confirmed Butler's fears, voiced as early as spring 1885, three months before
Stead's revelations, that the emerging social purity movement was dominated by 'a crowd of repressionists who are now going in a distinctly wrong
direction'.[53]

By 1886, Butler and her colleagues had resigned from the National
Vigilance Association and regrouped around the Personal Rights

---

[51] *Ibid.*, 252; Alan Hunt, *Governing Morals: A Social History of Moral Regulation* (Cambridge: Cambridge University Press, 1999): 175.
[52] *Ibid.*, 178–9.   [53] Bland, *Banishing the Beast*, 99.

Association, founded to campaign for purity whilst resisting the new emphasis upon coercion. As Butler's veteran feminist colleague Elizabeth Wolstenholme Elmy observed, the mainstream purity movement's attempts to repress prostitution re-introduced the Contagious Diseases Acts through the back door. Women thrown out of brothels were often subsequently sent to prison on vagrancy charges, where, once again, they were medically examined:

Have you protested against the arbitrary arrest and examination of women as 'unconstitutional and unjust' solely because they were inspected in the name of public health? Do such things become constitutional and just because they are done in the name of public morals? I say advisedly 'arrest and examination' because under the Prisons Act, such examinations are perfectly possible. In the name of public morality and social purity our mistaken friends will have brought us back to that cruel oppression of women which they denounced and resisted when enforced in the alleged interest of the public health.[54]

The Personal Rights Association's suspicions that the new militancy was merely introducing another form of the state harassment of prostitutes which in practice differed very little from that imposed by the Contagious Diseases Acts soon came to dominate criticisms of social purity during the 1900s. The repressive tendencies that so troubled Elmy and Butler intensified in 1901, when the National Vigilance Association, the London Public Morality Council and Westminster City Council banded together to recommend to the Home Secretary that 'vigorous action should at once be taken to clear the streets of prostitutes', initiating a five-year period of the most intense repression since 1885.[55] As the campaign for the second Criminal Law Amendment Act got underway in 1907, mainstream social purity's reliance upon coercion became yet more apparent. The Personal Rights Association was joined by the Legitimation League, a coalition of 'free lovers' and sex-radicals, by the Humanitarian League discussed above in chapter 1, and by the radical feminists at *The New Freewoman* and *The Egoist* to protest against social purity's victimisation of prostitutes.[56] Social purity recusant Sylvia Pankhurst summarised growing disquiet: 'It is a strange thing that the latest Criminal Law Amendment Act, which was passed ostensibly to protect women, is being used almost exclusively to punish women.'[57]

[54] Elizabeth Wolstenholme Elmy, *Journal of the Personal Rights Association*, 15 January 1886.
[55] See Bland, *Banishing the Beast*, 109.
[56] For the Legitimation League and its journal, *The Adult*, see Bland, *Banishing the Beast*, 105, 156–9.
[57] Sylvia Pankhurst, 'Protecting Women?', *Woman's Dreadnought*, 19 December 1914, 156.

Such, then, is the backdrop to Bloom's curiously anachronistic plan to reintroduce a discredited law, a law, furthermore, which social purity movements initially succeeded in banishing from the statute books, only to impose a very similar system of surveillance and punishment in its place. The most cursory of readings of *The Egoist* in the aftermath of the 1912 Criminal Law Amendment Act would have alerted Joyce to the irony, had he not appreciated it before, and in 'Eumaeus' he enfolds this irony into the texture of exhaustion and redundancy that the chapter's style articulates. We have already seen how Joyce orchestrates a competition of intertexts between the tired, mid-Victorian didactic novel *The Lamplighter* and the technologically contemporary mutoscope in order to call attention to the belatedness of the 'young person' archetype social purists continued to defend. In 'Eumaeus', Bloom's thoughts on prostitution reform, lazily reheated from a distantly remembered controversy of his youth, make a very similar point, since through them Joyce slyly alludes to the circularity of the mainstream social purity movement's progress from 1885 repeal to 1912 repression. Exhausted and drained by his adventures in Nighttown, ill-informed and consequently lacking the usual compassionate social vision which lends his 'reformer' identity a little credibility, Bloom proposes to implement a system of regulation and harassment ostensibly resisted by the contemporary social purity movement yet frequently covertly practised. Through Bloom, a would-be reformer who, in this case if not in others, voices a reactionary sexual politics which uncomfortably collided with the coercive strategies of contemporary vigilantes, Joyce argues for the retrograde and compassionless nature of purity ideology.

Bloom's reactionary endorsement of this simultaneously bygone and ongoing drive to reform prostitution through coercion is, however, significantly compounded by his furtive complicity in the vice he would regulate. As we have seen, Butler and her fellow repealers repeatedly insisted that those who proposed state regulation were covertly participating in vice; by their secret patronisation of prostitutes, by their concern to guarantee a 'safe' pool of women for public use, or even by their deployment of the speculum examination, a medical technique easily construed as 'instrumental rape'. Such an accusation of complicity is subversively revisited in 'Eumaeus', where Bloom's sudden enthusiasm for regulation is directly prompted by the appearance of a prostitute who lurches into the cabman's shelter and fixes him and the other men with her glassy stare. This woman is, of course, the same 'frowsy whore with black straw sailor hat askew' (*U* 11: 1252) who comes 'glazily into the day' (*U* 11: 1253) along Ormond

Quay towards Bloom at the close of 'Sirens'. There, Bloom recognises the woman as a former sexual partner – 'When first he saw that form endearing? Yes, it is. I feel so lonely. Wet night in the lane' (*U* 11: 1253–4), and recalls her unusual solicitation:

Psst! Any chance of your wash Knew Molly. Had me decked. Stout lady does be with you in the brown costume. Put you off your stroke, that. Appointment we made knowing we'd never, well hardly ever. Too dear too near to home sweet home. (*U* 11: 1256–9)

Fear of recognition and exposure both puts Bloom 'off his stroke' and causes him to take shelter from the possibility of recognition by looking into Lionel Marks' shop window. His anxiety lest he be seen is swiftly telegraphed: 'Heehaw shesaw', 'Sees me, does she?', 'Let her pass' (*U* 11: 1255, 1259, 1264).

The threat is recapitulated in 'Eumaeus', where, meeting the woman again, Bloom once more defensively averts his eyes, 'scarcely knowing which way to look' (*U* 16: 707) and feigns absorption in a discarded blush-pink copy of *The Evening Telegraph*. This prostitute, with her 'kind of demented glassy grin showing that she was not exactly all there' (*U* 16: 724), poses in her blatant derangement a particularly explicit challenge to a sexual politics of reform which positioned the prostitute woman as a spectacle and forced her to submit to inspection by either the state or purity vigilantes. Instead, she 'peered askew around the door' (*U* 16: 705), puts Bloom 'on tenterhooks' (*U* 16: 720), and views 'with evident amusement the group of gazers round the skipper Murphy's nautical chest' (*U* 16: 726–7). In a disquieting instance of female retaliatory spectatorship, she looks back, deploying a gaze which intimidates Bloom and the other men in the cabman's shelter, and Bloom's knee-jerk response to this scopic intimidation is to insist to Stephen upon the necessity for policing prostitutes. His theory therefore appears to be a defensive strategy, as Butler's libertarian repealers theorised, designed to mask his own complicity. Bloom is one of the men 'ultimately responsible for her condition' he guiltily mentions, and he significantly supports regulation as he rests in the cabman's shelter, exhausted by his adventures in Nighttown and terrified by a familiar prostitute 'reconnoitring on her own' (*U* 16: 705). The positioning of so reactionary an argument within 'Eumaeus' suggests that Bloom's unconvincing attempt to assume the reformer's mantle is a paranoid reaction to what has happened to him in 'Circe'. There, Bloom is subjected to those intimate and degrading inspections he later argues should be confined to prostitute women.

IV

Derided by a mob of 'antiBloomites' (*U* 15: 1753) for a variety of sexual transgressions, including employing 'a mechanical device to frustrate the sacred ends of nature' (*U* 15: 1741–2), Bloom is denounced as 'a vile hypocrite, bronzed with infamy'(*U* 15: 1757), 'a disgrace to Christian men' (*U* 15: 1754), 'a stinking goat of Mendes' (*U* 15: 1755), and, perhaps most damningly, 'as bad as Parnell was' (*U* 15: 1762). In his defence, he calls upon 'Dr Malachi Mulligan, sex specialist, to give medical testimony on my behalf' (*U* 15: 1772–3). Mulligan reveals a variety of sexual stigmata; Bloom is 'bisexually abnormal' (*U* 15: 1775–6), suffers from 'hereditary epilepsy...the consequence of unbridled lust' (*U* 15: 1777–8) and is 'prematurely bald from selfabuse' (*U* 15: 1780–1) and 'a reformed rake' (*U* 15: 1781). A 'pervaginal examination' (*U* 15: 1784) and the application of 'the acid test to 5427 anal, axillary, pectoral and pubic hairs' (*U* 15: 1784–5) reveals his patient '*virgo intacta*' (*U* 15: 1785–6). The fantasy-world of 'Circe' thus intriguingly transforms Bloom from a middle-class man suggesting a strategy of prostitution reform into that most potent late-Victorian spectacle of sexual degradation, a woman with her legs in stirrups having her body 'read' for legal evidence of sexual transgression. Since the gynaecological examination of prostitute women under the Contagious Diseases Acts was central to the campaign against regulation, it came to symbolise the dehumanising effects of coercive prostitution policies.[58] Bloom's internal examination at this point in 'Circe' is therefore Joyce's most visceral and startling assault upon the already precarious boundaries separating reformer from reformed. It stands as a synecdoche for the elaborate drama of surveillance, exposure and role-reversal which the entire chapter scripts.

This drama is strikingly focused at the moment when Bloom encounters brothel madam Bella Cohen. Joyce presents Bella as a phantasmagoric manifestation of that emasculating gaze employed earlier by Mulligan: 'Her eyes are deeply carboned' (*U* 15: 2746), 'her eyes rest on Bloom with hard insistence' (*U* 15: 2751–2), 'Her falcon eyes glitter' (*U* 15: 2753). Even Bella's fan uses the suggestive idiom of sight, 'Married, I see' (*U* 15: 2755), whilst Bloom

---

[58] Bloom's ordeal incidentally recalls a number of controversial vaginal inspections forced upon the virtuous. Most notoriously, W. T. Stead uncomfortably glossed over Eliza Armstrong's subjection to two similar 'instrumental rapes' for his own protection: besides the 'momentary surprise' of the midwife's examination, he assured the jury, Eliza did not experience 'the slightest inconvenience' (quoted in Walkowitz, *City of Dreadful Delight*, 112). Similarly, the case of a Mrs Percy, a music-hall entertainer from Aldershot wrongly registered as a prostitute who refused to submit to examination and who was driven to commit suicide after repeated complaints of police harassment, was widely publicised by repealers. See Walkowitz, *Prostitution*, 110.

protests 'We are observed' (*U* 15: 2800–1). Predictably, then, Bloom's responses display an anxiety about being surveyed: 'Rain, exposure at dewfall on the searocks, a peccadillo at my time of life' (*U* 15: 2794–5) he explains, a reference to 'Nausicaa' which curiously transfers Gerty's seashore 'exposure' to himself. This confusion anticipates how Bloom's transformation into spectacle is emphatically feminised:

(*He knots the lace. Bella places her foot on the floor. Bloom raises his head. Her heavy face, her eyes strike him in midbrow. His eyes grow dull, darker and pouched, his nose thickens.*)

BLOOM

(*mumbles*) Awaiting your further orders we remain, gentlemen . . .

BELLO

(*with a hard basilisk stare, in a baritone voice*) Hound of dishonour!

BLOOM

(*infatuated*) Empress! (*U* 15: 2829–37)

This moment of transsexual transformation is choreographed as a contest of gazes which Bloom has no chance of winning. Bella's 'eyes strike him in midbrow', Bloom's 'eyes grow dull, darker', cowed before this scopic interrogation, then 'Bello' fixes Bloom with a 'hard basilisk stare'. Accordingly, Bloom's feminisation is imaged as a form of psychological myopia. S/he falls to the ground before Bello with 'her eyes upturned in the sign of admiration' (*U* 15: 2851), eyes that then 'shut tight' with 'trembling eyelids' (*U* 15: 2853–4), and 'creeps under the sofa and peers out through the fringe' (*U* 15: 2871) to communicate her submissiveness through her glance. Bloom's surrender of the supposedly 'masculine' power of spectatorship is integral to his transformation into a prostitute woman. Joyce here emphasises the extent to which the prostitute was culturally produced as spectacle, as Bloom's sex change transforms him into the kind of abject sight he has previously attempted to regulate.

Bloom's treatment pointedly rehearses the motif of Gothic exploitation invariably produced by prostitution reformers. In social purity cautionary tales, as has been explored above in chapter 2, prostitution was melodramatically figured as a coerced state of 'white slavery', rather than one of a number of limited economic choices. Social purists insisted that young girls were commonly entrapped into houses of ill-fame by false promises, drugging or kidnap, and kept there by confiscation of property, threats and 'loans' of sexually flamboyant clothes of a higher quality than they could otherwise afford. If the woman later tried to leave, she would lose any possessions she brought to the house, and could theoretically be pursued for debt or theft of the socially stigmatising brothel clothes she left in.[59] This melodrama begins to operate as Bello tells Bloom

As they are now so will you be, wigged, singed, perfumesprayed, ricepowdered, with smoothshaven armpits. Tape measurements will be taken next to your skin. You will be laced with cruel force into vicelike corsets of soft dove coutille with whalebone busk to the diamondtrimmed pelvis, the absolute outside edge, while your figure, plumper than when at large, will be restrained in nettight frocks, pretty two ounce petticoats and fringes and things stamped, of course, with my houseflag. (*U* 15: 2972–80)

Thus attired, Bloom is subjected to the stock ordeal of brothel initiation; the certification and auctioning of virginity. The 'virgo intacta' Bloom becomes Bello's 'new attraction in gilded heels' (*U* 15: 3083), up for auction before a crowd of bystanders:

What offers? (*he points*). For that lot . . . (*he bares his arm and plunges it elbowdeep into Bloom's vulva*) There's fine depth for you! What, boys? That give you a hardon? (*he shoves his arm in a bidder's face*). (U 15: 3087–91)

The scene pastiches many social purity accounts of white slavery, most famously Stead's 'Maiden Tribute', promoted with placards crying out 'Five pounds for a virgin warranted pure' and describing the underworld 'traffic in maidenheads'.[60] Such accounts sensationally focused upon the key moment of virgin-purchase which Bello pornographically stages. As Bello's comments 'you male prostitute' and 'Sauce for the goose, my gander O' (*U* 15: 3177–9) indicate, this section of 'Circe' is scripted as revenge-fantasy. Bloom's visceral and shocking transformation into the somatic spectacle of the prostitute tropes for the chapter's sustained drive to interrogate the fragile boundary separating the reformer from the target of reform.

v

Bloom's mutation into the target of purity inquisition is not, however, limited to his fantasised incarnation as one of the prostitutes vigilantes attempted to 'rescue', reform and thereby survey. 'Circe's' fantasy sequences vertiginously veer between these scenarios of abjection and scenarios of

---

[59] Bristow *Vice and Vigilance*, 189–191 outlines the common myths about the entrapment of 'respectable' girls produced by the National Vigilance Association and others. He also gives details of other coercive techniques exposed by purity campaigners such as Alfred Dyer: 'More than the doors that opened only from the street, the confiscation of street clothes or the inevitable debts, the threat of turning a girl over to the police for illegally registering was the pimp's main weapon' (89).

[60] Walkowitz, *City of Dreadful Delight*, 82.

power and triumph, most notably when Bloom is declared leader of his utopian 'new Bloomusalem in the Nova Hibernia of the future' (*U* 15: 1544–5). Whilst the abjection scenarios clearly articulate a collapsing inwards of the categories of 'reformer' and 'reformed' by transforming Bloom into white-slave trafficker or prostitute, so too does this fantasy of public office. Bloom places himself at the centre of a lavish pageant of power, acclaimed by sumptuously dressed supporters; '*Timothy Harrington, late thrice Lord Mayor of Dublin, imposing in mayoral scarlet, gold chain and white silk tie*' (*U* 15: 1377–9), 'WILLIAM, ARCHBISHOP OF ARMAGH (*in purple stock and shovel hat*) (*U* 15: 1479–80), '*The princess Selene, in moonblue robes, a silver crescent on her head*' (*U* 15: 1509–10). Bloom himself is resplendent '*in a crimson velvet mantle trimmed with ermine*' (*U* 15: 1444), '*in dalmatic and purple mantle*' (*U* 15: 1477), in '*a mantle of cloth of gold*' (*U* 15: 1490), a ruby ring on one hand and the Koh-i-Noor diamond on the other. The streets of Dublin are festooned with '*Venetian masts, maypoles and festal arches*' (*U* 15: 1398), '*a streamer bearing the legends* Cead Mille Failte *and* Mah Ttob Melek Israel' (*U* 15: 1399–1400), '*imperial eagles hoisted, trailing banners and waving oriental palms*' (*U* 15: 1409), '*twentyeight Irish representative peers, sirdars, grandees and maharajahs bearing the cloth of estate*' (*U* 15: 1416–17) and '*an arch of triumph*' (*U* 15: 1441). This pomp and finery defensively emphasises Bloom's body as a legitimate public spectacle, as windows and balconies are lined with 'sightseers, chiefly ladies' (*U* 15: 1401). A warning sign, however, that this fantasy is about to be ruptured is given when John Howard Parnell declares 'Illustrious Bloom! Successor to my famous brother!' (*U* 15: 1513–4), a threat stated more explicitly when 'the mob' rephrase the comparison: 'Lynch him! Roast him! He's as bad as Parnell was. Mr Fox!' (*U* 15: 1762). The reference to Parnell alludes to another, closely affiliated dimension to the social purity agitation against public manifestations of vice; one Stephen Dedalus earlier encounters in *A Portrait of the Artist as a Young Man*. Bloom's abrupt trajectory from adored leader of men to bedraggled criminal in the dock, on trial for a host of past sexual misdemeanours, retraces a familiar *fin de siècle* story significantly inscribed by another strand of the social purity campaign.

Social purist Hugh Price-Hughes heralded the new campaign in February 1886 at a rally to celebrate Stead's release from jail:

Hitherto it has been held that a man's public life had no connection with his private life. In this reform they must begin at the fountainhead. They must begin by cleansing the House of Commons. They should lay it down as a great political principle that no man who believed that the daughters of the poor should be sacrificed to the lusts of his own sex should be fit to make the laws of England.

They should raise the purity of public opinion until it becomes impossible for an immoral man to occupy any public position in the country, from the village police station to the throne of England.[61]

This attempt to 'raise the purity of public opinion' captured the purity imagination, and, in alliance with the White Cross Leagues and the Church of England Purity Society, the National Vigilance Association insisted that 'aspirants for municipal, or other honours of this kind shall not only be personally free from reproach, but shall have healthy moral sympathies'.[62] It even formed a standing committee to

remorselessly exclude from all honourable office, either municipal or parliamentary, any man with any taint whatsoever upon his moral life...Until you make it impossible for a man whose reputation has been sullied, to seek as a candidate for any honour whatever in public life, we shall have to fight with this vice continuously and for ever.[63]

The most conspicuous casualties of this crusade to sanitise public office were Charles Stewart Parnell and the Liberal MP unfortunate enough to be cited as the co-respondent in a divorce case in the immediate aftermath of Stead's release. Sir Charles Dilke was accused of adultery with Virginia Crawford, the twenty-three year old daughter of one of his previous mistresses and wife of one of his parliamentary colleagues, Donald Crawford MP. As Judith Walkowitz notes, although most newspapers seized the opportunity of transforming the scandal into good copy, Stead's relentless persecution of Dilke in the *Pall Mall Gazette* was probably decisive in ruining his political career.[64] Stead mercilessly focused upon the 'perverse' sexual practises allegedly forced upon Virginia Crawford, whose voluble testimony vied with 'The Maiden Tribute' for sensationalism. Not only did she name Dilke as her first seducer, she added he had coerced her into three-in-a-bed sex sessions together with his maidservant Fanny, compared her sexually to her mother, and taught her 'five different kinds of French vice' so that she 'knew more than a woman of thirty'.[65] Dilke refused to testify, and Virginia Crawford's transparent eagerness to escape her marriage and shield her current lover, a Colonel Foster, created sufficient doubt to lead the court to dismiss the evidence against Dilke, yet grant Donald Crawford

[61] Hugh Price-Hughes, *The Sentinel*, February 1886, 20–1.
[62] *The Vigilance Record*, October 1888, 100.
[63] Birmingham and Midlands Counties Vigilance Association, *Occasional Paper*, 1893, 2. The Association was a local branch of the National Vigilance Association.
[64] Walkowitz, *City of Dreadful Delight*, 126.
[65] Roy Jenkins, *Victorian Scandal: A Biography of the Right Honourable Gentleman Sir Charles Dilke* (New York: Chilmark Press, 1965), 219.

a *decree nisi* nonetheless.[66] Social purist Alfred Dyer denounced the verdict as 'an extraordinary and ignominious piece of shuffling': Virginia Crawford had committed adultery with Dilke, but he not with her.[67] Outraged at this fresh example of the double standard, Stead repeatedly reminded his readers that Dilke was guilty not merely of adultery, but also 'the last outrages of depraved and unnatural vice', and declared 'the man against whom so frightful an accusation could lie is a worse criminal than most of the murderers who swing at Newgate'.[68] The campaign set the tone for purity response to the Parnell scandal three years later, again with Stead and Price-Hughes at the fore.[69]

Social purity's high-profile campaign against sexually compromised politicians supplies yet another dimension to the rhythm of acclamation and exposure, power and abjection which shapes Bloom's fantasies of reform in 'Circe' and 'Eumaeus'. Joyce's fascination with the Parnell scandal has been discussed at length above and does not need to be further substantiated, but his similar interest in the Dilke case is evident in his library, which contained an anonymous pamphlet, *Nouveau Scandale de Londres: L'Affaire Crawford* (Paris: 1886).[70] Appropriately, then, Bloom is a retentive reader of such accounts of high jinks in high life, musing upon the parallel between the two notorious divorce scandals of his youth and his own troubled marriage. He poignantly relates the Parnell scandal to his own experience – 'it was simply a case of the husband not being up to the scratch, with nothing in common between them beyond the name, and then a real man arriving on the scene' (*U* 16: 1379–81) – even claiming a spurious parallel between Kitty O'Shea and Molly: 'she also was Spanish or half so, types that wouldn't do things by halves, passionate abandonment of the south, casting every shred of decency to the winds'(*U* 16: 1409–10). Significantly, Bloom is so preoccupied by the divorce trial as media event that snippets from the Parnell and Dilke scandals coalesce in his memory to form a confused continuous narrative. Bloom remembers the allegation that Parnell escaped detection by scrambling down a fire escape attached to Katherine O'Shea's bedroom, and connects this spectacle to the media circus: 'a fact the weeklies, addicted to the lubric a little, simply coined shoals of money out of' (*U* 16: 1378–9). He recalls Parnell's 'letters containing

---

[66] *Ibid.*, 320.
[67] *The Sentinel*, April 1886, 7. To *The Times*, this verdict was 'very singular and to ordinary minds not very comprehensible', *The Times*, 13 February 1886.
[68] *The Pall Mall Gazette*, 16 February 1886.   [69] See chapter 3 above.
[70] Richard Ellmann, *The Consciousness of Joyce* (New York: Oxford University Press, 1977), 121. The initial 'scandale de Londres' was, of course, the 'Maiden Tribute' furore.

the habitual mushy and compromising expressions leaving no loophole to show that they openly cohabited two or three times a week at some well-known seaside hotel' (*U* 16: 1486–9), but moves seamlessly on to 'Then the *decree nisi* and the King's proctor tries to show cause why and, he failing to quash it, *nisi* was made absolute' (*U* 16: 1490–2). This addition alludes not to Parnell, but to Dilke: unusually, after the *decree nisi* was granted, Dilke unsuccessfully invoked the Queen's Proctor to overrule the divorce before it became absolute.⁷¹ A paragraph later, Bloom recalls another page-turning detail from *Crawford* v. *Crawford*: Donald Crawford testified in court that he had received anonymous letters warning 'Beware the member for Chelsea', and, when he confronted his wife, she confessed to him 'on her knees' in the marital bedroom.⁷² From these details Bloom produces a tightly scripted melodrama:

the legitimate husband happened to be a party to it owing to some anonymous letter . . . drawing attention to their illicit *proceedings* and leading up to a domestic rumpus and the erring fair one begging forgiveness of her lord and master on her knees and promising to sever the connection and not receive his visits any more. (*U* 16: 1533–9)

Bloom's confusion of Dilke with Parnell indicates how he views these divorce scandals not so much as individual dramas, but as generic narratives of melodramatic exposure.

A familiar pattern here emerges. In 'Eumaeus', Bloom casts himself as a prostitution reformer; in 'Circe' he is subject to precisely the 'reforms' he recommends. In 'Eumaeus' Bloom is a passive consumer of divorce-court narratives in part manufactured by the new social purity consensus; in 'Circe' his fantasies cast him as the target of purity's inspections. 'Eumaeus' retrospectively underlines this shift in perspective from spectator to spectacle. It seems curious that Bloom, a cuckolded husband, chooses to identify with the dashing lover rather than the 'legitimate husband', recalling with pride how 'He, B, enjoyed the distinction of being close to Erin's uncrowned king in the flesh . . . even when clothed in the mantle of adultery' (*U* 16: 1495–8). Whilst this identification might seem illogical or masochistic, it also suggests how Parnell/ Dilke's status as sexually exposed for Bloom overrides his identity as a married woman's lover. Bloom too is terrified

---

⁷¹ Trevor Fisher, *Scandal: The Sexual Politics of Late-Victorian Britain* (Gloucester: Alan Sutton Press, 1995), 107–9.

⁷² As Trevor Fisher notes, the anonymous letters read out in court, which taunted Donald Crawford 'Fool, looking for the cuckold when he has flown, having defiled your nest', combined with reports of Virginia Crawford's own histrionic conduct, contributed to the atmosphere of staged melodrama which surrounded the case. Fisher, *Scandal*, 101.

lest his sexuality be exposed to public ridicule, and his identification with Parnell/ Dilke unmistakeably taints his vision of his 'new Bloomusalem in the Nova Hibernia of the future', a dream of self-aggrandisement which is tellingly introduced by his remark to Zoe, 'Why, look at our public life!' (*U* 15: 1361). Bloom's rhetorical question is also a plea. His fantasy of assuming public office seems to hark back to a time where, as Hughes put it, 'it was held that a man's public life had no connection with his private life', since the pageant, ostentatious dress and ceremony he deploys can be read as a sustained attempt to divert public attention from the kinds of private spectacles exemplified by Parnell's flight down the fire escape, or Dilke's disconcertingly modern tabloid romps with Virginia Crawford and his maidservant Fanny. Nonetheless, such private spectacles intrude, as the 'new Bloomusalem' episode is shadowed on either side by courtroom-drama scenes highly suggestive of these contemporary scandals.

Once arrested by the two night watch for 'unlawfully watching and besetting', Bloom is placed on trial before a jury of his 'Hades' peers, and attempts to defend himself with 'I am a man misunderstood. I am being made a scapegoat of. I am a respectable married man' (*U* 15: 775–6). However, Bloom's assertion of private matrimonial respectability is queried by the first witness against him, Philip Beaufoy, who demands 'Why, look at the man's private life! Leading a quadruple existence! Street angel and house devil. Not fit to be mentioned in mixed society!' (*U* 15: 853–4). Beaufoy's declamation closely shadows social purity's rhetorical insistence upon exposing the discontinuity between the public and private lives of sexually transgressive politicians. This discontinuity is substantiated by Mary Driscoll who, whilst 'indignantly' (*U* 15: 687) refuting the second watch's suggestion that she is 'of the unfortunate class' (*U* 15: 865), nonetheless fixes Bloom in the familiar role of upper-class seducer attempting to debauch the daughters of the poor.[73] As Joyce surely appreciated, the evidence of domestic servants was an ubiquitous feature of *fin-de-siècle* sex trials, ranging from the mysterious Fanny, sensationally produced during *Crawford v. Crawford*, to the cook who claimed to witness Parnell scrambling down the fire escape, or the chambermaids who attested to stained bedlinen in hotel rooms occupied by Oscar Wilde and Lord Alfred Douglas.[74] Mary's

[73] 'The Maiden Tribute' relied heavily upon class rhetoric, arguing for 'the responsibility of the dissolute rich for the ruin of the daughters of the poor' and declaring 'the hour of democracy has struck'. Stead's appeal to respectable working-class outrage was also mobilised by purity lecturers such as Josephine Butler and James Wookey, who denounced a degenerate upper class for abusing poor girls whilst placing their own daughters under rigid protection. See Bristow, *Vice and Vigilance*, 110–11.

[74] The chambermaid Jane Cotter and housekeeper Mrs Perkins at the Savoy Hotel were crucial witnesses in Wilde's trial for violation of the infamous Labouchere Amendment to the Criminal Law

account of furtive below-stairs ambushes is substantiated by witnesses Mrs Yelverton Barry, Mrs Bellingham and the Honourable Mrs Mervyn Talboys, who attest to other instances of sexual subterfuge where Bloom has written a suggestive 'anonymous letter in prentice backhand...signed James Lovebirch' (*U* 15: 1016–20), or 'addressed me in several handwritings with fulsome compliments as a Venus in furs' (*U* 15: 1045–6) or 'observed me from behind a hackney car and sent me in double envelopes an obscene photograph, such as are sold after dark on Paris boulevards, insulting to any lady' (*U* 15: 1064–6). These attenuated advances burlesque Bloom's usual tendency to secrecy, and the women respond by contemplating a variety of shame punishments. 'Geld him. Vivisect him' (*U* 15: 1105), urges Mrs Bellingham, vivisection being, significantly, a practice rich in cultural resonances since it opened up the private zones of an animal's body to medical inspection, and was therefore vigorously opposed by many campaigning feminists also opposed to the state-licensed medical invasions of the Contagious Diseases Acts.[75] Mrs Talboys similarly declares 'I'll flog him black and blue in the public streets...He is a wellknown cuckold...Take down his trousers without loss of time' (*U* 15: 1115–18). Whilst these punishments obviously allude to pornographic classics such as Leopold von Sacher-Masoch's *Venus in Furs*, they crucially involve exposure. Proposals to flog Bloom 'in the public streets', 'vivisect him', remove his trousers or perform a 'pervaginal examination' involve opening up the body to public inspection, thereby making a figurative exposure startlingly literal. Joyce thus transforms into fantasy the courtroom dramas which proved so fruitful for social purity campaigners during the closing decades of the nineteenth century, positioning Bloom as an abject spectacle of degradation.

VI

It would seem, then, that Bloom travels far from his first tentative identification with reformers like W. T. Stead as he furtively enters Nighttown, terrified of being recognised and keen to claim the convenient alibi of secretary of the Magdalen Asylum and rescuer of fallen women. Joyce takes this initial identification and subjects it to a series of dazzling modulations, as

Amendment Act, 1885. Cotter testified she had seen young men sleeping in Wilde's bed, and more sensationally still, Perkins testified to 'fecal stains' on the bedlinen. Richard Ellmann, *Oscar Wilde* (London: Penguin, 1988), 432.

[75] For an analysis of feminist purity resistance to vivisection, and contemporary understandings of its metaphoric relationship to the treatment of prostitute women, see Coral Lansbury, 'The Anti-Vivisection Movement in England: Gynaecology, Pornography', *Victorian Studies* 28: 3 (1984), 413–37.

the Bloom who masquerades as a vice crusader becomes ensnared in a bewildering hall of mirrors, where the disciplinary looks he would bestow betray their libidinous subtexts and are thereby returned. Joyce exploits Bloom's vice-crusading alias to dramatise the self-reflexive paradox of social purity spectatorship. Monto may be an enticing spectacle of vice, drawing the social reformer's gaze, but it is simultaneously a place where that reformer is conspicuous and liable to be scrutinised himself. W. T. Stead may have been celebrated for his moral bravery in exposing the London underworld and thus forcing the passage of the 1885 Criminal Law Amendment Act, but he was also suspected of an unwholesome absorption in his subject and eventually imprisoned for child abduction. The prostitution reform literature Stead and others produced may have been 'pornography' in the primary 1909 sense of 'a description of prostitutes or prostitution, as a matter of public hygiene', but its frequently sensational, often prurient tone meant it also veered upon 'pornography' as we understand it today. Bloom's wild oscillations between the roles of vice crusader and target of vice crusades, his transformations from 'midnight-mission' worker to furtive brothel client intimidated by the two watch of 'Circe's' night patrol, from prostitution reformer to prostitute, from retentive reader of divorce-court reports to prisoner in the dock arraigned for sexual misdeeds, from public hero to abject victim of his own notoriously known private life, dramatise these fluidities and ambiguities to highlight suggestive continuities between purity and prurience.

'Circe' is therefore Joyce's most sustained and vigorous critique of the social purity movement, a critique nuanced yet also startlingly explicit. Composed as the New York Society for the Suppression of Vice's prosecution of *The Little Review* was drawing to its inevitable close, the strategies of pastiche and provocation that Joyce directed towards social purity from the start of his writing career take on hyperbolic force. In 'Scylla and Charybdis', Joyce responded to the threat of suppression by larding the chapter with thinly veiled allusions to the contemporary scandals which compromised theosophy's loudly proclaimed alliance with the social purity movement. With 'Nausicaa', he went further still, pointedly associating his 'young person' with popular pornography, and simultaneously sullying and querying her innocence. In 'Circe', the chapter's setting in the most notorious zone of commercial sex in the United Kingdom offers the scope for a singular blatancy of attack. For 'Circe' inscribes a resonant continuum between the hyper-reality of 1904 Monto, with its squalid slums and flaunting brothels, and the fantasy-scenes which purport to display the 'nighttown' of Bloom's unconscious. Perversely, Joyce insisted upon 'Circe' as the most realistic chapter of *Ulysses*, contemplating returning to Dublin to write it 'at source', gleaning the names of individual prostitutes and madams from *Thom's Directory* and telling Arthur Power 'In my Mabbot Street scene I approached reality closer in my opinion than anywhere else in the book.'[76] Yet, the kind of 'reality' Joyce means – the gritty urban realism which so occupied contemporary reformers – happily coexists in 'Circe' with flamboyant hallucinations, from Paddy Dignam's transformation into a dog, to Virag's ability to unscrew his head and place it under his arm. This curious interplay informs Joyce's assault upon the vice societies, since, as Joyce surely understood, the social purity crusades against prostitution drew attention to the faultline dividing reality from fantasy. The precariousness of this boundary was epitomised in Stead's 'Maiden Tribute', an unstable text which disconcertingly mediated between what Stead designated 'the horrible realities which torment those whose lives are passed in the London inferno', and the melodramatic, frequently prurient fantasies which so compromisingly underpinned his own motives and narrative. 'Circe's ironic proximity to such reform texts and practices uncovers what many suspected lay buried in social purity's unconscious, dramatising the movement's 'feverish sin-stained dreams'.

---

[76] Arthur Power, *Conversations with James Joyce*, ed. Clive Hart (Chicago: University of Chicago Press, 1974), 75.

Afterword

When Joyce wrote to Carlo Linati in September 1920 protesting about his long struggles with censorship, it would seem his complaints were oddly disingenuous. He may well have despaired that 'as I hear, a great movement is being prepared against the publication' (*L* 1: 147), yet to become the target of this 'great movement' was equally a role he anticipated, provoked and, eventually, profited from. For Joyce accompanied his protest with one of several intricate 'schema' for *Ulysses*, emphasising the novel's Odyssean parallels and creative techniques. Although he would later regret this defence, contemporary commentators such as Valery Larbaud, Stuart Gilbert and Ezra Pound seized upon it, responding to *Ulysses*' courtroom travails by producing critical appendices insisting on the novel's formal, schematic structure, its status as 'high art', its consanguinity to the classics, and its Homeric chapter titles.[1] As Hugh Kenner explains, such appendices 'were constrained to demonstrate that the Blue Book of Eccles was something more than a cloud of verbal gas with dirty words in it': they were intended to shield *Ulysses* against allegations of obscenity.[2] Not only, then, did the interventions of the vice societies catapult Joyce's work towards notoriety; furthermore, they helped to assure Joyce's status:

---

[1] Joyce sent a copy of the same schema to Valery Larbaud in 1921 to help him with his introductory lecture on *Ulysses*, but later noted it was 'in order to help him confuse the audience a little more. I ought not to have done so', Richard Ellmann, *James Joyce* (Oxford: Oxford University Press, 1983), 519. For uses of the schema, see Ezra Pound, 'Mr Villerant's Morning Outburst', *The Little Review* 5: 7 (November 1918): 11; Valèry Larbaud, 'James Joyce', *La Nouvelle Revue Française*, 18 (April 1922), 386; Paul Vanderham situates Pound as the instigator of what he calls 'the critical censorship of *Ulysses*', *James Joyce and Censorship: The Trials of Ulysses* (London: Macmillan, 1998), 28.
[2] Hugh Kenner, 'Review of *Ulysses on the Liffey*', *James Joyce Quarterly*, 11 (1973), 276–9.

ULYSSES

Suppressed four times during serial publication in *The Little Review*, will be published by 'Shakespeare and Company' complete as written.

This edition will be private and limited to 1,000 copies.

100 copies signed on Dutch hand-made paper	350 fr.
150 copies on verge d'Arches	250 fr.
750 copies on hand made paper.	150 fr.[3]

As the Prospectus for Shakespeare and Co.'s first edition insists, social purity censorship and the cultural prestige signalled by limited editions, signed copies and hand-made paper were intimately entangled.

These attempts to manipulate the 'artistic merit' defence have, however, produced a distorted perspective, where Joyce is too glibly identified with the 'visionary, self-denying artist, who works in constant jeopardy of suppression by a philistine public'.[4] For this persuasive stereotype of artistic grace under fire carries overtones of passivity which cannot readily be applied to any aspect of Joyce's creative practice. Instead, Joyce responded to those 'watch warriors of the vigilance committee' (*FW* 34: 4) with an explosive combination of exasperation, pastiche, belligerence and wit. As we have seen time and again, social purity campaigns, in all their diversity, form part of the intricate cultural context of Joyce's fiction, whether those campaigns be to remove 'penny dreadfuls' from schoolboys, deter young women from emigrating, prevent adolescent masturbation, raise the nation to a higher plane of celibate spirituality, close down mutoscope parlours or police the dangerous and often exhilarating red-light zones of the metropolis. Joyce cannibalises these populist moral crusades, surely immediately recognisable to contemporary readers, and regurgitates them into fiction, where, broken apart, broken down and reassembled, they become their own critique. Through this bricolage process, he insinuates the complex network of moral panics and cultural anxieties lurking beneath social purity's various attempts to 'protect' those overwhelmed by that 'contagion of satyriasis which infects alike our books, our journals, engravings and photographs, and extends from our fine art exhibitions down to our allumette boxes'.[5]

Whilst this creative and imaginative relationship to the social purity campaigns clearly modifies any understanding of Joyce as simply a passive victim

---

[3] Prospectus for *Ulysses*, Shakespeare and Co., 8 Rue DuPaytren, Paris, 1921. Loaned to the British Library from a private collection and featured in *Imaging Ulysses: Richard Hamilton's Illustrations to James Joyce*, exhibition, 2 February – 19 May 2002.
[4] Walter Kendrick, *The Secret Museum: Pornography in Modern Culture* (New York: Viking, 1987), 149.
[5] *The National League Journal*, November 1882.

of philistine censorship, Joyce's sustained pastiche of the purity movement has two further, tangential implications.[6] The first concerns Joyce's much-disputed and problematic relationship to 'emancipated women', particularly the women's suffrage movement developing alongside his creative career. Joyce's frustrating ambivalence towards gender is evidenced in a series of bewilderingly inconsistent pronouncements which deliberately resist easy interpretation. 'Throughout my life women have been my most active helpers', Joyce acknowledged in gratitude to women like Harriet Shaw Weaver, Dora Marsden, Sylvia Beach, Margaret Anderson and Jane Heap, yet still insisted to Mary Colum, 'I hate intellectual women.'[7] Such striking ambivalence can be glimpsed through Joyce's shifting interpretations of Ibsen, a dramatist he praised in 1900 for his 'extraordinary knowledge of women'.[8] In 1936, he declared '[Ibsen] was no more a feminist than I am an archbishop', whilst, to Arthur Power he claimed

the purpose of *The Doll's House*, for instance, was the emancipation of women, which has caused the greatest revolution in our time in the most important revolution there is – that between men and women; the revolt of women against the idea that they are the mere instruments of men.[9]

Such bewildering statements have troubled attempts to unravel Joyce's relationship to contemporary sexual politics, and several feminist critics have accordingly been trapped into 'putting Joyce on trial for evidence of misogynist address', or, conversely, refuting the misogyny charge.[10] How to make sense of Joyce's disconcertingly inconsistent comments on feminism and women, ranging from youthful enthusiasm to misogynist middle age, is a question which continues to perplex.[11]

This resistant ambivalence demands a fresh perspective, since to speak of a monolithic feminism during Joyce's lifetime is, then as now, to oversimplify a complex debate. As we have seen, mainstream feminism was inextricably bound up with a social purity movement which grew increasingly conservative and coercive during the decades following 1885. Whilst early purity feminists like Josephine Butler left the National Vigilance Association in protest, the alliance between social purity and first wave feminism

---

[6] Kendrick, *The Secret Museum*, 149. [7] Ellmann, *James Joyce*, 634, 529.

[8] James Joyce, 'Ibsen's New Drama', *The Fortnightly Review*, n.s., 67 (1 April 1900), 582.

[9] Arthur Power, *Conversations with James Joyce*, ed. Clive Hart (Chicago: University of Chicago Press, 1974), 34.

[10] Margot Norris, 'Joyce's "Mamafesta": Mater and Material, Text and Textile', in *Gender in Joyce*, ed. Jolanta W. Wawrzycka and Marlena G. Corcoran (Gainesville: University Press of Florida, 1997), 2.

[11] For a perceptive overview of the history of feminist criticism on Joyce, see Norris, 'Joyce's "Mamafesta" ', 1–8.

was consolidated during the 1900s, as the suffrage movement appropriated
purity rhetoric to demand 'Votes for Women and Chastity for Men' and
to insist female enfranchisement would 'stop the White Slave Traffic'.[12]
The largest suffrage organisation, the Women's Social and Political Union
campaigned alongside the National Vigilance Association for the second
Criminal Law Amendment Act (1912), and Christabel Pankhurst intensified her organisation's reliance on purity arguments to win the vote with
her polemical attack on 'male vice' and sexually transmitted disease, *The
Great Scourge and How to End It* (1913). The feminist mainstream thus
emphasised sexual danger at the expense of pleasure, focusing on male sexual abuse, drawing attention to venereal disease statistics and venerating
celibacy. Pankhurst was perhaps the most notorious exponent of this strand
of feminism, but her beliefs were endorsed by a number of other prominent
suffragists, such as Cicely Hamilton, Charlotte Despard, Lucy Re-Bartlett
and Frances Swiney, who speculated, for instance, that male sexual excess
had turned semen into 'a racial poison'.[13] Such statements, although undoubtedly extreme, offer a glimpse of an established anti-sex strain running
through suffrage feminism and resting upon a sexual politics of female vic-
timhood exploited by social purists. Joyce's antipathy towards social purity
goes some way towards supplying a context for his ambivalence towards
'the emancipation of women' he at times supported, at times decried.

To assess Joyce's contested and paradoxical relationship to 'feminism',
we must rehistoricise contemporary debates over sexuality, suffrage and
'the woman question' to acknowledge how feminism, then as now, was not
a monologue but a complex debate between distinct and often competing
strands. Joyce's sporadic aversion towards 'emancipated' or 'intellectual'
women, despite his friendship for and gratitude to a coterie of women
who must be classed as such, can be particularised as hostility towards one
particular and dominant strand, the purity feminist mainstream. After all
'A Feminist' (*U* 15: 1465) is only explicitly named once in *Ulysses*, adding
her assent to a chorus who proclaim Bloom 'the world's greatest reformer'
(*U* 15: 1459). Purity feminism, whilst dominating the suffrage movement,
was not, however, the only form of expression for those concerned with
'the emancipation of women', as this study has repeatedly noted. Renegade
suffragists like Teresa Billington-Grieg and Dora Marsden, and radicals
like Jane Heap and Stella Browne were amongst social purist's staunchest

---

[12] Alan Hunt, *Governing Morals: A Social History of Moral Regulation* (Cambridge: Cambridge University Press, 1999), 179.
[13] See Lucy Bland, *Banishing the Beast: English Feminism and Sexual Morality 1885–1914* (London:
Penguin, 1995), 245–7 for a detailed discussion.

critics, and for them 'the emphasis upon chastity was anathema'.[14] These women joined a tradition of feminist purity dissidence first established by Josephine Butler, Elizabeth Wolstenholme Elmy and others who broke away in the 1880s to form the Personal Rights Association, designed to shield women from the coercive 'protection' the National Vigilance Association had in mind. Responses to Pankhurst's *The Great Scourge and How To End It* offer a glimpse into the depth of the fissure. *The Shield*, the journal of the Personal Rights Association, decried 'the note of sex-antagonism', whilst the socialist weekly *The Clarion* complained the 'scolding article' was 'utterly valueless and likely to discredit the cause we believe in'.[15]

These dissident 'emancipated women' were, instead, eager to engage with the taboo questions of sexual politics; contraception and abortion, women's capacities for orgasm and sexual pleasure, 'free unions' and marriage, homosexuality and the new science of 'sexology'. They have emerged here as Joyce's natural allies in the battle against the vice crusaders; those exposing the reactionary sexual politics behind the 'epidemic of terrible rumours' about white slavery, the writers of the articles on birth control, 'free love', and 'The Chastity of Continence' which ran alongside *A Portrait* in *The Egoist*, the editors of the journal 'making no compromise with the public taste' which doggedly continued to publish *Ulysses* despite three confiscations by the New York Society for the Suppression of Vice. These radical feminists, keen to push sexual politics beyond 'Votes for Women and Chastity for Men', were those 'most active helpers' Joyce acknowledged, who so diligently published his work in *The Egoist* and *The Little Review* alongside their lively polemic. It was a debt Joyce would wryly acknowledge in *Finnegans Wake*, pointedly reversing Ezra Pound's significant title change: 'I'm so keen on that New Free Woman with novel inside' (*FW* 145: 28). Joyce's ambivalence towards 'women's emancipation' can be understood in the context of this explicit polarity between social purity feminism and the more marginal radical feminism given a voice in *The New Freewoman*. Whilst his opposition to the former is manifest, his political and literary affiliations to the latter are also clear.

Joyce's creative appropriation of social purity discourses also informs a second contested debate; the disputed question of his status as a 'colonial', 'postcolonial' or even, in Joyce's own happy coinage, a 'semicolonial' (*FW* 152: 16) writer. For Joyce's interest in social purity underlines

---

[14] Rebecca West in *The Clarion*, 26 September 1913.
[15] *The Shield*, April 1914, 3; *The Clarion*, 26 September 1913.

a fascinating cultural anomaly. Although social purity concerns over sexual exploitation, masturbation, prostitution, 'obscene literature' and 'demoralising' popular entertainments were undoubtedly shared by the Irish Catholic Church, and although Catholic Ireland's 'proud reputation for chastity' was repeatedly commended by social purists, there was no home-grown, Catholic, nationalist purity league to rival the Dublin White Cross Vigilance Association until after the foundation of the Free State.[16] Until then, the National Vigilance Association's satellite organisation virtually monopolised purity work in Ireland, despite its evangelical Protestantism, Unionist political allegiances, and its viceregal patrons, the Earl and Countess Aberdeen. The National Vigilance Association's 'Dublin branch' sent reports back to London boasting of its close ties with the Dublin Metropolitan Police; patrols 'acted always with the fullest recognition and co-operation on the part of the Police Authorities', and frequently 'desired to express their gratitude to the Chief Commissioner of Police, Mr Harrell, and to those working under him for their constant help and advice'.[17] This close alliance with a police force which was often perceived as 'the visible presence of an alien administration', as Joseph O'Brien puts it, goes some way towards explaining why Catholic nationalist opinion was hostile enough for Michael McCarthy to complain that 'The Dublin White Cross Vigilance Association are the sort of people who are stoned in Phoenix Park on a Sunday.'[18] Social purity's increasing reliance upon legal coercion, its collaboration with the state, its love of surveillance and its status as an unofficial branch of the police force must have compromised its position in Dublin. The movement's religious, political and state affiliations suggest that, in the absence of a contemporary Catholic vigilance crusade, social purity activities are arguably another of Joyce's many examples of British cultural imperialism and Irish 'grateful oppression'.

---

[16] Ellice Hopkins, *The Purity Movement* (London: Hatchards, 1885), 16. As noted above, whilst the Irish Vigilance Association, a Catholic organisation loosely modelled on the Dublin White Cross Vigilance Association, was founded in 1911, it did not flourish in either members or activities until after it moved into close alliance with the Free State administration. See above, Introduction, note 62.

[17] *The Vigilance Record*, March 1887; March 1888. Rule Seven of the Dublin White Cross Vigilance Association counselled members to remember 'the object is to endeavour to carry out the provisions of the CRIMINAL LAW [*sic*] and therefore to co-operate with the police', *The Vigilance Record*, April 1891. The annual report for 1898 praised 'the excellent work of the Metropolitan Police', adding 'our inspector is constantly patrolling the city in cooperation with the Police', the Dublin White Cross Vigilance Association, *Report for Year Ending 31 Dec. 1898* (Dublin: White Cross Publications, 1899), 5.

[18] Joseph O'Brien, *Dear, Dirty Dublin: A City In Distress 1899–1916* (London: University of California Press, 1982), 180; Michael McCarthy, *Priests and People in Ireland* (London: Hodder and Stoughton, 1908), 293.

If Joyce's fiction, as Emer Nolan and Vince Cheng have so persuasively argued, explores the devastating effects upon Dublin's citizens of Ireland's status as a British colony, then social purity discourses and practices render the sense of colonial subjection they identify startlingly personal. For, as Whately Cook Taylor protested in 1874, the year of the foundation of the Social Purity Alliance, 'Hitherto, whatever the laws have touched, they have not invaded the sacred precinct.'[19] Taylor's 'sacred precinct' was, of course, the private spheres of the body and the home, and social purity ideology, propaganda and legislation would make porous the boundary between the public and the private. This porosity takes on a devastating resonance within the culture Joyce describes, since a form of moral regulation closely entangled with the state invades the occluded sphere of the bedroom. Joyce's sensitivity to such an invasion is implicit in the ways the police, an ubiquitous marginal presence in his fiction, are repeatedly associated with sexuality.[20] In 'Two Gallants', the informer Corley 'often to be seen walking with policemen in plain clothes, talking earnestly' (*D* 45), uses sex in order to gain access to his servant-girlfriend's employer's store of fine cigars and gold sovereigns. In 'Lestrygonians', the political resonances of Corley's ploy are brought to the fore as Bloom speculates 'those plainclothes men are always courting slaveys' (*U* 8: 445–6) in order to gain access to the secrets of political households: 'And who is the gentleman does be visiting there? Was the young master saying anything? Peeping Tom through the keyhole' (*U* 8: 447–9). Even Bloom's loss of virginity to the prostitute Bridie Kelly took place whilst 'together they hear the heavy tread of the watch as two raincaped shadows pass the new royal university' (*U* 14: 1064–7). These intimations of a particularly pervasive form of policing shadow social purity's political resonances in Joyce's deposed capital. For, since purity campaigns encouraged precisely this kind of state intervention into a sphere previously designated private, it internalised and intensified the condition of being policed. What Joyce's use of social purity intertexts suggests is the claustrophobic nature of the policing strategies so in evidence within the public spaces of Dublin. The colonial undertones Nolan and Cheng detect extend into the most intimate private spaces of all, those of the body and the erotic imagination.

[19] Quoted in Jeffrey Weeks, *Sex, Politics and Society* (London: Longman, 1981), 83.
[20] O'Brien, *Dear, Dirty Dublin*, 180 notes that the police were indeed an ubiquitous presence in Dublin, the most intensely policed of all cities in the British Isles, despite the lack of a professional criminal class which might justify a force of over 1,100 men. Their presence is documented by Joyce, who ascribed the symbol 'Constables' to the 'Lestrygonians' episode, Don Gifford, *Annotations to James Joyce's 'Ulysses'* (Berkeley: University of California Press, 1989), 156, and includes at least two police informers, Corley and the unnamed narrator of 'Cyclops' within *Ulysses*.

The implications of Joyce's subversion of social purity for these wider questions of feminism and colonial identity disturb the accepted narrative about his response to suppression. This narrative argues that censorship is external to Joyce's fiction, a restraint imposed from without by a philistine 'public opinion' once the work of creation was complete and therefore to be loftily transcended by frustrated genius. The disillusioned artist retreated to an apolitical, experimental High Modernist aestheticism, a disdain the 'self-doomed, unafraid' Joyce himself brashly proclaimed in 1904:

> Unfellowed, friendless and alone,
> Indifferent as the herring-bone,
> Firm as the mountain-ridges where
> I flash my antlers on the air. (*Poems* 99)

Yet this longstanding and still entrenched view of Joyce the apolitical writer in splendid isolation, preoccupied with style rather than the substance of ideology and history is still, as Cheng notes, insidious, since it deflects attention from 'the manifestly political content and ideological discourse of Joyce's work onto his unarguably potent role and influence in stylistic innovation'.[21] To explore Joyce's creative appropriation of the social purity crusades is to assail this false dichotomy and demonstrate how the prolonged conflict with censorship does not stand outside his creative practice, but, rather, lies at its heart. The forgotten cultural ephemera here retrieved – 'penny dreadfuls', white slave scares, theosophy scandals, masturbation tracts, mutoscopes and 'midnight missions' – form part of an encyclopaedic allusiveness woven into the fabric of the fiction, yet offer more than 'local colour' and suggest more than Joyce's well-documented delight in an eclectic popular culture. Together they reveal a sustained, complex and politically freighted assault upon a movement responsible for the international proscription of *Ulysses*, and thus partly productive of his notoriety. The threat or expectation of censorship is not incidental but integral to Joyce's aesthetic.

[21] Vincent Cheng, *Joyce, Race and Empire* (Cambridge: Cambridge University Press, 1995), 2.

Select bibliography

Anderson, Margaret, *My Thirty Years' War*. New York: Covici, Friede, 1930.
Anonymous, *The Garment of Purity*. London: King, Sell and Routon, 1896.
   The Modern Eveline. Paris: Charles Carrington, 1904.
   The White Slave Traffic. London: C. Arthur Pearson, 1910.
   The Dangers of False Prudery. London: National Vigilance Association, 1912.
   ['By the Author of The White Slave Traffic']. In the Grip of the White Slave Trader.
     London: C. Arthur Pearson, 1912.
Anthony, Barry, 'Shadows of Early Films'. In *Sight and Sound* 59: 3 (1990), 194–7.
Attridge, Derek, *Joyce Effects: On Language, Theory and History*. Cambridge: Cambridge University Press, 2000.
Attridge, Derek and Marjorie Howes, *Semicolonial Joyce*. Cambridge: Cambridge University Press, 2000.
Balides, Constance, 'Scenarios of exposure: Women in the cinema of attractions'. In *Screen* 34: 1 (Spring 1993), 19–37.
Barker, James, *A Secret Book for Men*. Brighton: n.p., 1888.
Bartley, Paula, *Prostitution: Prevention and Reform in England, 1860–1914*. London: Routledge, 2000.
Beach, Sylvia, *Shakespeare and Company*. Lincoln: University of Nebraska Press, 1991.
Beisel, Nicola, *Imperilled Innocents: Anthony Comstock and Family Reproduction in Victorian America*. Princeton: Princeton University Press, 1997.
Bennett, Paula and Vernon A. Rosario, eds., *Solitary Pleasures: The Historical, Literary and Artistic Discourses of Autoeroticism*. London: Routledge, 1995.
Bernheimer, Charles, *Figures of Ill-Repute: Representing Prostitution in Nineteenth-Century France*. London: Duke University Press, 1997.
Besant, Annie, *The Path of Discipleship*. London: Theosophical Publishing Society, 1896.
Billington-Greig, Teresa, 'The Truth about White Slavery'. In *The English Review*, June 1913, 405–19.
Bland, Lucy, *Banishing the Beast: English Feminism and Sexual Morality 1885–1914*. London: Penguin, 1995.
Bland, Lucy and Laura Doan, *Sexology Uncensored: The Documents of Sexual Science*. Cambridge: Polity Press, 1998.

Boyer, Paul, *Purity in Print: The Vice Society Movement and Book Censorship in America*. New York: Charles Scribner's Sons, 1968.

Braude, Ann, *Radical Spirits: Spiritualism and Women's Rights in Nineteenth-Century America*. Boston: Beacon Press, 1989.

Briggs, Austin, ' "Roll Away the Reel World, the Reel World": "Circe" and Cinema'. In *Coping With Joyce: Essays from the Copenhagen Symposium*. Ed. Morris Beja and Shari Benstock. Columbus: Ohio State University Press, 1989, 149–56.

'The Mutoscope Crank'. In *James Joyce Broadsheet* 51 (October 1998), 3.

Bristow, Edward, *Vice and Vigilance: Purity Movements in Britain since 1700*. Dublin: Gill and Macmillan, 1977.

Prostitution and Prejudice: The Jewish Fight Against White Slavery 1880–1939. Oxford: Clarendon Press, 1982.

Brown, Susan Sutliff, 'The Joyce Brothers in Drag: Fraternal Incest in *Ulysses*'. In *Gender in Joyce*. Ed. Jolanta W. Wawrzycka and Marlena G. Corcoran. Gainesville: University Press of Florida, 1997, 8–28.

Brown, Richard, *James Joyce and Sexuality*. Cambridge: Cambridge University Press, 1985.

Brown, Richard and Anthony, Barry, *A Victorian Film Enterprise: The History of the British Mutoscope and Biograph Company 1897–1915*. Trowbridge: Flicks Books, 1999.

Bryson, Mary E., 'Metaphors for Freedom: Theosophy in the Irish Literary Revival'. In *Canadian Journal of Irish Studies* 3: 1 (June 1977), 32–40.

Budgen, Frank, *James Joyce and the Making of Ulysses*. Bloomington: Indiana University Press, 1960.

Bulfin, William, *Tales of the Pampas*. London: Overseas Library, 1900.

Bullen, Robert, *Our Duty as Teachers with Reference to Social Purity*. London: n.p., 1886.

Burch, Noel, *Life to those Shadows*. Trans and ed. Ben Brewster. Berkeley: University of California Press, 1990.

Burfield, Diana, 'Theosophy and Feminism: Some Explorations in Nineteenth-Century Biography'. In *Women's Religious Experience*. Ed. Pat Holden. London: Croom Helm, 1983, 35–54.

Callanan, Frank, *T. M. Healy*. Cork: Cork University Press, 1995.

Chandos, John, *Boys Together: English Public Schools 1800–1864*. London: Yale University Press, 1984.

Chandrasekhar, Sripati, *A Dirty, Filthy Book: The Writings of Charles Knowlton and Annie Besant*. Berkeley: University of California Press, 1981.

Chant, Laura, *Why We Attacked The Empire*. London: Horace Marshall and Son, 1895.

Cheng, Vincent, *Joyce, Race, and Empire*. Cambridge: Cambridge University Press, 1995.

Chesterton, G. K., 'A Defence of Penny Dreadfuls'. In *The Defendant*. London: 1901, 3–18.

Clarke, Bruce, *Dora Marsden and Early Modernism: Gender, Individualism, Science*. Ann Arbor: University of Michigan Press, 1996.

Coates, James, ed., *Has W. T. Stead Returned? A Symposium*. London: L.N. Fowler, 1913.

Collinson, Joseph, *Facts About Flogging*. London: Humanitarian League, 1905.

Comolli, Jean-Louis, 'Machines of the Visible'. In *The Cinematic Apparatus*. Ed. Stephen Heath and Teresa de Laurentis. New York: St Martin's Press, 1980, 121–42.

Comstock, Anthony, *Traps for the Young*. Ed. Robert Bremner. Cambridge, Mass.: Harvard University Press, 1967.

Connelly, Mark Thomas, *The Response to Prostitution in the Progressive Era*. Chapel Hill: University of North Carolina Press, 1980.

Coote, William, 'Law and Morality'. In *Public Morals*. Ed. James Marchant. London: Morgan and Scott, 1902.

  A Vision and its Fulfilment. London: National Vigilance Association, 1902.

  The Romance of Philanthropy. London: National Vigilance Association, 1916.

Cousins, Margaret [Gretta] and James, *We Two Together*. Madras: Ganesh, 1950.

Cranston, Sylvia. *HPB: The Extraordinary Life and Influence of Helena Blavatsky*. New York: G. P. Putnam's Sons, 1993.

Davidoff, Leonora, 'Gender and Class in Victorian England: The Diaries of Arthur J. Munby and Hannah Cullwick'. In *Feminist Studies* 5 (Spring 1979), 87–141.

Davies, M., *Mystic London, or, Phases of Occult Life in the Metropolis*. London: Tinsley Bros., 1875.

De Grazia, Edward, *Girls Lean Back Everywhere: The Law of Obscenity and the Assault on Genius*. London: Constable, 1992.

Denzin, Norman, *The Cinematic Society: The Voyeur's Gaze*. London: Sage Publications, 1995.

Despard, Charlotte, *Theosophy and the Women's Movement*. London: Theosophical Publishing Society, 1913.

Devlin, Kimberley, 'The Romance Heroine Exposed: "Nausicaa" and *The Lamplighter*'. In *James Joyce Quarterly* 22: 4 (1985), 383–396.

Diner, Hasia, *Erin's Daughters in America: Irish Immigrant Women in the Nineteenth Century*. Baltimore: Johns Hopkins University Press, 1983.

Doane, Mary Ann, 'Film and the Masquerade: Theorising the Female Spectator'. In *Screen* 23: 3–4 (Sept.–Oct. 1982), 74–87.

Dromer, Kirsten, *English Children and Their Magazines, 1751–1945*. New Haven: Yale University Press, 1988.

Duane, Patrick A., 'Penny Dreadfuls, Boys' Literature and Crime'. In *Victorian Studies* 22: 2 (1979), 133–151.

  'Boys' Literature and the Idea of Empire, 1870–1914'. In *Victorian Studies* 24: 1 (1980), 80–121.

Dublin White Cross Vigilance Association, *Report for Year Ending 31 Dec. 1898*. Dublin: White Cross Publications, 1899.

Dyer, Alfred, *The European Slave Traffic in English Girls: A Narrative of Facts*. London: Dyer Brothers and Co., 1881.

  Plain Words to Young Men upon an Avoided Subject. London: Dyer Brothers and Co., 1886.

Eglinton, John. *Irish Literary Portraits*. London: Macmillan, 1935.
   A Memoir of A. E. London: Macmillan, 1937.
Ellmann, Richard, *The Consciousness of Joyce*. New York: Oxford University Press, 1977.
   James Joyce. Oxford: Oxford University Press, 1983.
   Oscar Wilde. London: Penguin, 1988.
Ernst, Morris L., *To The Pure: A Study of Obscenity and the Censor*. London: Cape, 1929.
Everard, Revd. G., *A Strange Companion*. London: White Cross Society, 1884.
Fawcett, Millicent, *The White Slave Trade: Its Causes and the Best Means of Preventing It*. London: National Vigilance Association, 1899.
Fell, John, ed., *Before Hollywood: Turn of the Century American Film*. New York: Hudson Hills Press, 1987.
Finegan, John, *The Story of Monto*. Dublin: Mercier Press, 1979.
Fisher, Trevor, *Scandal: The Sexual Politics of Late-Victorian Britain*. Gloucester: Alan Sutton Press, 1995.
Foster, Roy, 'Protestant Magic'. In *Paddy and Mr Punch: Connections in English and Irish History*. London: Penguin, 1993.
Foucault, Michel, *The History of Sexuality*, 1. *The Will to Knowledge*. Trans. Robert Hurley. London: Penguin, 1990.
Gay, Peter, *The Bourgeois Experience: Victoria to Freud*, 1. *Education of the Senses*. New York: Oxford University Press, 1984.
Gibbons, Luke, *Transformations in Irish Culture*. Cork: Cork University Press, 1996.
Gibson, Ian, *The English Vice: Beating, Sex and Shame in Victorian England and After*. London: Duckworth, 1979.
Gilbert, Stuart, *James Joyce's 'Ulysses'*. New York: Knopf, 1930.
Graham-Yooll, Andrew, *The Forgotten Colony: A History of the English Speaking Communities in the Argentine*. London: Hutchinson, 1981.
Greenwood, James, *The Wilds of London* (1874). Reprinted New York: Garland, 1985.
Groden, Michael, *Ulysses in Progress*. Princeton: Princeton University Press, 1977.
Gunning, Tom, 'The Cinema of Attraction: Early Film, its Spectator and the Avant-Garde'. In *Wide Angle* 8: 3–4, (Fall 1986), 63–70.
   'Phantom Images and Modern Manifestations: Spirit Photography, Magic Theater, Trick Films and Photography's Uncanny'. In *Fugitive Images: From Photography to Video*. Ed. Patrice Petro. Bloomington: Indiana University Press, 1992, 42–71.
Guy, Donna, *Sex and Danger in Buenos Aires: Prostitution, Family and Nation in Argentina*. London: University of Nebraska Press, 1991.
Hall, Lesley, 'Forbidden by God, Despised by Men: Masturbation, Medical Warnings, Moral Panic and Manhood in Great Britain, 1850–1950'. In *Forbidden History*. Ed. John C Fout. Chicago: Chicago University Press, 1991.
Haney, Robert W., *Comstockery in America: Patterns of Censorship and Control*. Boston: Beacon Press, 1974.

Hanscombe, Gillian and Smyers, Virginia L., *Writing for Their Lives: The Modernist Woman*. London: Women's Press, 1987.

Hansen, Miriam, *Babel and Babylon: Spectatorship in American Silent Cinema*. Cambridge: Harvard University Press, 1991.

Harris, Reader A., *An Address to Men Only*. London: n.p.. 1899.

Henke, Suzette, 'Gerty MacDowell: Joyce's Sentimental Heroine'. In *Women in Joyce*. Ed. Suzette Henke and Elaine Unkeless. Urbana: University of Illinois Press, 1982, 123–49.

Hickson, Alisdare. *The Poisoned Bowl: Sex and the Public School*. London: Duckworth, 1996.

Hiley, Nicolas, 'Can't you find me something nasty?: Circulating Libraries and Literary Censorship in Britain from the 1890s to the 1910s'. In *Censorship and the Control of Print in England and France 1600–1910*. Ed. Robin Myers and Michael Harris. Winchester: St Paul's Bibliographies, 1992, 123–47.

Hime, Maurice, *Schoolboys' Special Immorality*. London: White Cross League, 1901.

Hobson, Barbara Meil, *Uneasy Virtue: The Politics of Prostitution and The American Reform Tradition*. London: University of Chicago Press, 1990.

Hollingsworth, Keith, *The Newgate Novel, 1830–1847: Bulwer, Ainsworth, Dickens and Thackeray*. Detroit: Wayne State University Press, 1963.

Holman, Roger, ed., *Cinema 1900/1906: An Analytical Study*. Brussels: International Federation of Film Archives, 1982.

Hopkins, Ellice, *Wild Oats and Acorns*. London: White Cross League, 1883.
The Purity Movement. London: Hatchards, 1885.
True Manliness. London: White Cross Society, 1885.
Who Holds the Rope? London: White Cross Society, 1886.
The Power of Womanhood, or, Mothers and Sons. London: White Cross Society, 1899.

Howe, Joseph, *Excessive Venery, Masturbation and Continence. The Etiology, Pathology and Treatment of the Diseases Resulting from Venereal Excesses*. London and New York: E. B. Treat, 1883.

Howell, Philip, 'Venereal Disease and the Politics of Prostitution in the Irish Free State'. Forthcoming in *Irish Historical Studies*.

Hunt, Alan, 'The Great Masturbation Panic and the Discourses of Moral Regulation in Nineteenth- and Early Twentieth-Century Britain'. *Journal of the History of Sexuality* 8: 4 (1998), 575–615.
Governing Morals: A Social History of Moral Regulation. Cambridge: Cambridge University Press, 1999.

Hutch, Richard, 'Helena Blavatsky Unveiled'. In *The Journal of Religious History* 11: 2 (1980), 318–30.

Hynes, Samuel Lynn, *The Edwardian Turn of Mind*. Princeton: Princeton University Press, 1968.

International Mutoscope Syndicate, *The Age of Movement*. London: International Mutoscope Syndicate, 1901.

Irish Vigilance Association, *Constitution*. Dublin: Brindley and Son, n.d.

Jackson, John Wyse and McGinley, Bernard, *James Joyce's 'Dubliners': An Annotated Edition*. London: Sinclair Stevenson, 1993.

Jeffries, Sheila, *The Spinster and her Enemies*. London: Pandora Press, 1985.

Jenkins, Ralph, 'Theosophy in Scylla and Charybdis'. In *Modern Fiction Studies* 15: 1 (1969), 35–48.

John, Juliet, ed., *Cult Criminals: The Newgate Novels, 1830–1847*. London: Routledge, 1998.

Joyce, Stanislaus, *My Brother's Keeper*. Ed. Richard Ellmann. London: Faber and Faber, 1958.

    The Complete Dublin Diary of Stanislaus Joyce. Ithaca: Cornell University Press, 1975.

Kearns, Kevin, *Dublin Tenement Life: An Oral History*. Dublin: Gill and Macmillan, 1994.

Kendrick, Walter, *The Secret Museum: Pornography in Modern Culture*. New York: Viking, 1987.

Kenner, Hugh, *The Pound Era*. London: Pimlico, 1991.

Kershner, R. B., *Joyce, Bahktin and Popular Literature: Chronicles of Disorder*. London: University of North Carolina Press, 1989.

Kirk, Edward, *A Talk With Boys About Themselves*. London: n.p., 1905.

Lamos, Colleen, 'James Joyce and the English Vice'. In *Novel: A Forum on Fiction* 29: 1 (1995), 19–26.

    Deviant Modernism. Cambridge: Cambridge University Press, 1998.

Leadbeater, Charles W., *The Astral Plane*. London: Theosophical Publishing Society, 1895.

    The Aura: An Inquiry into the Nature and Function of the Luminous Mists Seen Around Human and Other Bodies. London: Theosophical Publishing Society, 1897.

Leonard, Garry, *Advertising and Commodity Culture in Joyce*. Gainesville: University of Florida Press, 1998.

Lidderdale, Jane and Nicholson, Mary, *Dear Miss Weaver: Harriet Shaw Weaver 1896–1961*. London: Faber and Faber, 1970.

Lowe-Evans, Mary. *Crimes Against Fecundity: James Joyce and Population Control*. Syracuse: Syracuse University Press, 1989.

    'Sex and Confession in the Joyce Canon: Some Historical Parallels'. In *Journal of Modern Literature* 16: 4 (Spring 1990), 563–76.

Luddy, Maria, *Women and Philanthropy in Nineteenth-Century Ireland*. Cambridge: Cambridge University Press, 1995.

Lyons, F. S. L., *Charles Stewart Parnell*. London: Fontana, 1991.

Lyttelton, Revd. Edward. *The Causes and Prevention of Immorality in Schools*. London: Social Purity Alliance, 1887.

Maddox, Brenda. *Nora*. London: Minerva, 1988.

Marcus, Stephen, *The Other Victorians: A Study of Sexuality and Pornography in Mid-Nineteenth-Century England*. London: Weidenfeld and Nicolson, 1970.

Mason, Michael, *The Making of Victorian Sexuality*. Oxford: Oxford University Press, 1994.

Mayne, Alan, 'Representing the Slum'. In *Urban History Yearbook* 17 (1990).

Mayne, Judith, *The Woman at the Keyhole: Feminism and Women's Cinema*. Bloomington: Indiana University Press, 1990.

McCarthy, Michael, *Priests and People in Ireland*. London: Hodder and Stoughton, 1908.

McKirdy, Olive Christian, *The White Slave Market*. London: Stanley Paul, 1912.

Mead, G. R. S. and Herbert Burrows, *The Leadbeater Case: The Suppressed Speeches of Herbert Burrows and G. R. S. Mead*. Manchester: E. E. Marsden Press, 1908.

Mendes, Peter, *Clandestine Erotic Fiction in English 1800–1930*. London: Scholar, 1993.

Miles, Eustace, *A Boy's Control and Self-Expression*. Cambridge: E. P. Dutton and Company, 1904.

Miller, Andrew and James Eli Adams, *Sexualities in Victorian Britain*. Bloomington: Indiana University Press, 1996.

Miner, Maude, *The Slavery of Prostitution*. New York: Macmillan, 1916.

Mitchell, Sally, *The New Girl: Girls' Culture in England, 1880–1915*. New York: Columbia University Press, 1995.

Moore, George, 'The New Censorship of Literature'. In *New York Herald*, 28 July 1889.

Mort, Frank, 'Purity, Feminism and the State'. In *Crises in the British State 1880–1930*. Ed. M. Langan and B. Schwartz. London: Hutchinson, 1985, 209–25.

  Dangerous Sexualities: Medico-Moral Politics in England since 1830. London: Routledge and Kegan Paul, 1987.

Mulvey, Laura, 'Visual Pleasure and Narrative Cinema'. In *Screen* 16: 3 (Autumn 1975).

Musser, Charles, *The Emergence of Cinema: The American Screen to 1907*. Berkeley: University of California Press, 1994.

National Vigilance Association, *Minutes*. Callmark GB/ 106/ 4/ NVA. In Fawcett Library, London Guildhall University.

  Pernicious Literature. London: National Vigilance Association, 1889.

  Annual Reports, London: National Vigilance Association: 1885–1920.

Nelson, Claudia, 'Mixed Messages: Authoring and Authority in British Boys' Magazines'. In *The Lion And The Unicorn* 22: 1 (January 1997), 1–24.

New York Society for the Suppression of Vice. *Annual Reports*, New York: New York Society for the Suppression of Vice, 1879–1925.

Niver, Kemp R., *Biograph Bulletins 1896–1908*. Los Angeles: Locare Research Group, 1971.

Nolan, Emer, *James Joyce and Nationalism*. London: Routledge, 1995.

Nolan, Janet, *Ourselves Alone: Women's Emigration from Ireland 1885–1920*. Kentucky: University Press of Kentucky, 1989.

Norris, Margot, 'Joyce's "Mamafesta": Mater and Material, Text and Textile'. In *Gender in Joyce*. Ed. Jolanta W. Wawrzycka and Marlena G. Corcoran. Gainesville: University Press of Florida, 1997, 1–8.

O. Baylen, Joseph, 'Stead's Penny Masterpiece Library'. In *Journal of Popular Culture* 9: 3 (1975), 710–25.

O'Brien, Joseph. *Dear, Dirty Dublin: A City In Distress 1899–1916*. London: University of California Press, 1982.

O'Broin, Leon, *Frank Duff: A Biography*. Dublin: Gill and Macmillan, 1982.

O'Donovan, Jeremiah, 'The Awakening of Brian Joyce'. In *The Irish Homestead*, December 1901, 14.

'Rose Brolley'. In *The Irish Homestead*, December 1902, 21–2.

O'Farelly, Agnes, 'The Reign of Humbug', *Gaelic League Pamphlets*, no. 10. Dublin: Gaelic League, 1900.

Oldstone-Moore, Christopher, 'Hugh Price Hughes and the Nonconformist Conscience'. In *Eire-Ireland* 30: 4 (1996), 122–35.

O Súilleabháin, Sean, *Irish Wake Amusements*. Cork: Mercier Press, 1967, 23–45.

Owen, Alex, *The Darkened Room: Women, Power and Spiritualism in Late-Victorian England*. London: Virago, 1989.

Pankhurst, Christabel, *The Great Scourge and How to End It*. London: E. Pankhurst, 1913.

Parent-Duchâtelet, Alexandre-Jean-Baptiste, *De la prostitution dans la ville de Paris, considérée sous le rapport de l'hygiène publique, de la morale et de l'administration*, 1. Paris: J.-B. Ballière et Fils, 1857.

Parker, Alison, *Purifying America: Women, Cultural Reform and Pro-Censorship Activism 1873–1933*. Chicago: University of Illinois Press, 1997.

Partridge, Eric, *A Dictionary of Slang and Unconventional English*. London: Routledge, 1938.

Pearson, Michael, *The Age of Consent: Victorian Prostitution and its Enemies*. Newton Abbott: David and Charles, 1972.

Petrow, Stefan, *Policing Morals: The Metropolitan Police and the Home Office 1870–1914*. Oxford: Oxford University Press, 1994.

Platt, Len, 'The Voice of Esau: Culture and Nationalism in "Scylla and Charybdis"'. In *James Joyce Quarterly* 29: 4 (1992), 737–50.

Plunkett, Horace, *Ireland in the New Century*. London: Dublin, 1904.

Pound, Ezra, *The Letters of Ezra Pound 1907–1941*. Ed. D. D. Paige. London: Faber and Faber, 1962.

Power, Arthur, *Conversations with James Joyce*. Ed. Clive Hart. Chicago: University of Chicago Press, 1974.

Prunty, Jacintha, *Dublin Slums 1800–1935: A Study in Urban Geography*. Dublin: Irish Academic Press, 1998.

Pure Literature Society, The, *Annual Reports*, London: Pure Literature Society, 1875–1899.

Richards, Grant, *Author Hunting: Memoirs of Years Spent Mainly in Publishing*. London: Unicorn Press, 1960.

Richards, Grant, *Memoirs of a Misspent Youth, 1872–1896*. London: Grant Richards, 1932.

Richards, Thomas, *The Commodity Culture of Victorian England: Advertising and Spectacle*. Stanford: Stanford University Press, 1990.

Rockett, Kevin, Luke Gibbons and John Hill, *Cinema and Ireland*. London: Routledge, 1988.

Roe, Clifford G., *The Great War on White Slavery*. New York: 1911.

The Horrors of the White Slave Trade: The Mighty Crusade To Protect the Purity of our Homes. London and New York: n.p., 1912.

The Girl Who Disappeared. Chicago: Bureau of Moral Education, 1914.

Rosario, Vernon A., *The Erotic Imagination: French Histories of Perversity*. Oxford: Oxford University Press, 1997.

Rose, Jonathan, *The Intellectual Life of the British Working Classes*. London: Yale University Press, 2001.

Rosen, Ruth, *The Lost Sisterhood*. London: Johns Hopkins University Press, 1982.

Ryan, John F., 'Gerald O'Donovan: Poet, Novelist and Irish Revivalist'. In *The Journal of the Galway Archaeological and Historical Society* 48 (1996), 1–47.

Salmon, G. A., 'What Boys Read'. In *The Fortnightly Review* 45 (February 1886), 254–63.

Salt, Henry, *The Flogging Craze: A Statement of the Case Against Corporeal Punishment*. London: Allen and Unwin, 1916.

Scholes, Robert, 'Grant Richards to James Joyce'. In *Studies in Bibliography* 16 (1963), 139–160.

Senn, Fritz, 'Nausicaa' in *James Joyce's 'Ulysses': Critical Essays*. Ed. Clive Hart and David Hayman. Berkeley: University of California Press, 1974, 277–311.

Sibly, F. Arthur, *Private Knowledge for Boys*. Gloucester: Stonehouse Press, 1912.

Silver, Carole, *Strange and Secret People: Fairies and Victorian Consciousness*. Oxford: Oxford University Press, 1999.

Solomon-Godeau, Abigail. *Photography at the Dock: Essays on Photographic History, Institutions and Practices*. Minneapolis: University of Minnesota Press, 1991.

Stansell, Christine, *City of Women: Sex and Class in New York 1789–1860*. New York: Alfred A. Knopf, 1986.

Stead, William Thomas, 'The Maiden Tribute of Modern Babylon'. In *The Pall Mall Gazette*, 6–10 July 1885.

Letters from Julia, or, Light from the Borderland. London: Grant Richards, 1897.

The Discrowned King of Ireland. London: Review of Reviews, 1891.

A Plea for the Revival of Reading with a Plan of Campaign. London: Review of Reviews, 1906.

Thacker, Andrew, 'Dora Marsden and *The Egoist*: "Our War is With Words"'. In *English Literature in Transition* 36: 2 (1993), 179–96.

Tickner, Lisa, *The Spectacle of Women: Imagery of the Suffrage Campaign*. London: Chatto and Windus, 1989.

Tillett, Gregory, *The Elder Brother: A Biography of Charles Webster Leadbeater*. London: Routledge and Kegan Paul, 1982.

Theosophist, The, *Five Years of Theosophy: Mystical, Philosophical, Theosophical, Historical and Scientific Essays Selected from 'The Theosophist'*. No named editor. London: Reeves and Turner, 1885.

Travellers' Aid Society, The, *Minutes and Annual Reports*, 1885–1904. Callmark 1/ TAS/ Box 201. Fawcett Library, London Guildhall University.

Ullman, Sharon R., *Sex Seen: The Emergence of Modern Sexuality in America*. Berkeley: University of California Press, 1997.

Valente, Joseph, 'The Novel and the Police (Gazette)'. In *Novel: A Forum on Fiction* 29: 1 (1996), 7–21.

Vanderham, Paul, *James Joyce and Censorship: The Trials of Ulysses*. London: Macmillan, 1998.

Varley, Henry, *Private Address to Boys and Youths on an Important Subject*. London: Christian Commonwealth, 1884.

Verschoyle, John, 'The Condition of Kerry'. In *Living Age*, 171 (1886), 545–567.

Walkowitz, Judith R., *Prostitution and Victorian Society: Women, Class and the State*. Cambridge: Cambridge University Press, 1980.

 City of Dreadful Delight: Narratives of Sexual Danger in Late-Victorian London. London: Virago, 1998.

Walters, Ronald G., *Primers for Prudery: Sexual Advice to Victorian America*. Baltimore: Johns Hopkins University Press, 2000.

Ward, Margaret, 'Conflicting Interests: The British and Irish Suffrage Movements'. In *Feminist Review* 50 (1995), 129–40.

 Hanna Sheehy-Skeffington: A Life. Cork: Attic Press, 1997.

Washington, Peter, *Madame Blavatsky's Baboon*. London: Secker and Warburg, 1993.

Weeks, Jeffrey, *Sex, Politics and Society*. London: Longman, 1981.

Wicke, Jennifer, *Advertising Fictions: Literature, Advertisement and Social Reality*. New York: Columbia University Press, 1988.

Williams, Linda, 'Corporealised Observers: Visual Pornographies and the "Carnal Density of Vision" '. In *Fugitive Images: From Photography to Video*. Ed. Patrice Petro. Bloomington: Indiana University Press, 1995, 3–41.

Williams, Linda, *Hard Core: Power, Pleasure and the 'Frenzy Of The Visible'*. London: Pandora, 1990.

Wills, Clair, 'Joyce, Prostitution and the Colonial City'. In *The South Atlantic Quarterly* 95: 1 (Winter 1996), 79–95.

Wilson, J. M., *Sins of the Flesh: A Sermon Preached in Clifton College Chapel*. London: Social Purity Alliance, 1883.

Winslow, L. S. Forbes, *Spiritualistic Madness*. London: Bailliere, Tindall and Cox, 1877.

Woodhouse, J. R., 'Victorian Verecundity: D'Annunzio's Prudish Public'. In *Moving in Measure: Essays in Honour of Brian Moloney*. Ed. Judith Bryce and Douglas Thompson. Hull: Hull University Press, 1989, 107–21.

Yeats, W. B., *A Critical Edition of the Major Works*. Ed. Edward Larrissy. Oxford: Oxford University Press, 1997.

Index